Religions of Asia

NINIAN SMART

Religions of Asia

PRENTICE HALL
Englewood Cliffs, N.J. 07632

Prentice Hall Inc
A Division of Simon & Schuster
Englewood Cliffs, New Jersey 07632

10 9 8 7 6 5 4 3 2 1

ISBN 0–13–772427–6

This book was designed and produced by
CALMANN & KING LTD., London

Designed by Andrew Shoolbred
Picture research by Sara Waterson
Maps by Hardlines, Oxford

Typeset by Fakenham Photosetting Ltd., Norfolk
Printed in Singapore

Frontispiece: A Buddhist monk with a begging bowl in a street in
Osaka, Japan.

Cover: Ganden Lamo Thangka, 20th century Tibetan School of
Painting, artist unknown, from Kopan Monastery, Kathmandu,
Nepal. This painting shows the Tushita Pure Land at the top with
the figure of Maitreya from whose heart emanates the main central
figure of Lama Je Tsong Khapa, the 14th century Tibetan master
who founded the Gelugpa tradition of Buddhism. Courtesy Tibet
Image Bank, photograph by Robin Bath.

Contents

Preface

In this book I explore the history, traditions, and practices of the religions of Asia. The story of these religions is told tradition by tradition and for each I have included quotations from important sacred texts and definitions of key terms. In examining the traditions I have used two vital theoretical approaches.

One is the seven-dimensional model incorporating important characteristic categories, such as ritual, social organization, and religious experience, in order to ensure a balance in the treatment of each religion. Often writers on religion have been lopsided in their approach, through getting too preoccupied with some particular aspect, such as doctrine.

Second, I emphasize the patterns of action and response during the colonial period controlling the ways religions reshaped themselves in responding to the challenges of external powers and the demands of modernization. Without neglecting the ancient sources of religion, I also emphasize modern times.

I have been much assisted in preparing this volume by Rosemary Bradley and Melanie White, of Calmann and King, who have been full of help and good advice.

Ninian Smart
July 29, 1992
Tremezzo, Italy

CHAPTER ONE

Overview of Asian Religions

Asian Religions

By Asian religions we here mean those which prevail in India and Central Asia, in Southeast Asia, and in East Asia: that is, in the whole region to the south of Siberia, from Afghanistan to Japan, and from Sri Lanka to Mongolia. The most important of these, from a traditional perspective, are Buddhism, Hinduism, Jainism, and Sikhism, originating in India; Confucianism and Taoism, indigenous to China; Shinto, native to Japan. But Islam and Christianity are important too, especially the former. It dominates Indonesia, Pakistan, and Bangladesh, as well as Afghanistan and parts of Central Asia, while the Republic of India contains about as many Muslims as either Pakistan or Bangladesh (approximately 100 million each). While Islam is a Western religion in the sense that it draws heavily on its predecessors, Judaism and Christianity, and originated in the same cultural area, a chapter on its Asian manifestations is included.

Similarly, Christianity and other Western worldviews, notably Marxism, have had a dramatic impact on Asia, due primarily to the expansion of the colonial West, from the fifteenth century to the twentieth. It is not possible to depict modern China without describing Maoism, or Southeast Asia without sketching in varieties of Marxism, or any of the countries in the region without describing the ways in which they reacted to the incursions of Western science and Christian missions. These are considered in the chapter on Asian Islam, while in the initial overview of Asian religions particular attention will be paid to the impact of the West in modern times, thus setting the scene for the delineation of the sweep of Asian religious history, in which the colonial period proved to be dramatically important. Moreover, Chapter 9, on Confucianism, will incorporate an account of some important modern rivals and alternatives, notably Maoism.

So our accounts of the various religions and worldviews will pay particular attention to their modern manifestations. Religions may sometimes claim to

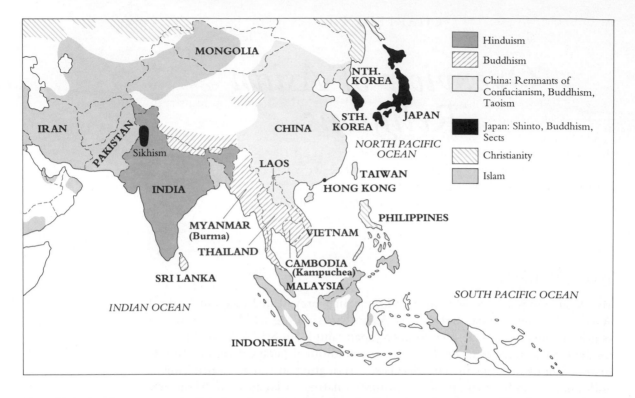

Map of Asia showing the approximate distribution of Hinduism, Buddhism, Confucianism, Taoism, Shinto, Sikhism, and Islam in the world today.

remain fixed and unalterable, but in fact they do change, if only to retain an earlier spirit among altered circumstances. Not changing when circumstances change is itself a sort of changing. And in underlining the vitality of modern forms of religion we can remind ourselves that it is only modern religions that we ever meet. We encounter, not Paul or Confucius, but modern Christians and Confucianists; not the Buddha or Rāmānuja, but modern Buddhists and Hindus. All this does not mean that ancient history is not important: of course it is, not just because the men and women who lived in those days are just as important as we are, but also because the religions that were shaped in the past provide the materials out of which their modern manifestations are constructed.

The understanding of Asian religions and ideologies is vital to our grasp of today's world. First of all, they constitute a dynamic ingredient in the evolution of the civilizations of the region. You cannot have a feel for China's heritage without knowing about Confucianism and the spirit of Taoism. India's rich culture is permeated by the Hindu tradition, and owes much to Buddhism, Jainism, and Sikhism, not to mention Islam. And so on with the other great cultures of the area such as those of Tibet, Korea, Japan, and Thailand: these all have powerful religious ingredients. Second, nowadays even the West contains the vital presence of Asian cultures: there are Chinese, Japanese, Korean, and Vietnamese populations in California, Australia, Canada, New York State, and so on. Third, a major part of the industrial and technological dynamic of modern capitalism flows out of the Pacific rim and Asia in general: the values driving these forces owe something to the spiritual past – this is very evident in Japan and Korea, for instance. Even in China, where traditional religion has been swamped by Maoism, the seeds of the past are beginning to sprout again. Fourth, political life is increasingly determined by revivalist religious forces, like those of Islam in Indonesia, Hinduism in the Republic of India, Buddhism in Sri Lanka, and so on.

There are methods of understanding religions and worldviews, and we shall sketch these later in this chapter (see page 28). Briefly, they involve the use of imagination and a balanced and what we shall call "dimensional" approach to people's ideas and practices:

Imagination because we have to enter other people's worlds (as a Native American proverb has it, "Never judge a person till you have walked a mile in his moccasins");

Dimensional because we have to see a religion in its various dimensions – its experiences, its stories, its ethics, its art, its rituals, its institutions, its doctrines. Being informed about these things is important, to give food to the imagination. First, we will look briefly at the history of religion in Asia.

An Overview of Asian Religious History

The Indian subcontinent, stretching from the Himalayan mountains in the north to the island of Sri Lanka in the south, is crucial to the history of Asian religion, because one of its great religions, namely **Buddhism**, spread into virtually every country of South, Central, and East Asia. Buddhism remains the predominant religion of Sri Lanka, Burma (now Myanmar), Thailand, Cambodia (Kampuchea), Laos, Vietnam, Korea, and Japan, as well as Tibet and Mongolia. It suffused Chinese culture, and once was a main shaper of Indian culture. It was important, before Islam, in Indonesia, and also in Central Asia (notably in what today is Afghanistan). It remains vigorous in Nepal and along the foothills of the Himalayas. And so to understand much of Asian civilization it is important to understand Buddhism.

Buddhism emerged in the fifth century C.E., with the teaching of the Buddha. It had as its background a mixture of religions then forming in the valley of the Ganges river. Among these was its rough contemporary **Jainism**, which had ancient roots among the beliefs and practices of ascetics and recluses who taught a variety of philosophies. Buddhism also took up themes from the religion known as Brahmanism, which itself was to become a principal ingredient in that complex of practices and beliefs which came together to form what we know today as **Hinduism**. Hinduism inherited the ancient compositions collected together as the Vedic hymns, reflecting the religion of Indo-Europeans who had entered India much earlier, in the middle of the second millennium B.C.E. At about the time of the Buddha and a little after, the Brahmin class, who were hereditary priests, formulated doctrines about the sacred power Brahman which sustained the cosmos. These ideas were expressed in the famous texts known as the *Upaniṣads* (Upanishads).

In the third century B.C.E. the emperor Aśoka, who came to the throne probably in 268, patronized Buddhism and sent out missions from his capital Pataliputra on the Ganges, to various countries including Sri Lanka, which became an important center for the editing and bringing together of Buddhist texts. Eventually Buddhism began to divide into differing forms. The main variety in Sri Lanka and throughout Southeast Asia was the so-called Theravāda or Doctrine of the Elders. This does not involve the cult of a supreme God, but focuses upon the path which, trodden over innumerable lives, can lead to sainthood and the attainment of *nirvāṇa* – a timeless transcendent state which ensures an end to rebirth in the round of becoming. The form of Buddhism which came to prevail in China, Korea, and Japan is known as the Great Vehicle or Mahāyāna, and is more expansive and embracing. It includes a wealth of varieties, the two most important of which are Ch'ān or Zen (these are both renditions, one in Chinese and the other in Japanese, of an Indian term for meditation), and Pure Land Buddhism, which stresses the worship of Buddha figures, notably that of the Buddha Amitābha, who has fashioned a paradise or Pure Land for those who call upon him in faith. The idea of the person called a Bodhisattva is also important in Mahāyāna thought. This is someone who is destined to achieve enlightenment, who puts off his or her ultimate release in order to work ceaselessly for the good of others and who uses his or her vast store of surplus merit, acquired through these good deeds, to help others along the path to ultimate liberation. Buddhism entered China in the first century C.E. and thence migrated into Korea and Japan, as well as Vietnam.

Meanwhile in India a mingling of various movements, under the aegis of the Brahmins, came to form what we can recognize as Hinduism. There emerged a well-articulated caste system, involving not only the four main classes of the Aryans (Brahmins, warriors, merchants, and laborers) but innumerable subdivisions by region and occupation, as well as the "fifth class" or untouchables (subjugated tribal peoples and workers in unclean occupations, such as butchers and sweepers). At the same time there came to be a variety of devotional movements, addressed to varying depictions of God, such as Viṣṇu, Śiva and Dūrgā, the Goddess, as well as the avatars or incarnations of Viṣṇu, such as Rāma and Krishna (Kṛṣṇa). Some famous scriptures emerged, notably the Song of the Lord or *Bhagavadgītā*, part of the great epic called the *Mahābhārata*. Woven from many myths, temples, statues, philosophies, meditation, yoga, asceticism, sacred rituals, pilgrimages, and devotion, Hinduism gradually emerged as a vast federation of religious themes and movements. As it developed, Buddhism faded, so that by 1000 C.E. it was greatly weakened and hardly survived in India the impact of conquering Islam, from the eleventh century onwards.

Meanwhile Jainism survived, within the fabric of Hinduism. Its primary value was *ahiṃsā* or non-injury to living beings. By austere living a person could attain final liberation and the cessation of reincarnation. This emphasis on rebirth is common to all major Indian religions – Hinduism, Buddhism,

Jainism, and Sikhism. The Jaina ideal is that of such leaders as Mahāvīra whose lives are of such exemplary austerity that they end their days without eating, starving themselves to death, harming no animals as they stand immobile till their decease. The community has been a prosperous one, because lay people tend to be merchants, since farming involves the killing of insects and other living beings. Their temples are often spectacular, and their network of monasteries and convents provides the matrix for the community.

From the eighth century onward Buddhism spread into Tibet. By the sixteenth century the spiritual ruler there was also the monarch: the succession of Dalai Lamas has continued into modern times. From Tibet the complex form of Buddhism often known in the West as Lamaism (from *lama*, a monk) spread into Mongolia.

Meanwhile, India experienced a number of Muslim invasions, culminating in the establishment of the Mughal empire, ruling from Delhi, in the sixteenth century. Islam made quite a lot of headway in India, partly converting from untouchables, who had much to gain, partly spreading because of the example of Sufi (mystic) holy men and women, partly gaining from the empire's Islamic status. Arising within the rift created by the clash of Hindu and Islamic ideals and practices was the Sikh religion, going back to Nānak (1469–1504), who sought a synthesis of the theistic beliefs of each faith. Later **Sikhism** was solidified into a martial religion, based in the Punjab, by Guru Gobind Singh (died 1708).

The gradual conquest of India by the British culminated in the establishment of the Indian empire (or Rāj) in 1858. The introduction of English-speaking higher education, the creation of the rail system, the establishment of an effective civil service – these and other measures brought into being a more unified India. The criticism of Hindu practices by missionaries and to some extent by the government led to a reaction which in effect expressed a revitalized Hinduism based on an adaptation of traditional Indian philosophy. This was formulated most clearly at the end of the nineteenth century by the reformer Swami Vivekānanda and in the twentieth century by a number of Indian writers in English, notably Sarvepalli Radhakrishnan. This modern Hindu ideology saw all religions as pointing to the same truth and Hinduism as a pioneer of such embracing toleration. This served as a main basis for Indian nationalism. Though India and Pakistan split apart at independence in 1947, the ideology served the Republic of India well, with its sizeable Muslim and other minorities.

Theravāda Buddhism was also faced with the Western modernist challenge during the latter part of the nineteenth century and the twentieth century. It too was revitalized, through the editing and publication of the Pali canon (i.e. scriptures written in the Pali language) and through a new awareness of Buddhism's consonance with science and modern ethics. Thailand, the only country not to be conquered by a Western power, helped to maintain Buddhist practice, through the example of an enlightened monarchy.

The Three Religions (San-chiao) of China as personified in K'ung, Lao-tzu and the Buddha. Chinese painting late 15th–early 16th century Ming Dynasty (1368–1644). Hanging scroll, ink and color on silk, 57¾ × 29 ins (146.7 × 73.6 cm).

In the first century C.E. Buddhism had reached China via Central Asia and the Silk Route, which conveyed merchandise between East and West north of Tibet into China. Later Buddhism also reached China by sea via Canton. There it encountered established Chinese worldviews, including most notably the philosophy of Confucius, Taoism, and popular religion, all somewhat intermingled. The ideas of K'ung, known to the West as Confucius (a Latin version of his full name, created by early Catholic missionaries from the West), which appeared in the fifth century B.C.E., took an increasing hold on the Chinese imagination, and came to dominate the imperial examination system, for entry into the civil service. The books K'ung edited, from before his time, together with classical texts recording his own philosophy, were the basis for mainstream Chinese education until the beginning of the twentieth century (the old imperial examination system was replaced in 1905). **Confucianism** was the dominant government ideology during most of Chinese history. However, to some degree it was merged with traditional practices such as the reverencing of ancestors, seen as invisible members of continuing society.

Taoism or the philosophy of the Tao or Way, that is the Way of the cosmos or underlying principle in all natural events, dates from the same time as Confucius, that is the sixth to fifth centuries B.C.E. and was ascribed to the sage Lao-tzu. It contrasted with the formalism of K'ung, who considered that correct behavior or *li*, including the performance of rituals, was the key to the good ordering of society. Taoism by contrast stressed conformity to the Way of the world, naturalness, and spontaneity. To be vital, one should act naturally, without effort – in brief one should act without acting. Through the centuries, this philosophy fed anarchistic and rebellious elements in Chinese society. It was reinforced by religious Taoism, which postulated a hierarchy of gods and a kind of celestial civil service. It fostered alchemy and other methods of prolonging life. While both Taoism and Confucianism were sometimes in conflict with Buddhism, from the eleventh century C.E. onward the three religions complemented each other in Chinese life.

The modern era was traumatic for China. Western powers and later Japan came to control much of China's trade and occupied many seaports. The empire was on the verge of being dismembered, and its spiritual resources for various reasons were not adequate to adapt to a new nationalist and modernizing mode. The dissolution of the old order in 1911 led to a period of anarchy and civil war, finally resolved by the victory of Maoist communism in 1949. This led in due course to the suppression of most traditional religious life, both in China proper and in Chinese-occupied Tibet and Mongolia. A new factor in Chinese life, from the nineteenth century, was the creation of a significant diaspora of Chinese abroad, in such countries as Singapore, Malaysia, and Indonesia.

In the second and first centuries B.C.E. Korea had been directly under Chinese domination. So in succeeding centuries it was under the influence of Chinese Buddhism and Confucianism. Korea was important in developing new forms of Confucian thought and a distinctively Korean form of Meditation Buddhism. In modern times its development was distorted by Japanese occupation, from 1910, and the division into the communist North and the American-influenced South, at the end of World War II. Protestantism has made substantial gains since then, and Korea is, apart from the Philippines, the most Christianized country in Asia.

Japan was also in the orbit of the influence of Chinese culture. Buddhism spread to Japan from the late fifth century C.E. onward, and then evolved dramatically from the twelfth to the sixteenth century, especially in the development of Japanese Pure Land schools and Zen. The Japanese reacted to the West first by closing off the country and then in the Meiji era (from 1868) by opening up in a planned and vigorous manner, turning itself rapidly into a modern industrial power. The changes helped to create new religious movements, and to bring about a nationalist spirit within the traditional cult of the gods, known as **Shinto**.

It may be seen that the differing regions reacted very differently to the impact of the West and modernity. India updated its Hindu philosophy but in a way that also left intact nearly all Hindu practice. The Buddhist countries of Southeast Asia were much affected by socialist experiments. China reasserted its strength through the militarism of a largely foreign ideology, namely Marxism. Japan farsightedly imported modernism, but merged it with some elements of traditional religion and culture. Some areas such as Tibet, and for a while Korea, experienced foreign colonialism, but Asian rather than European.

Meanwhile, Islam in many areas grappled with the challenge of modernity in varied ways – through a moderate ideology in Indonesia, synthesizing Islamic and minority values, through revived Islam in Pakistan, and through struggles against Marxism in Central Asia, notably in Afghanistan.

Ways of Exploring Religion

Exploring religions needs imagination. As we have noted already, it involves walking in other people's moccasins. Of course we need information, both historical and dimensional (looking at the various dimensions of a religion). But information without empathy can be wooden. To give our explorations spirit and meaning we have to look at the world from the viewpoint of the typical believer. This is true in other human sciences: to understand history in general the standpoint of the actors is important. But it is especially true of the modern study of religion.

Particularly in the period since the 1960s we have evolved a way of exploring religion and religions which emphasizes the imaginative and rounded treatment of human beliefs and practices. This modern style of religious studies takes seriously the plural character of humankind's religions. In the old days Catholics tended to study the Catholic tradition, Jews Judaism, Muslims Islam – and then mainly from the point of view of affirming the preferred values of these traditions. There is nothing wrong in this, but it is incomplete from the angle of trying to understand humanity and humanity's history. To grasp the nature of Sri Lankan life you have to know something of Theravāda Buddhism; to think through the policies of contemporary Iran you need to understand Shi'a Islam; to grasp the nature of Japanese history you should have an understanding of Shinto and Mahāyāna Buddhism. And so on. To realize the multicolored fabric of human spirituality you need an approach to the major religions at least.

To walk in others' moccasins means taking seriously what believers take seriously, whether we believe in their values or not. In exploring Hinduism we need to see, for instance, the beauty and power of Viṣṇu and Śiva and of the great Goddess. We need to imagine how it is to believe in *karma* and reincarnation (even if we do not believe in these things ourselves). In other words we must imagine that the gods of others are our gods, and others' ideals of freedom are our ideals. We can express this by saying that whether or not God exists, he or she is *real* to the believers: they can experience their god or goddess, and the experience has an effect upon them. We are interested in our exploration more in the power of a faith than in judging whether it is true. Of course we are likely to be interested in the latter question, but it has to be laid on one side while we are entering into a faith. We suspend our own beliefs in entering the beliefs (and of course practices) of others. One scholar expressed this whole idea, perhaps a little misleadingly but certainly forcibly, by saying that the believer is always right.

Empathetic imagination is important widely in education. To understand the opposite sex we must exercise imagination (we are not often asked to exercise it in much of the educational system, alas). We can reinforce imagination by talking to a friend of another faith, or going to her or his shrine and meeting other members of the faith. There are also various films and other devices for making religions alive – insights come from reading novels like *The Brothers Karamazov* (for Russian Eastern Orthodoxy) by Fyodor Dostoyevsky and *A Passage to India* (for Hinduism and Islam in India) by E. M. Forster. Travel helps, if sensitively prepared. The contemplation of the material dimension of a religion – its artworks, buildings, icons, and so on – can be illuminating. The austerity of Scottish Calvinism is revealed in some of its churches; the serenity of ideal Buddhism is seen in the face of many Buddha-statues; the awesome simplicity of Islamic faith is perceived in beautiful mosques; the power of the numinous Christ is felt in the icon of the Ruler of All; the fascination and strength of female deity is felt through statues of Kali.

In working backwards in time through the histories of faiths we necessarily make great use of texts, including those that may be deemed in a religion to be sacred or canonical (that is, authoritative as to doctrine and practice). Because we use texts, we often get only a partial view of the past – we gain access often to the religion of the elite, excluding many men and most women. Texts also tell us more about doctrines and stories than about other aspects of a religious movement. We need to remember these points in treating the past. Nevertheless texts, and also the languages they are written in, remain vital. While we cannot possibly master all the languages of religions, from Arabic to Sanskrit, Greek to Chinese, Zulu to Japanese, we can at least be sensitive to them and know something of the key terms. In this book we include for each religion a list of some of the important words. The illustrations give an impression of the material manifestations of the religions.

To get a balanced view of the past it is useful to consider various crucial periods. Very often a religion's roots and ingredients may go very far back before the period of its classical formation. Thus the roots of Christianity lie in part, of course, in the Jewish religion represented by the Hebrew Bible or Old Testament (as Christians called, and call, it). But the period when Christianity took on its characteristic form, as Catholicism and Orthodoxy, in the Western and Eastern parts of the Roman empire, was in the early fourth century C.E. It then emerged in its early classical form, with essential doctrines such as the Trinity, and the rich worship of its churches, together with the burgeoning of monasticism. Similarly, Judaism as we know it – the Judaism of rabbis and synagogues and Talmudic commentaries and the elaboration of the Law or Torah – was formed during much the same period. It is often said that Hinduism started with the ancient hymns of the Veda. But though the hymns became an important ingredient in the elaborated system of Hinduism, it is misleading to say that Hinduism began so early. It was not till the early centuries C.E. that it developed its typical characteristics – temples, philosophies, *Gītā*, caste, divine statues, yoga, and pilgrimages, etc. It is true that sometimes religions were formed swiftly by their founders – notably Islam. But often the founder lived at some time distant from the classical growth of his faith or the faith about him (or her, in a few cases, such as Christian Science, which had a woman founder).

Often the period of the formation of a religion represents the fusion of diverse elements. Christianity absorbed much of Greek and Roman culture, in particular that spiritual system of practices and ideas known as Neoplatonism, with its strong contemplative and mystical elements. These are combined for instance in the thought of the highly influential Augustine (354–430). Neoplatonist ideals reinforced the monastic ideal, which centered on the life of interior prayer.

Other infusions create new rhythms in a religious tradition. Thus the embracing of feudalism in the early Middle Ages, together with the adoption of much of the thought of Aristotle, created medieval Catholicism. Then in due course the Reformers, in the early and the middle sixteenth century, went back beyond the formulations of classical Christianity and formed a new version based upon the teachings of the New Testament reinterpreted in a new age.

In brief, to understand the rhythms of a religion we need to note how each stage represents a new infusion. Religions blend anew, and create forms adequate for diverse ages and cultural conditions. They are not static entities. However traditional, they need to revitalize traditions.

As well as historical explorations there is a need for a balanced perspective as represented by the dimensional approach. The focus of each religion – God, Viṣṇu, Buddhahood, the Goddess – is filtered through a multi-dimensional glass. We now turn to these dimensions. The scheme presented here has seven dimensions: it is a convenient way of analyzing the nature of a tradition or subtradition (for every tradition sooner or later divides up into denominations, movements, sects – in a word, subtraditions). The dimensions are: (1) the practical and ritual dimension; (2) the experiential and emotional dimension; (3) the narrative or mythic dimension; (4) the doctrinal and philosophical dimension; (5) the ethical and legal dimension; (6) the social and institutional dimension; and (7) the material dimension.

The Practical and Ritual Dimension

Every tradition has some practices to which it adheres – for instance regular worship, preaching, prayers, and so on. They are often known as rituals (though they may well be more informal than this word implies). This practical and ritual dimension is especially important with faiths of a strongly sacramental kind, such as Eastern Orthodox Christianity with its long and elaborate service known as the Liturgy. The ancient Jewish tradition of the Temple, before it was destroyed in 70 C.E., was preoccupied with the rituals of sacrifice. Thereafter the study of such rites was seen as equivalent to their performance, so that study itself became almost a ritual activity. Likewise, sacrificial rituals are important among Brahmin forms of the Hindu tradition.

The ritual dimension: Easter celebrations in Moscow.

Also important are other patterns of behavior which, while they may not strictly count as rituals, fulfill a function in developing spiritual awareness or ethical insight. These include practices such as yoga in the Buddhist and Hindu traditions, methods of stilling the self in Eastern Orthodox mysticism, meditations which can help to increase compassion and love, and so on. Such practices can be combined with rituals of worship, where meditation is directed toward union with God. They can count as a form of prayer. In such ways they overlap with the more formal or explicit rites of religion.

The Experiential and Emotional Dimension

We only have to glance at religious history to see the enormous vitality and significance of experience in the formation and development of religious traditions. Consider the visions of the Prophet Muhammad, the conversion of Paul, the Enlightenment of the Buddha. These were seminal events in human history. And it is obvious that the emotions and experiences of men and women are the food on which the other dimensions of religion feed: ritual without feeling is cold, doctrines without awe or compassion are dry, and myths which do not move hearers are feeble. So it is important in understanding a tradition to try to enter into the feelings which it generates – to feel the sacred awe, the calm peace, the rousing inner dynamism, the perception of a brilliant emptiness within, the outpouring of love, the sensations of hope, the gratitude for favors which have been received. One of the main reasons why music is so potent in religion is that it has mysterious powers to express and engender emotions.

Writers on religion have singled out differing experiences as being central. For instance, Rudolf Otto (1869–1937) coined the word "numinous." For the ancient Romans there were *numina* or spirits all around them, present in brooks and streams, and in mysterious copses, in mountains and in dwelling-places; they were to be treated with awe and a kind of fear. From this word, Otto derived his adjective, to refer to the feeling aroused by a *mysterium tremendum et fascinans*, a mysterious something which draws you to it but at the same time brings a fear permeated by awe. It is a good characterization of many religious experiences and visions of God as Other. It captures the impact of the prophetic experiences of Isaiah and Jeremiah, the manifestation of God appearing to Job, the conversion of Paul, the overwhelming vision given to Arjuna in the Hindu Song of the Lord (*Bhagavadgītā*). At a gentler level it defines the spirit of loving devotion, in that the devotee sees God as merciful and loving, yet Other, and to be worshiped and adored.

But the numinous is rather different in character from those other experiences which are often called "mystical." Mysticism is the inner or contemplative quest for what lies within – variously thought of as the Divine Being within, or the eternal soul, or the Cloud of Unknowing, emptiness, a dazzling darkness. There are those, such as Aldous Huxley (1894–1963), who have thought that the imageless, insight-giving inner mystical experience lies at the heart of all the major religions.

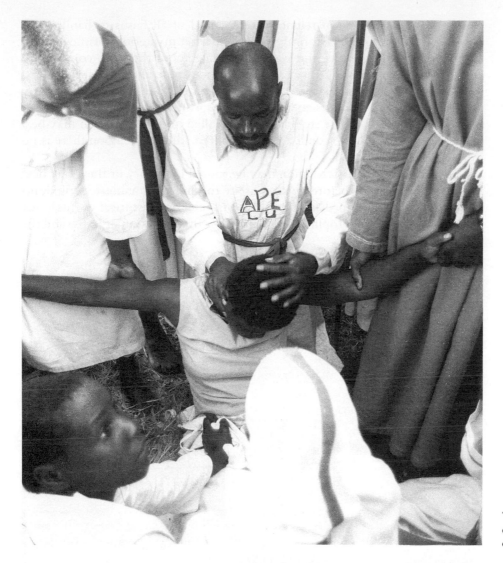

The experiential
dimension: casting out
demons.

There are other related experiences, such as the dramas of conversion,
being "born again," turning around from worldly to otherworldly existence.
There is also the shamanistic type of experience, where a person goes upon a
vision quest and acquires powers to heal, often through suffering himself or
herself and vividly traveling to the netherworld to rescue the dying and bring
them to life again. Shamans are common to many small-scale societies and
peoples that make their living by hunting, but many of the marks of the
shamanistic quest have been left upon larger religions.

The Narrative or Mythic Dimension
Often experience is channeled and expressed not only by ritual but also by
sacred narrative or myth. This is the third dimension – the mythic or narra-

tive. It is the story side of religion. It is typical of all faiths to hand down significant stories: some historical; some about that mysterious primeval time when the world was in its timeless dawn; some about things to come at the end of time; some about great heroes and saints; some about great founders, such as Moses, the Buddha, Jesus, and Muhammad; some about assaults by the Evil One; some parables and edifying tales; some about the adventures of the gods; and so on. These stories are often called myths. The term may be a bit misleading, for in the context of the modern study of religion there is no implication that a myth is false.

The seminal stories of a religion may be rooted in history or they may not. Stories of creation are before history, as are myths which indicate how death and suffering came into the world. Others are about historical events – for instance the life of the Prophet Muhammad, or the execution of Jesus, and the

The mythic dimension: a brahmin worshipping Kṛṣṇa.

Enlightenment of the Buddha. Historians have sometimes cast doubt on some aspects of these historical stories, but from the standpoint of the student of religion this question is secondary to the meaning and function of the myth. To the believer, very often, these narratives *are* history.

This belief is strengthened by the fact that many faiths look upon certain documents, originally maybe based upon long oral traditions, as true scriptures. They are canonical or recognized by the relevant body of the faithful (the Church, the community, Brahmins and others in India, the Buddhist Sangha or Order). They are often treated as inspired directly by God or as records of the very words of the founder. They have authority, and they contain many stories and myths which are taken to be divinely or otherwise guaranteed. But other documents and oral traditions may also be important – the lives of the saints, the chronicles of Sri Lanka as a Buddhist nation, the Hasidic stories of famous holy men of eastern Europe, traditions concerning the life of the Prophet (*hadith*), and so forth. These stories may have lesser authority but they can still be inspiring to the followers.

Stories in religion are often tightly integrated into the ritual dimension. The Christian Mass or communion service, for instance, commemorates and presents the story of the Last Supper, when Jesus celebrated with his disciples his forthcoming fate, by which (according to Christians) he saved humankind and brought us back into harmony with the Divine Being. The Jewish Passover ceremonies commemorate and make real to us the events of the exodus from Egypt, the sufferings of the people, and their relationship to the Lord who led them out of servitude in ancient Egypt.

The Doctrinal and Philosophical Dimension

Underpinning the narrative dimension is the doctrinal dimension. Thus, in the Christian tradition, the story of Jesus' life and the ritual of the communion service led to attempts to provide an analysis of the nature of the Divine Being which would preserve both the idea of the Incarnation (Jesus as God) and the belief in one God. It should also make sense of the coming of the Holy Spirit who guides and inspires the Church. The result was the doctrine of the Trinity, which sees God as three persons in one substance. Similarly, with the meeting between early Christianity and the great Graeco-Roman philosophical and intellectual heritage it became necessary to face questions about the ultimate meaning of creation, the inner nature of God, the notion of grace, the analysis of how Christ could be both God and human being, and so on. These concerns led to the elaboration of Christian doctrine. In the case of Buddhism, to take another example, doctrinal ideas were more crucial right from the start, for the Buddha himself presented a philosophical vision of the world which itself was an aid to salvation.

In any event, doctrines come to play a significant part in all the major religions, partly because sooner or later a faith has to adapt to social reality and so to to the fact that much of the leadership is well educated and seeks some kind of intellectual statement of the basis of the faith.

The doctrinal dimension: the Buddha in his form as teacher.

It happens that histories of religion have tended to exaggerate the importance of scriptures and doctrines. This is not too surprising since so much of our knowledge of past religions must come from the documents which have been passed on by the scholarly elite. Also, and especially in the case of Christianity, doctrinal disputes have often been the overt expression of splits within the fabric of the community at large, so that frequently histories of a faith concentrate upon these hot issues. This is clearly unbalanced; but I would not want us to go to the other extreme. There are scholars today who have been much impressed with the symbolic and psychological force of myth, and have tended to neglect the essential intellectual component of religion.

The Ethical and Legal Dimension

Both narrative and doctrine affect the values of a tradition by laying out the shape of a worldview and addressing the question of ultimate liberation or salvation. The law which a tradition or subtradition incorporates into its fabric can be called the ethical dimension of religion. In Buddhism for instance, there are certain universally binding precepts, known as the Five Precepts or virtues, together with a set of further regulations controlling the lives of monks and nuns and monastic communities. In Judaism we have not merely the Ten Commandments but a complex of over six hundred rules imposed upon the community by the Divine Being. All this Law or Torah is a framework for living for the Orthodox Jew. It also is part of the ritual dimension, because, for instance, the injunction to keep the Sabbath as a day of rest is also the injunction to perform certain sacred practices and rituals, such as attending the synagogue and maintaining purity.

Similarly, Islamic life has traditionally been controlled by the law or *sharī'a*, which shapes society in its religious and political aspects, as well as the moral life of the individual – prescribing daily prayers, giving alms to the poor, and so on, and that society should have various institutions, such as marriage, modes of banking, etc.

Other traditions can be less tied to a system of law, but still display an ethic which is influenced or controlled by the myth and doctrine of the faith. For instance, the central ethical attitude in the Christian faith is love. This springs not just from Jesus' injunction to his followers to love God and their neighbors: it also flows from the story of Christ himself who gave his life out of love for his fellow human beings. It also is rooted in the very idea of the Trinity, for God from all eternity is a society of three persons, Father, Son, and Holy Spirit, kept together by the bond of love. The Christian joins a community which reflects, it is hoped, the life of the Divine Being, both as Trinity and as suffering servant of the human race and indeed of all creation.

The Social and Institutional Dimension

The dimensions outlined so far – the experiential, the ritual, the mythic, the doctrinal, and the ethical – can be considered in abstract terms, without being

The ethical dimension: Zen monks exhibit discipline and the desire for orderly work as they set out to tidy the grounds of their monastery,

embodied in external form. The last two dimensions have to do with the incarnation of religion. First, every religious movement is embodied in a group of people, and that is very often rather formally organized – as Church, or Sangha, or *umma*. The sixth dimension therefore is what may be called the social or institutional aspect of religion. To understand a faith we need to see how it works among people. This is one reason why such an important tool of the investigator of religion is that subdiscipline which is known as the sociology of religion. Sometimes the social aspect of a worldview is simply identical with society itself, as in small-scale groups such as tribes. But there is a variety of relations between organized religions and society at large: a faith may be the official religion, or it may be just one denomination among many, or it may be somewhat cut off from social life, as a sect. Within the

The social dimension: a Jewish family celebrating their first Passover since arriving in Israel.

organization of one religion, moreover, there are many models – from the relative democratic governance of a radical Protestant congregation to the hierarchical and monarchical system of the Church of Rome.

It is not, however, the formal officials of a religion who may in the long run turn out to be the most important persons in a tradition. For there are charismatic or sacred personages, whose spiritual power glows through their demeanor and actions, and who vivify the faith of more ordinary folk – saintly people, gurus, mystics, and prophets, whose words and example stir up the spiritual enthusiasm of the masses, and who lend depth and meaning to the rituals and values of a tradition. They can also be revolutionaries and set religion on new courses. They can, like John Wesley, become leaders of a new denomination, almost against their will; or they can be founders of new groups which may in due course emerge as separate religions – an example is Joseph Smith II, prophet of the new faith of Mormonism. In short, the social dimension of religion includes not only the mass of persons but also the outstanding individuals through whose features glimmer old and new thoughts of the heaven toward which they aspire.

The Material Dimension
This social or institutional dimension of religion almost inevitably becomes incarnate in a different way, in material form, as buildings, works of art, and

other creations. Some movements, such as Calvinist Christianity, especially in the time before the present century eschew external symbols as being potentially idolatrous; their buildings are often beautiful in their simplicity, but their intention is to be without artistic or other images which might seduce people from the thought that God is a spirit who transcends all representations. However, the material expressions of religion are more often elaborate, moving, and highly important for believers in their approach to the divine. How indeed could we understand Eastern Orthodox Christianity without seeing what icons are like and knowing that they are regarded as windows onto heaven? How could we get inside the feel of Hinduism without attending to the varied statues of God and the gods?

Other important material expressions of a religion are those natural features of the world which are singled out as being of special sacredness and meaning – the river Ganges, the Jordan, the sacred mountains of China, Mount Fuji in Japan, Eyre's Rock in Australia, the Mount of Olives, Mount Sinai, and so forth. Sometimes of course these sacred landmarks combine with more direct human creations, such as the holy city of Jerusalem, the sacred shrines of Banaras, or the temple at Bodh Gaya which commemorates the Buddha's Enlightenment.

The material dimension: the Holy city of Banaras. Note that the Hindu temples are overshadowed by a mosque built by Aurangzeb as a sign of the ultimate triumph of Islam.

Uses of the Seven Dimensions

To sum up: we have surveyed briefly the seven dimensions of religion which help to characterize religions as they exist in the world. The point of the list is so that we can give a balanced description of the movements which have animated the human spirit and taken a place in the shaping of society, without neglecting either ideas or practices.

Naturally, there are religious movements or manifestations where one or other of the dimensions is so weak as to be virtually absent: nonliterate small-scale societies do not have much means of expressing the doctrinal dimension; Buddhist modernists, concentrating on meditation, ethics, and philosophy, pay scant regard to the narrative dimension of Buddhism; some newly formed groups may not have evolved anything much in the way of the material dimension. Also there are so many people who are not formally part of any social religious grouping, but have their own particular worldviews and practices, that we can observe in society atoms of religion which do not possess any well-formed social dimension. But of course as a phenomenon within society they reflect certain trends which in a sense form a shadow of the social dimension (just as those who have not yet got themselves a material dimension are nevertheless implicitly storing one up, for with success come buildings and with rituals icons, most likely).

If our seven-dimensional portrait of religions is adequate, then we do not need to worry greatly about further definition of religion. In any case, I shall now turn to a most vital question in understanding the way the world works, namely to the relation between more or less overtly religious systems and those which are commonly called secular: ideologies or worldviews such as scientific humanism, Marxism, existentialism, nationalism, and so on. In examining these worldviews we shall take on some of the discussion about what count as religious questions and themes. It is useful to begin by thinking out whether our seven-dimensional analysis can apply successfully to such secular worldviews.

The Nature of Secular Worldviews

Nationalism

Although nationalism is not strictly speaking a single worldview or even in itself a complete worldview, it is convenient to begin with it. One reason is that it has been such a powerful force in human affairs. Virtually all the land surface of the globe, together with parts of the world's water surface, is now carved up between sovereign states. Nationalism has given decisive shape to the modern world, because its popularity in part stems from the way in which assembling peoples into states has helped with the processes of industrialization and modern bureaucratic organization. Countries such as Britain, France, the United States, Germany, and Italy pioneered the industrial revolution, and the system of national governments spread from western to eastern Europe after World War I and from Europe to Asia, Africa, and elsewhere

A Japanese naval officer indicates his nationalist dedication by wrapping his country's flag around his head before donning his helmet for combat.

after World War II. Ethnic identity was sometimes demarcated by language and therefore cultural heritage, sometimes by religion, sometimes both, and sometimes simply by shared history. Examples of each of these categories can be seen in the cases of Germany (shared language), the two parts of Ireland (distinctive religion), Poland (both distinctive language and religion), and Singapore (shared history of Chinese, Malay, and other linguistic groups). Colonialism often helped to spread nationalism by reaction: the British conquest of India fostered an Indian nationalism, and there are signs of national awakenings in parts of the former Soviet Union, once colonized by Tsarist Russia, and in Tibet, conquered by China.

The nation-state has many of the appurtenances of a religion. First of all (to use the order of the dimensions of religion in the previous section), there are the *rituals* of nationhood: speaking the language itself; the national anthem; the flying and perhaps saluting of the flag; republic and memorial days, and other such festivals and holidays; the appearance of the head of state at solemn occasions; military march-pasts; and so on.

The experiential or *emotional* side of nationalism is indeed powerful – for the sentiments of patriotism, pride in the nation, love of its beauties and powers, and dedication to national goals, can be very strong. Especially in times of national crisis, such as war, such sentiments rise to the surface. But they are reinforced all the time by such practices as singing the national anthem and other patriotic songs.

The *narrative* dimension of nationalism is easily seen, for it lies in the history of the nation, which is taught in the schools of the country, and which in some degree celebrates the values of the great men and women of the nation. History is the narrative that helps to create in the young and in citizens at large a sense of identity, of belonging, of group solidarity.

Of *doctrines* nationalism is somewhat bereft, unless you count the doctrine of self-determination. But often, too, nations appeal to principles animating the modern state, such as the need for democracy and the rights of the individual in a freedom-loving nation, etc.; or a nation may appeal to the doctrine of a full-blown secular ideology, such as Marxism. Or it may hark back to the teachings of its ancestral religion, and so represent itself as guarding the truths and values of Christianity, Buddhism, or a revived Hinduism.

The *ethical* dimension of nationalism consists in those values which are instilled into citizens. Young people are expected to be loyal people, taxpayers, willing to fight if necessary for the country, law-abiding, and good family people (supplying the nation with its population). There is of course a blend between ethical values in general and the particular obligations to one's own kith and kin, one's fellow nationals.

The *social* and *institutional* aspect of the nation-state is of course easily discerned. It culminates in a head of state who has extensive ceremonial functions. The state has its military services, which also perform ceremonial as well as fighting tasks. There are public schools, with the teachers imparting the treasured knowledge and rules of the nation. Even games come to play an institutional role. In some countries loyalty to religion or to a secular ideology blends with loyalty to one's nation, and those who do not subscribe to it are treated as disloyal.

Finally, there is of course much *material* embodiment of the nation in its great buildings and memorials, its flag, its great art, its sacred land, its powerful military hardware.

In all these ways, then, the nation today is like a religion. If you have a relative who has died for a cause, it is most likely that he/she died for his/her country, rather than for a religion.

It is, then, reasonable to treat modern nationalism in the same terms as religion. It represents a set of values often allied with certain essentially modern concerns: the importance of economic development; the merits of technology; the wonders of science; the importance of either socialism or capitalism, or some mixture, in the process of modernization; the need for the state to look after the welfare of its citizens; the importance of universal education; and so on.

There are some growing limitations on nationalism: the fact that in many countries there are now increasing ethnic mixes, the growth of transnational corporations, the developing economic interdependence of nations, the impossibility of older ways of conceiving sovereignty in the context of modern warfare, and so on. But nevertheless, nationalism remains a very strong and alluring ingredient in the world, and many of the trouble spots are so because of unfulfilled ethnic expectations and ethnic rivalries – for example in Sri Lanka, Kurdistan, Afghanistan, and elsewhere.

The Dimensions of Marxism

Although Marxism suffered some staggering blows in 1989, with the crumbling of the regimes in East Germany, Poland, Czechoslovakia, Hungary, Romania, and Bulgaria, not to mention its loss of control in the Soviet Union and Yugoslavia in 1991, it nevertheless has left an important mark on history, and in Asia its powers are still considerable. In China the version known as Maoism, which is basically Marxism as adapted to Chinese conditions, still is the fundamental ideology and practice of the regime – perhaps not in its full form as when Mao Zedong was alive, but at least in a modified way. Forms of Marxism also dominate in North Korea and parts of Southeast Asia.

The *rituals* of Chinese Marxism combine with those of nationalism, celebrating the revival of China in the face of colonial oppression, with parades, the use of the color red (by chance an auspicious color in traditional China), slogans, the deployment of the Red Army on ceremonial occasions, and so on. The *emotions* it encourages are those of patriotism, internationalism, and

A new god: a wall poster in Peking showing Chairman Mao. During the Cultural Revolution the people of China were encouraged to see the Chairman as a super-human figure, and his words in the form of the "Little Red Book" as holy writ.

31

revolutionary commitment. Its *ethics* point to hard work, solidarity, being a good citizen, limiting families for the sake of the state, plain living, and so on. The *institutions* which sustain it are the Party and the Army. Its *philosophy* is that of Marx as modified by Mao (who was somewhat influenced by Taoist ideas). Its *myth* is the heroic story of the Chinese Communist Party and especially the heroic Long March which saved the movement in the 1930s and which made its leaders into military heroes and sufferers for the cause. Its *material* manifestations are seen in socialist realist art, with its pious themes and glorification of the Party, as well as in scenes of pilgrimage such as Tiananmin Square in Beijing (tarnished, however, by the massacre in June 1989) and the caves of Yenan where Mao and his comrades lived after the Long March. The music of the Revolution is military and rousing.

And so Marxism can often take on the form of a religion, which, when combined with patriotism, can be powerful. But it is a militant worldview, which tries to suppress traditional religions. To varying degrees Buddhism, Confucianism, Taoism, Islam, and Christianity, as well as many elements of folk religion, have been submerged in modern China. As it turns out, of course, it is not easy to change human minds, and people go on believing and practicing even under oppression. As the pro-democracy movement of the spring of 1989 demonstrated, the human spirit takes a lot of quenching. Even so, Chinese Marxism still functions as a patriotic and overarching ideology.

The Dimensions of Scientific Humanism

Some other secular worldviews are less clearly like traditional religions in so far as they tend not to wield the symbols of power. For instance, scientific humanism is influential among many intellectuals in the West, and expresses something of the worldview of ordinary folk in secularized circumstances. It holds to human and democratic values, and it stresses science as the source of knowledge. It repudiates the doctrines of religion, especially of Jewish and Christian theism. It sees human individuals as of ultimate value.

Though to a greater or lesser extent our seven-dimensional model may apply to secular worldviews, it is not really appropriate to try to call them religions. For the adherents of Marxism and humanism wish to be seen as very different from those who espouse religions – they conceive of themselves, on the whole, as antireligious. However, we have seen enough of the seven-dimensional character of the secular worldviews (especially nationalism and state Marxism) to emphasize that the various systems of ideas and practices, whether religious or not, are competitors and mutual blenders, and can thus be said to play in the same league. They all help to express the various ways in which human beings conceive of themselves, and act in the world.

Patterns of the Present

Still vitally important and in many ways dominant in our contemporary world is the civilization of the West. The countries of Scandinavia and western Europe are all democratic and capitalist, though with socialist admixtures; and the same can be said of North America and Australasia. These countries have been deeply affected by Christianity and most of all by varieties of Protestantism, from the state-supported types like Lutheranism and Anglicanism to the radical kinds like Anabaptism and the Quaker tradition. But also vital in this bloc is the intellectual rejection of religion among scientific humanists, and in many countries the alienation of the working classes from religion. So we cannot simply call this Western bloc of countries Christian. (In any case there are minority faiths, from Judaism to Hinduism.) But it has had the imprint of Europe's major faith. We can call it the "Transchristian West," meaning that it contains and yet also transcends Christian values. As mother of so much in modern culture and knowledge it remains powerful, despite the end of the colonial period in which so many Western countries carved empires for themselves in Asia, Africa, America, and the Pacific. The first then of our cultural blocs is what I have called the *Transchristian West*.

Another region which overlaps greatly with it in religious and political attitudes is the *Latin South* – namely Latin America from Mexico to the Argentine, and partly embracing the Caribbean. Though it is Catholic like southern Europe, it has not had quite the same experiences, for it was born of the synthesis between Iberian and indigenous cultures, and underwent the colonial period. It thus has a different attitude toward capitalist democracy, and is often suspicious of its northern manifestations.

Another region with strong links to the Transchristian West is what may be called the *Marxist Area*, where an attempt to create a Marxist civilization is in process of collapsing, save perhaps in China and some other parts of Asia. Traditionally in this area, during the post-revolutionary period, religions were suppressed. But the collapse of the eastern European regimes in 1989 has changed this and faiths such as Polish Catholicism are vigorously pursued. Some of the countries are making good progress toward a Western system, but the values of Marxism are by no means extinguished in the former Soviet Union, and have been somewhat reinforced in China after the Tiananmin Square massacre in June 1989. Marxism has also crumbled in some outriding nations such as Ethiopia and Mozambique, but at present remains fast in Cuba.

In South and Southeast Asia various countries have been able to maintain important parts of their traditions and also to incorporate some elements of modern capitalism and democracy – countries such as India, Nepal, Myanmar, Sri Lanka, Thailand. They may have Muslim minorities (very large in the case of India), but they are predominantly non-Muslim in character, maintaining the traditional religions of *Old South Asia*.

To the east is another area where indigenous traditions have maintained themselves, though with infusions of Western ideas and practices. Here we have Japan, South Korea, Taiwan, Hong Kong, and Singapore. They maintain in some degree the three religions of the old China, with that special evolution which is Japanese religion, including indigenous Shinto. They have in recent times had a spectacular economic success. We shall call this bloc *Old East Asia*.

Slicing through the South Asian region is that vast crescent which constitutes the Islamic cultures of the world: Indonesia, Malaysia, Bangladesh, Pakistan, Afghanistan, Iran, Iraq, and so on through the Arab countries to secular (but historically Islamic) Turkey and to the countries of West Africa as far as northern Nigeria. This region contains many smaller countries, and outside it there are further important Islamic populations. We can call it the *Islamic Crescent*.

East of it are the Pacific islands, from huge New Guinea to the Melanesian, Micronesian, and Polynesian groups. Very scattered and not heavily populated, they nevertheless constitute an alternative style. They are in many ways allied to other small-scale societies in the Philippines, Australia (the Aboriginals), North America (Native Americans), and elsewhere. We may refer to these as *Small-Scalers*; and they can be found in all regions of the world. They are important from various points of view, and we may sometimes have to draw attention to their plight amid the large-scale and often cruel forces of the modern world.

Finally, there are the multitudinous variations of Black culture in Africa south of the Sahara (roughly speaking). Here we have complex and differing kinds of classical African religions often in deep interplay with kinds of missionary religions, resulting in a whole flock of new religious movements and forms of independent Churches. This region we can call *Black Africa* (though it also contains that troublesome component, South Africa, with its potent white minority).

These regions – the Transchristian West, the Marxist Area, the Latin South, Old South Asia, Old East Asia, the Islamic Crescent, the Small-Scalers, and Black Africa – together constitute our world. They are woven together by modern communications and are coalescing into a single global economy. It is from this postcolonial perspective that we conceive the present and the past. But in now trying to see the way human spiritual and material history was before our time, we have to shake our heads and rid them of the knowledge we now have: for the civilizations as they grew did so in relative isolation, and they had no advance insight into how human history was to turn out. As the Children of Israel entered the Promised Land they could foresee neither Pilate nor Yasser Arafat; and as artisans produced wondrous figures in the cities of the Indus Valley, they could not foresee the *Gītā* or Gandhi.

So now we turn to look, within this overall pattern of world religions, at the major religious traditions of Asia, beginning with Hinduism and then Buddhism in South Asia.

CHAPTER TWO

The Hindu Tradition

India's Diversity

India is often referred to as a subcontinent. Its area is fairly well defined, because it resulted from the drift of part of the old continent of Gondwana-land northwards, where it slowly but inexorably collided with the southern part of what was then Asia. By consequence the great ranges of the Hima-layas rose up, to form a barrier, scarcely penetrable except to the northwest, which was to enable Indian culture to emerge largely on its own. In thinking about the area we should not be mesmerized by modern political divisions. India, in the historical sense of the term, comprises everything now included in the modern states of Pakistan, India, Bangladesh, Nepal, Bhutan, and Sri Lanka.

Over time, Hinduism has become the main force in Indian life, together with Islam. During the most glorious period of Indian civilization, roughly speaking during the first thousand or more years of the Common Era, there was a mixed Hindu-Buddhist Indic culture, with other smaller religious elements, such as Jainism and, in the far southwest, Christianity, woven into its fabric. This Indic civilization had within it fabulous diversity, made richer by the fact that only at certain periods was India under the domination of a single major empire, and that it was typically fragmented into various states and tribal enclaves. Its diversity partly came from its languages, ranging from the Indo-European tongues of north India (such as Gujerati, Hindi, and Bengali) to the Dravidian languages (Tamil, Telugu, Kannada, Malayalam) of the south. As these languages developed they became vehicles of differing kinds of piety. And beyond the variety of tongues there were differences of climate and terrain, from the mountains and green forests of Sri Lanka and Kerala to the dry deserts of Rajasthan, and from the steamy heat of the monsoons to the colder drizzles and snows of the Himalayan foothills.

Even to talk of a single something called Hinduism can be misleading, because of the great variety of customs, forms of worship, gods, myths,

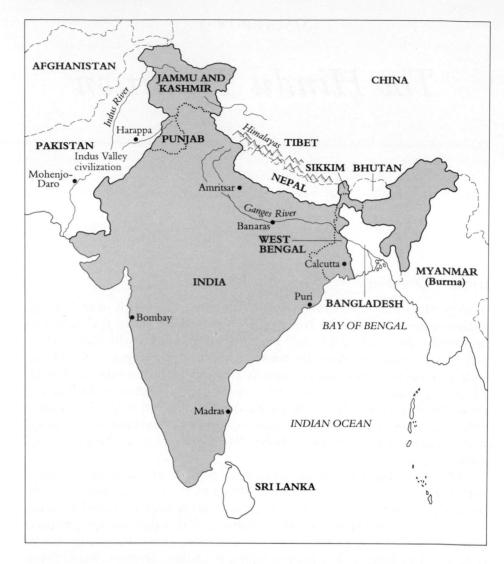

Map showing the
Indian subcontinent.

philosophies, types of ritual, movements, and styles of art and music contained loosely within the bounds of the religion. Some scholars would like to
jettison the term. Yet in modern times there is a much better defined sense
than before of what is in the Hindu tradition. It is as if many Hinduisms had
merged into one. It is now much more like the trunk of a single mighty tree;
but its past is a tangle of most divergent roots.

   In tracing the formation of religious ideas and practices in India, and
particularly those of the Hindu tradition, it is useful to divide the history of
the subcontinent into five periods: early, preclassical, classical, medieval, and
modern. The early period of the Indus Valley civilization and its aftermath
lasted from about 3000 B.C.E. down to the culture reflected in the early sacred
text known as the *Rig Veda*, around 1000 B.C.E.

The next phase, which may be called preclassical, covers the formative and creative recasting and development of worldviews, including the composition of the texts known as Upanishads (800–400 B.C.E.), the teachings of Mahāvīra the Jain (see Chapter 4) and Gautama the Buddha (c. 500 B.C.E., see Chapter 5), and the spread of the religions of the Brahmins, the Buddhists, the Jains, and others. Roughly speaking this is the period of a thousand years from 1000 B.C.E. to near the turn of the millennium (say 100 C.E.).

Then we come to the great classical period of Indic civilization, lasting until about 1000 C.E., which contains the development of most of the patterns of classical Hindu religiosity and the great flourishing and then the decline (in India) of Buddhism. It was a Hindu-Buddhist civilization, with many other motifs woven into it.

Then, from 1000 onward till the dawn of the modern period (roughly 1750), we have the formation of a Hindu and Muslim (see Chapter 7) civilization in the Indian subcontinent: it saw the reign of the great Mughals from Delhi, the consolidation of traditional Hinduism, the final withering of Buddhism in India, the rise of the Sikhs (see Chapter 8), and the attempt by Akbar (ruled 1562–1605) to establish a pluralistic ideology accepting the truth of India's many faiths. This "medieval" period ended with the increased incursions of Europeans, above all the British, who came to dominate the area.

The modern era, after 1750, saw the coming of missionaries, the founding of the British Rāj, and the development of railroads, higher education, modern industry, and a relatively centralized administration. It saw the renewal of Hinduism, Islam, and other religions, and the struggle for independence which ended with the partition of India into the states of India and Pakistan, and the subsequent splitting of Pakistan into (West) Pakistan and Bangladesh. It saw the resurgence of Buddhism in Sri Lanka and the forcible modernization of Tibet by China. Above all it brought a new understanding of Hinduism.

During the various periods there arose empires which sometimes unified most of India and sometimes did not – such as the Indus Valley civilization which lasted till about 1500 B.C.E. in the early period; the Mauryan empire toward the end of the preclassical period, especially under the pro-Buddhist emperor Aśoka (reigned 269–232 B.C.E.); the Gupta and Kushan empires during the classical period; and the Mughal empire during premodern times. Especially during the Gupta period, the spread of Sanskrit culture across the whole of India helped unify the subcontinent.

In all sorts of ways, however, it is not possible to look on South Asia – the Indian subcontinent – as a single unit. Regional empires and monarchies and other groupings were quite as normal as the unitary state.

The Ingredients of Indian Religion

If the history of India and its neighbors up to the modern period has been complex, so have the many doctrines, rituals, experiences, and customs which characterize Indian thinking. To a Western reader in particular, and to many South Asians who have been alienated from their heritage by modern education, they are in part unfamiliar. So it is useful to list some of the main ingredients of religious practices and beliefs during the classical period. A survey of these ingredients will constitute the grammar of Indian religions, just as the gods, holy figures, temples, and statues constitute their vocabulary, and will be followed by discussions in depth of Hinduism in this and the next chapter, and then of Jainism in Chapter 4.

If we were miraculously transported back to the sacred cities along the holy river Ganges during the classical age of Indian culture, we would be struck, doubtless, by the splendor of temples, the variety of human types, from proud Brahmins, with their partly shaved heads, to recluses with matted hair; from women in white, widowed and immersed in piety, to monks and nuns belonging to the Jain and Buddhist orders. Let us analyze the ingredients by reference to our seven dimensions.

Śiva dancing and so signifying the effortless joy of the act of creation.

Of the *ritual* and *practical* dimension, three important elements are: yoga or self-training; worship or *pūjā*; and sacrifice. The first is ancient in the tradition, and forms the basis of an inward search, and a training of the mind, taking somewhat differing forms according to the school or movement to which one belongs. Much later, during the premodern period, it was supplemented by that kind of gymnastics which in this century became popular in the West and which often is identified with yoga, although it is in fact far less significant than the spiritual side. The inward search is to discover the true Self or to attain liberation. It has been one of the main preoccupations of the Indian spiritual tradition.

Worship was in classical India directed toward a large number of gods, of whom Viṣṇu and Śiva emerged as dominant. Buddhist *pūjā* too, in its later stages, embodied fervent devotion or *bhakti* toward the Buddha conceived as a kind of God.

Sacrifices of all sorts existed in earliest India. Later, under the influence of Buddhism and Jainism sacrifice came to be largely confined to plant life and melted butter (ghee) and the like. The people in charge of sacrificial ritual were the Brahmins, who were the highest of the four classes which supplied the skeleton of the later fully elaborated caste system. From their expertise in sacrifices, the Brahmins came to dominate the rituals of temples, which did not exist in the earliest recorded Brahmin religion, i.e. in the Vedas. Temples were houses of the gods, in which their daily life was enacted, and where festivals abounded.

Pilgrimage is a less important element in the ritual dimension, but it was integral to Jainism, Buddhism, and the religion of the Brahmins, taking the faithful to sacred rivers, to holy temples, or the birthplaces of the great. There were treks, too, to the great mountains, to the source of the Ganges, and to the places where holy persons would meditate and practice austerities.

The Sanskrit for austerity is *tapas*, literally "heat," for austere self-mortification creates heat in the body, and with it power. *Tapas* as a practice came to form a vital part of some religious movements, notably Jainism. It is the polar opposite of Tantra, which uses magical and esoteric means of gaining liberation, sometimes through the performance of that which is normally forbidden – extramarital sex, meat-eating, and so forth – to express the ways in which the Tantric adept is above ordinary social laws.

So we can list as important practices, among the welter of Hindu, Buddhist, and other rituals, yoga, worship, sacrifice, pilgrimage, austerity, and Tantra. On the *experiential* and *emotional* level, the spirit behind such ritual practices varied. Poets and others expressed the feelings of devotional religion or *bhakti*, associated both with temple worship and with the fervor of pilgrimages and festivals. Behind yoga there was the spirit of meditation or *dhyāna*, with the hope of inner peace, bliss, insight, and what was called liberation. For the ascetic there was the sense of independence and power, so that the adept frightened the gods, according to myth: for the ascetic would gain more power than they.

The *mythic* dimension of Indian classical culture revolves around a thousand themes. There are millions of gods (traditionally 330 million), but there emerged the famous Hindu trio of Brahmā, Viṣṇu, and Śiva as the most important. Also vital are their female consorts, conceived as personal manifestations of *śakti* or creative force. In Indian civilization the female is thought of as active, the male more as passive. Sometimes, in the religious movement known as Śaktism (from *śakti*), the Supreme Being is conceived as female (Dūrgā or Kālī). Another theme is that of the *avatāra* or human incarnation of God, mostly of Viṣṇu, a theme which plays some part in the vast epics known as the *Mahābhārata* and the *Rāmāyana*. It is thought that the *avatār* figure comes down to restore proper teachings and behavior at the end of a period of decline, a theme which is found in the three major traditions of the Brahmins, Buddhism, and Jainism. In the case of the Buddha, he is not precisely a "descent" of God, but rather a superhuman person who enters the world to restore the Truth to humans.

God is described in numerous narratives as taking many forms, and gradually there grew up the view that the different gods were so many manifestations of the One Divine Being. This idea, first expressed in the *Rig Veda*, was among other things a way of synthesizing the myriad myths.

In all the major systems of belief in Indian culture there prevailed a sense of decline. The present age, or Kaliyuga, latest of the vast and endless cycles of time which go to make up the fabric of human existence, is one of increasing chaos and evil.

These ideas were to be interpreted in terms of the *doctrinal* and *philosophical* themes which characterize classical Indian culture. A pervasive theme is rebirth or reincarnation. Each individual living being traverses virtually endless time through many, many lives. The person's destiny is shaped by the deeds she or he has performed both before and in this life. This "law of *karma*" (action) binds living beings to the round of existence or *saṃsāra*. The desire to leave *saṃsāra*, or at least to overcome its cloying effects, calls for great efforts, which eventually may yield liberation of *mokṣa* when the individual leaves *saṃsāra*, or at least overcomes it by superior insight into the nature of the world.

God as creator is also implicated in the processes of *saṃsāra*: but he or she (or it) is often conceived also as lying beyond all description. This unspeakable Brahman lies beyond even God as she or he appears as a person. So in some philosophies there is that higher side of the Divine which has a correspondence with the inner side of the soul, the eternal *ātman* or Self which lies within every individual. By turning inward and practicing meditation a person may come to experience that inner eternal Self and at the same time achieve unity with the one Divine Being, Brahman. Many forms of belief in India have not accepted the idea of God, and so in them liberation is not communion with God but a lonely disappearance from the round of rebirth.

So there are various dominant doctrines of Indian culture during the classical age: the idea of reincarnation or rebirth, the possibility of ultimate liberation, the idea of a personal God who creates and recreates the cosmos, and for that matter destroys and redestroys it, the notion of an indescribable Brahman lying so to speak beyond the personal God, and the idea of something eternal within the migrating individual. The various philosophies of the Indian tradition are expressed through variations of the ways in which these ideas are put together.

As to the *ethical* dimension the Jain and Buddhist traditions place strong, though differently slanted, emphasis on the practice of non-injury to living beings. This had its effects on the Brahmins, who came to be vegetarian. It was part of an ethos of asceticism which permeated parts of classical Indian civilization. Such "giving up" often took the form of leaving the world to become a monk or nun; but an alternative was the system of four stages of life, which was often held up as the ideal of the pious householder. According to this scheme a man in his early life is a celibate student, learning at the feet of a Brahmin teacher; then he becomes a householder; thirdly, he begins to withdraw from family and public life; and finally he becomes a wandering, homeless recluse, or *sannyāsin*. This allows an ethic of compromise between living in the world and outside society. Increasingly, a person's moral and ritual duties came to be determined by his or her particular circumstances in life.

The pervasive belief in rebirth had its effects of course on the whole interpretation of moral life. It was typically thought in popular Indian traditions that one could improve one's position in life in the future – even to the extent of going to heaven – by accumulating merit. Such merit could be attained by charitable giving (to holy persons and for pious purposes, such as contributing to the beautification of temples); but above all by good deeds.

In brief, from an ethical angle, there are a number of fairly constant elements in Indian civilization: a tendency to respect the sanctity of all forms of life; a sense of the special character of the ascetic life; an emphasis on attaining merit; and the idea that much, in the practical life, depends on a person's place in life.

All this was integrated into the *social* and *institutional* dimension of classical Indian culture, of which the caste system came to be the most striking and pervasive feature. Its skeletal structure was formed during the early days of the Indo-European invasion of India, around 1500 B.C.E. The invaders, like others of the Indo-European linguistic group, were divided into three classes: the priests (Brahmins), the warriors (Kṣatriyas), and the artisans and others who served the top two classes (Vaiśyas). As they conquered the indigenous peoples a fourth class of servants and underlings (Śūdras) was added. Eventually, even further down, a fifth class of "untouchables" came to be recognized. Because Hindu ritual was much concerned with purity, the four- or five-class system itself came to be reinforced by the practical application of the concepts of purity and impurity: the upper-class Indian could be contaminated by contact with those lower down, and especially by the untouchables. This last class came to include a whole variety of tribal peoples who were absorbed into the fabric of the wider society. The first four classes are known

41

as the *varṇas* or (literally) "colors." This name probably derives from racial distinctions, the Indo-European invaders being originally of light complexion. This *varṇa* system was later reinforced and rendered much more complicated by subgroups known as *jātis* ("births" or "lineages").

The vast mosaic known as the caste system represents an elaborate hierarchy into which Indian society is formed; but the Buddhists and others never recognized the system, especially because, when men and women entered the monastic order, the Sangha, they were supposed to leave social distinctions behind them. This Order was, with its Jain counterpart, an important ingredient in Indian society in the classical period. Monasticism had some place in Hinduism also, as in the organization founded by the great reformer Śankara (late eighth century C.E.).

Various other kinds of holy persons were socially important too: the priestly Brahmins, who were highest in the Indian hierarchy; Buddhist and other monks; naked holy men and Jain monks; gurus or teachers of various kinds; *sannyāsins* or recluses of varying persuasions. Animals, too, above all the cow, could be a source of holy power and cleansing efficacy. Yet if many of these figures signified renunciation, erotic acceptance of the world was also part of the fabric of India. The family was a vital center of life and of domestic cults.

On the *material* and *artistic* level, the classical period saw the emergence of that typical feature of the Indian scene, the temple. (In the early period Brahmin religion used only temporary sacred grounds and structures.) As well as the shrines to the many gods, there were Buddhist and Jain temples. There were also sacred rivers, sources of purity and founts of merit; and holy mountains, homes of gods and sacred teachers. In the temples were images and icons, and in houses too there were little shrines. Many images were small and cheap, for the villager or the poor person; and some were made of clay and used temporarily for some great feast in the calendar of Indian religious life. They were "throwaway" sculptures. Perhaps most powerful of all symbols was a stone pillar with a rounded top, the *lingam*. In its simplicity and suggestive strength, it expressed and promised the fertile power of God.

We can schematize all this as follows:

DIMENSION	ITEMS
Ritual, practical	yoga, worship, sacrifice, pilgrimage, austerity, and Tantra
Experiential, emotional	*bhakti, dhyāna*, sense of empowerment
Narrative, mythic	myriad gods, the religious hero who restores the Truth, times in decline
Doctrinal, philosophical	rebirth, possibility of liberation, God as personal, Brahman as nonpersonal, an eternal soul or freedom-seeking nature within each person
Ethical, legal	reverence for animals, ascetic ethos, merit-making, ethics of one's station in life
Social, institutional	caste system, Sangha system, varieties of sacred or holy persons, sacred cow, family
Material, artistic	holy places (mountains and rivers), temples, images, *lingam*

These ingredients, combined in differing ways, represent many of the varieties of Indian religion. It was out of this classical material that the idea of Hinduism as such was composed in the modern, colonial period.

The Early Period

In 1924 there began a series of discoveries which has revealed a remarkable ancient culture, known as the Indus Valley civilization. This great and uniform civilization stretched from Gujarat in the south to the eastern Punjab in the north and from Sind in the west to the edges of Uttar Pradesh in the east. Its chief cities were at Mohenjo-Daro on the Indus and Harappa on the Ravi (or near it, for the riverbed has changed its course). They were rather uniformly laid out in grids of streets, with villas, houses, and small lanes occupying the various blocks; and with a higher acropolis containing what seems to be a temple complex and a granary, dominated by a large tank or bath. An excellent sewage system formed a network that covered the whole of each city. Outside the main walls (designed no doubt to resist flooding) were areas for the farmers and others who supplied services to the merchants and priests who, we may infer, controlled the civilization.

There are affinities to, and there were some contacts with, the Elamite and Sumerian cultures to the west; and from Elam the Indus Valley civilization may have derived its writing system. Alas, this is as yet not deciphered, or at

Mother goddess from the tombs at Mohenjo-Daro. In common with many ancient cultures, the Indus Valley civilization appears to have centered its rituals on the worship of female fertility goddesses.

least not in any agreed manner. The most likely thing is that the language was an early version of Dravidian, and that Dravidian-speakers, probably pastoralists, had moved southwards from Central Asia to the Indus region, where an urban and mercantile civilization had gradually been built up on the basis of villages. The Indus Valley civilization lasted essentially from about 2500 to 1500 B.C.E. It ended rather suddenly, possibly through some great natural disaster combined with conquest by outsiders. Many scholars have held that it was destroyed by the invading Aryans, speaking an Indo-European language, who came into India around 1500 B.C.E.

From the Indus Valley culture we have a wonderful harvest of seals, inscribed clearly with the ideographic script whose decipherment remains controversial. The seals lead us into a world of goddesses, snakes, tigers, water buffaloes, a unicorn, sacred peepul trees, bulls, and elephants. There is a cross-legged figure sometimes thought to be a forerunner of the Hindu god Śiva. The are also small figures of gods and goddesses, sometimes dancing. But what these seals and figurines mean is obscure. There are some mixed animal-human figures, and a wonderful figure of a priest or shaman, perhaps, with a neat beard and a band round his head. Many of these figures are suggestive: they link up with later Dravidian conceptions of a fertility goddess with both benign and fierce attributes. There are suggestions that perhaps sacrifice on the high places in the cities was important. There may have been great processions of the goddess and other deities, and maybe pilgrimages to the mountains from where the inhabitants of the civilization had come. It may be, too, that the figure often identified with Śiva was a fertility god. Perhaps there were myths of the divine couple. The buffalo also seems to have been the consort of the Great Goddess.

We have too little evidence to be sure of anything about the worldview or political structure of this great civilization. We can imagine that once the streets and alleyways of the cities teemed with life, each household no doubt engaging in domestic rites before sculptured figures, and that religious life also involved ablutions and perhaps, among the prosperous, the sacrifice of animals. Out in the surrounding countryside there were wide fields of grain, part of which was tribute to the city granaries. All this is likely to have been organized through religious allegiance rather than force, for we do not, strange to say, find evidence of weapons. On special feast days doubtless the high platforms with their bathing tanks would witness a priesthood skilled in sacrificial ritual, parading before the Goddess from whom the earth and the prosperities of the farming life emanated. From her too, no doubt, came domestic animals, and she gave protection against the tigers and snakes who lived on the earth and on the fringes of the villages.

The Preclassical Period

As time passed, the Dravidians moved south, and in due course made other powerful contributions to Indian religion and culture. The great Indus Valley civilization died. In its place there slowly arose a new mixture, composed of Aryan and various other ingredients. The invaders came from the northwest and settled in the region between the Indus, flowing southwest, and the Ganges going east. Eventually the heartland of this Aryan culture, of which Sanskrit was the sacred and later the literary language, spread down along the Ganges, where, by the sixth century B.C.E., various mercantile cities arose, such as Banaras (or Varanasi) and Pataliputra (modern Patna). Republics and kingdoms were in the making; and in this exciting climate of economic advancement and political consolidation there was a creative welter of religious movements. The Aryan priests, the Brahmins, brought with them a repertory of sacred lore and hymns composed over a period of five hundred years. The ascetic traditions were revitalized in the same period by Mahāvīra and the Buddha; and other worldviews, typically propounded by wandering teachers, contended both with these and with Brahmin orthodoxy. Among these doctrines were materialism, rejecting all ideas of transcendent powers and goals, and skepticism, rejecting all positions.

The Brahmins and Ascetics

Brahmin culture turned out to be the most persistent element in all Indian civilization. The Brahmins, who thought of themselves as animated by the power *brahman*, enjoyed tremendous prestige, and shared preeminence with other sacred persons, collectively known as *śramaṇas* or wandering ascetics. *Śramaṇas* thought of themselves as beyond ordinary social obligations: they had left the world behind. But the Brahmins were necessarily tied to the concerns of ordinary life in a rather direct way: many of them made their living by their expertise in ritual. This ritual, increasingly complicated, could bring for the person who paid for the sacrifice (in cows and other expensive commodities) prosperity and the assurance of worldly success. And the tradition of ritual which they brought with them was derived from the timeless past, from the age of the seers (*ṛṣis*) who heard the ultimate sacred sounds and brought them forth by a creative process to compose the collections of hymns known as the Three Vedas (to which a fourth, magical collection, the *Atharva Veda*, was added in the preclassical period, after 600 B.C.E.). Masters of the holy hymns and the sacred language, skilled in the intricacies and long performance of sacrificial rites, whether for kings and princes or for ordinary householders, the Brahmins were one of the main forces in the creation of Indian religion. So much so indeed that even today what we mean by "Hinduism" is largely their creation: Hindu orthodoxy is defined as the acceptance of the authoritative value of the revelation (*śruti*), which includes the Vedas.

The Early Vedic Period

In voyaging to the ancient past we are necessarily indebted mainly to texts. We have seen how hard it is to interpret the rich archeological findings of the Indus Valley civilization without the benefit of a deciphering of the script. In the case of the early Aryans in India, who infiltrated there in waves during the period from about 1500 B.C.E. onward, having originated (probably) in the region of southern Russia, we have texts which reflect their existence during the period of settlement. There are of course problems, for the texts, orally transmitted over many centuries, were gathered together subsequently for ritual purposes, and not in order to give us an historical record of early times. We have to make inferences from the hymns, and it is not always easy to do so. Imagine trying to reconstruct American or British life from a Catholic hymnbook. We could pick up hints, but often the references to Zion and Calvary would baffle us: were they contemporary references or not?

The hymns look back to a time when the plains of north India were being subdued by those who called themselves Aryans or "Noble People." Arrogant, aggressive, and confident, these folk were able with horses and chariots to conquer the native Dasyus, who were dark people, living in citadels, venerating *lingams*, tied in no doubt to a plethora of rituals to increase their crops and pastoral wealth. Many of them were descendants of those who had once occupied the Indus Valley cities. Much of their lore and elements of their speech were to be incorporated into the traditions and language of the Aryans.

Some of the many gods of the *Rig Veda* reflect the period of aggrandizement. There is the fierce, towering Indra, great warrior leader, incarnated in the thunderstorm and the lightning bolt. Over a quarter of the hymns in the collection are addressed to him. His main function is in leading the warriors, the Kṣatriya class, the second of the fourfold list of Vedic society. Not only does he fight human enemies but also the wicked demons, the antigods, who support them. But Indra is also in some sense creator, for in primordial times he prized apart heaven and earth, and freed from a cave the cows imprisoned there, the main symbol of Aryan wealth. In his creative act he discovered the Sun, which brings light and vision to all creatures.

Indra in his violence and creativity – and his exuberance, too, in drinking great drafts of the sacred and hallucinogenic drink of *soma* – gives us a feel for the rough warriors who led the migrations out of the plains southward and westward in search of new pasturelands and places to conquer. He hints at the ethos of the distant past, before the Aryans had settled in and become integrated into the landscape of north India, with its warm and rich forests, its cleared areas for cultivation, its expanding villages, and its cities in the making.

Indra's parting of the sky and earth sets the scene for conflicts between good and evil gods. The latter are often associated with human enemies; but even the divine Vedic world itself is riven with conflict, so that there are strains between a number of the mighty forces which are envisioned in the hymns. Even sacrifice, the central ritual, is seen as a mode of conflict: sacrificial rituals often incorporated contests of riddles and chariot races, as if inner combats were continuous with the ongoing struggle between the mobile horsemen of the Aryans and the settled culture of the despoiled indigenous inhabitants.

If Indra is rambunctious and somewhat chaotic, the god Varuṇa is, much of the time, the model of order. He presides over the orderliness of the cosmos, summed up as *ṛta*, an idea somewhat like the later Hindu concept of *dharma* as the sacred pattern underlying both cosmic and social life. He displaces Dyaus the old sky-god, who is the Vedic counterpart of the Greek Zeus and the Roman Jupiter. Varuṇa rules the heavens and especially the night sky, where the stars are perceived as his innumerable eyes. And so it is that he knows everything. He is the moral judge, since he knows all the secrets of human beings, and with his companion, Mitra, he presides over promises and contracts. He upholds truth. But he has dark and earthly associations too, and these become more vital in the later mythology of the classical period.

An important ritual god, personifying the phenomenon that is central to sacrifice, is Agni, god of fire. As the representative of earthly fire, Agni is the lowest of a threesome that also includes atmospheric fire or lightning (Indra) and the heavenly fire of the Sun (Surya). Alternatively, he may be identified with the fiery aspect of all three. By a splendid act of imagination, the people who defined their society through the Vedic hymns saw the continuity between the three levels of heaven, atmosphere, and earth. A night storm, especially in the warm climate of India, is terrifying; and earthly fire can be unpredictable and hard to maintain, especially when people are on the move.

Fire is important sacrificially in many cultures. The reason is that it performs at least two functions: it consumes or transforms that which is offered; and it wafts the offering upward to the gods, conceived as being "up there." When a person offers that which is valuable, it is important that he or she gives it away: it has to leave his or her zone and enter the god's zone. This is done by the smoke of offerings burnt as sacrifice. Already something is done, of course, in the case of animals; their life is destroyed, for instance by the letting of blood.

In the sacrifice, fire is created by one stick twirling in a hole in another. The sexual symbolism of this act – phallus in vagina – likens the making of fire to the stimulating of fertility in animals and human beings. In many ways fire is crucial to cosmic processes, but above all it is the consumer and conveyor of what is sacrificed, whether it be the horses of the ancient kingly sacrifices or the ghee and milk poured out daily in domestic rituals. It is the necessary adjunct of the long and complex Brahmin-controlled sacrifices that are made to bring prosperity. So it is not surprising that Agni the fire-god appears so frequently in the Vedic hymns.

Another important god in Vedic times, who later faded in actual religious practice, was Soma, god of the intoxicating juice that was prepared and consumed as part of the ritual. It stimulated visions, and it may be that some of the imagery of the hymns comes from the contents of such visions.

By comparison the gods who are so great later – Viṣṇu and Śiva – were minor. But Viṣṇu's importance is foreshadowed in the myth in which he takes three steps across the universe, establishing its bounds; the last step is indeed beyond human ken, for it paces out heaven. Those who reenact this creative act in ritual attain to a mastery of the cosmos. His companion Rudra, the Red One, is uncontrolled fire, dwelling in mountains and jungles, wild. Later he is to become the great god Śiva.

The hymns indicate that within the framework of a given celebration many of the gods – the more important ones described above, as well as others – were regarded as supreme. It is like a painting: the perspective and the frame isolate the painting from all others. So in a given hymn the given god is God. This has been called henotheism, from the Greek, meaning "one-God-at-a-time-ism." It is one way of combining a kind of theism or belief in God with the existence of different cults of gods; and it has been a characteristic of Indian religion since these early times.

The hymns of the *Rig Veda* and the other collections do not yield enough information for us to trace anything of the history of the early period, or indeed of anything before about 600 B.C.E. Their importance is less as historical data than as sacred texts, which came to be part of the later canonical revelation. Though there are continuities between the hymns and the more developed classical religion of India, there were also considerable transformations, which were brought about by the Brahmins' seeking control over, and being influenced by, non-Aryan forces in Indian society which brought with them new religious ideas. It was a series of blends between the Vedic tradition and such forces which prepared the way for the creation of classical Hinduism. But already the hymns prepared the way for Hindu monism and theism. For instance the famous hymn (*Rig Veda* X.129, verse 2) says:

Death then existed not nor life immortal;
Of neither night nor day was any token;
By its inherent force the One breathed windless.
No other thing than that beyond existed.

A New Beginning

In the hundred years or so around 500 B.C.E., a whole new range of ideas and practices became important. Principal among them was the idea of *saṃsāra*, the cycle of rebirth, which led to a quest for liberation through the practice of austerity or meditation or both. To be saved we need to wipe out the effects of our past actions or *karma*. It was this set of beliefs that formed the background of many of the new religious movements; and it was a set of ideas that penetrated into Brahmin religion as a new and great secret, in the teachings of the speculative texts known as the Upanishads.

Brahmanism, or the Religion of the Upanishads

To the east of the main Aryan area, the new religious revival represented by Buddhism, Jainism, and other movements was a challenge from a region where Brahmin control and presence were less fully felt. There was in Brahmin life a certain dilemma. The reason why Brahmins were in demand from kings and wealthy folk was their expertise in ritual: that implied secrecy. On the other hand, their doctrines needed to develop in debate with outsiders, such as these sophisticated new movements. They were scarcely in a position to speak too openly, beyond instructing those members of the community who belonged to the upper three classes (priests, warriors, and artisans): the "twice-born" who were born again through an initiation with the sacred thread and the status of full-fledged Aryans.

In some measure Brahmin ideas were opened up through the composition of the texts known as Upanishads. The principal ones were composed perhaps between 800 and 400 B.C.E., and in parallel with some of the new ideas prevalent in the śramanic movements. These works, partly verse and partly prose, were attached to the growing corpus of works in turn affixed to the Vedic hymn collections, and known as Brāhmaṇas and Āraṇyakas (Holy and Forest Treatises). The Upanishads are concerned essentially with the meaning of the sacrificial rites, and in the process they introduce profound metaphysical and religious ideas.

When we refer to "the Upanishads" we mean those original ones which form part of the revealed corpus of the Veda. In fact, Upanishads as a kind of literature continued to be composed right down to the sixteenth century. The term means "Secret Teachings," and it is assumed that they originated in oral interpretations of the sacred tradition imparted by gurus within the context of initiation.

The central concept in the Upanishads is that of *brahman*. This is sacred or divine power operative in the sacrifice and indeed within the Brahmin class

Brahmins reciting a fire ritual to ensure good harvest.

itself. What power? The new insight of these texts is that the whole cosmos is as it were a sacrifice, and *brahman* is the holy power which informs and animates the whole of reality. Consequently the word came to be used as a name of the divine Ultimate, or of God, and is commonly written in English with a capital, as Brahman. No longer was the sacred expertise of the Brahmins seen as something restricted to the operations of sacred liturgy. It was now seen in principle as knowledge about the whole universe. Some of the Upanishads see Brahman as a personal Lord or Īśvara, as in the *Īśa Upaniṣad*. Sometimes it is seen as without personal qualities, but lying "beyond" qualities and the reach of speech. Much of later Indian philosophizing concerns the question as to whether the Ultimate is personal or nonpersonal. Sometimes it is seen as both: nonpersonal in its own nature, but personal in relation to the universe and creatures.

Into the sacred world of Brahman and the Brahmin ideology there penetrated that other complex of ideas which I have called śramanic: ideas of reincarnation, liberation, yoga, and *tapas*. So many times we hear in ancient texts of Brahmins and *śramaṇas* as coupled together: they were the two classes of holy persons in the society of the sixth and fifth centuries B.C.E. It is not surprising that the Brahmins made a move toward synthesis. The results of such a move are to be found in the Upanishads.

First, there is presented as a new and secret teaching the idea of rebirth – or redeath as it is more grimly called – that the individual who has not gained the Ultimate will be subjected to repeated death.

Second, in the Upanishads we find the remarkable act of identification in which the inner, yogic quest is coupled by implication to the rituals of sacrifice through which Brahmins tried to control cosmic events. This act of identification is to say that Brahman is the same as the *ātman* or eternal Self which lies within the person. As the formula which is used has it, "That art

---

Īśa Upaniṣad

By the Lord all this universe must be enveloped,
Whatever moving thing there is in this moving world.
Renounce this and you may enjoy existence.
Do not covet anyone's wealth.
Even while doing deeds here
One may wish to live a hundred years;
Thus on thee – this is how it is –
The deed adheres, not on the person.

Those worlds are named after the antigods
Which are covered over by blind darkness.
Those people who kill the Self
Go to them, on descending.

Unmoving, the One is swifter than the mind.
The senses do not reach it, as it hurries on before.
Running past others. It goes, while standing still.
In it Mātariśvān places activity.

It moves, it moves not;
It is far and it is near;
It is within this universe
And it is outside of all this.

Now he who looks on all things
As in the Self, and on the Self
As in all beings – he
Does not shrink away from Him.

---

thou": in other words, that Ultimate Being out there, which lies behind and pervades the visible world as its ground and creator, is the same as that eternal something within you.

So the two paths, of ritual action and inner self-control, converge. The Upanishads, moreover, stress the unity of the world and with it the sacred Lord who controls it. But the many gods of the Vedic tradition are not simply swept aside: they are so many refractions of the One. The texts also make use of ideas which were later or at about the same time worked up into the philosophical system known as Sāṃkhya, which was closely associated with the practice of yoga and the Hindu tradition of thought known as Yoga Philosophy. Though yoga in the general sense crosses the boundaries of tradition, a particular formulation of its philosophy came to be accepted as orthodox and Hindu; and it was this system which coalesced in the medieval period with Sāṃkhya.

Sāṃkhya thought had affinities with the śramanic systems. It saw the world in terms of a unitary cosmos, known as *prakṛti* or nature, and many souls wandering through transmigration and so impaled on suffering. There was no God as such in this viewpoint, but the Upanishads saw the quest for liberation in terms of the attainment of unity with or close communion with the One Holy Power of Brahman.

If the central ritual idea of Brahmanism was *yajña* or sacrifice, the central idea of the inner quest was that of direct experience through meditation. A third ingredient can be seen glimmering through the texts. The beginnings of devotion are to be seen as directed toward a supreme Lord. This motif was to be taken up much more powerfully later on in the Indian traditions, both Buddhist and Hindu, as *bhakti*. The reliance on the Lord also foreshadows the message of the *Bhagavadgītā*. And so the main themes of the Hindu tradition are perceived at least in principle.

In the *Īśa Upaniṣad* ("Secret Teaching of the Lord") there is a famous vision of the cosmic Lord standing outside the cosmos, and a vision of the One somehow within us. The question which was later to exercise thinkers was whether Brahman and soul are strictly identical, in which case we all share the one Self, and the fact that we seem to be many individuals rests on an illusion; or whether we have separate selves which the one Lord indwells. But we still have some way to go from the Upanishads to classical Hinduism.

Classical Hinduism: its Main Shape

Devotion

Various forces were coalescing to provide a shape for the heterogeneous religions over which the Brahmins came to prevail. The cult of gods and goddesses, probably always important inside the home, began to acquire more public form. Perhaps in part under the stimulus of Buddhism, the Hindu temple came to play a leading role in Indian life. It provided a focus for ceremonial and a place for meeting with the great and lesser gods. The

(*left*) A typical
southern gopuram or
temple tower
decorated with the
gods, near
Kanchipuram.

(*right*) The descent
from heaven to earth
of the river Ganges,
with various mythic
figures, at
Mahabalipuram in
Tamil Nadu, South
India.

Brahmanical heritage in the old days had been without such icons and build-ings. The place of sacrifice had to be laid out, constructed, as befitted an originally nomadic way of life. There was no necessity that Brahmins should be involved in the *pūjā* of the temple; but it was an advantage to the priestly class that it should control so potent a means of focusing the people's piety and impulses to giving. So images and temples were the outer manifestation of a wider role for priests in the developing Hindu society.

This was a symptom of the growing importance not just of worship but more particularly that fervent sharing in the life of the God known as *bhakti* religion. Its features are already portrayed in one book of the great epic *Mahābhārata*, known as the Song of the Lord or *Bhagavadgītā*. This was composed possibly as early as 300 B.C.E. It has in it – as the most famed of India's philosophers, Sánkara, said – the essence of the Vedas. Its popularity gave it immense influence, and it inspired many imitations on behalf of Śiva and other gods. It came to be recognized as part of the sacred tradition or *smṛti*, which continues the more strictly authoritative *śruti* or revelation, con-sisting of the Vedic hymns and appended works down to the main classical Upanishads; in fact, in its conditioning of Indian religion, the *Gītā* is actually more influential than the Vedic hymn collections.

In the *Bhagavadgītā*, Viṣṇu as Lord and numinous creator of the universe reveals himself as also loving. His avatar Kṛṣṇa declares at the end: "Those

Hinduism some key terms

Arca Image which is occupied by a god once it is consecrated.

Ātman The Self of an individual which is eternal and in Advaita Vedānta is regarded as identical with Brahman (see below).

Avatāra Descent or incarnation of God (notably Viṣṇu) in such figures as Rāma, Kṛṣṇa, and the future Kālī.

Bhakti Warm devotion to God.

Brahman The sacred Power which is both in the sacrifical process and in the cosmos: hence the term is used of the Divine Being.

Dharma The pattern underlying the cosmos and manifest in the ethical and social laws of humankind.

Īśvara The Lord, that is, God considered as a person and (typically) as creator.

Jāti Caste, a group with whom the individual identifies in marriage and in eating: the fabric of *jātis* makes up the caste system.

Karma The law which governs the effects of deeds both in this life and in subsequent lives within the operation of rebirth or reincarnation.

Pūjā Worship.

Sannyāsin Holy person who has left ordinary duties as determined by *dharma* and *jāti* behind, often as a wanderer.

Yoga Methods of meditation, sometimes involving physical as well as mental discipline.

who worship me with complete discipline and who contemplate me, whose thoughts are constantly on me – these I soon raise up from the sea of death and rebirth." Arjuna, awaiting battle against his relatives, is given a firmer mind after his confusions and despair about the dread effects of battling against his kith and kin. There are many riches in the *Gītā* ("Song"), as it is often called for short; but the central value is that of loyalty and devotion to God, namely *bhakti*.

Viṣṇu, with his incarnations, and Śiva, great Yogin and destroyer of the world, stimulator of the divine *śakti* or power, emerge during this time as the twin great manifestations of the divine Being. They displace some of the older deities important in the Vedic scriptures. Followers of Viṣṇu were called *Vaiṣṇavas* and of Śiva were called *Śaivas* and included the important movements of Kashmiri and Tamil Śaivism. They are enclosed together in the world of traditional religion (*smārta*) as both rivals and cooperators. Viṣṇu is gentler, and much concerned with the periodic restoration of the Dharma through sending down his incarnations, of whom Rāma and Kṛṣṇa are the

A youthful Kṛṣṇa plays his flute to various women, symbolizing the souls of his devotees, near Brindaban.

two most important – Rāma the ideal king, Kṛṣṇa the glorious lover. Śiva is more numinous, wrathful, and destructive, but potent through yoga, and indissolubly linked to the Goddess.

The third main divinity of later Hinduism, the Goddess, was beginning to emerge into general recognition by the fourth century C.E., in such texts as the *Devīmāhātmyam*. She was always there, of course: already in the Indus Valley civilization, and in the villages and undercurrents of life below the surface of the rather macho society of the Vedic hymns; and in the many myths of the consorts of the gods, above all of the great Gods. In Tantric Hinduism she was destined to flower further. But we may say that for much of the Hindu tradition the three great deities are Śiva, Viṣṇu, and the Goddess, under her various names such as Dūrgā, Kālī, and Parvatī.

Below the ultimate Gods are the many deities of the incredibly rich narrative corpus of the Hindus: the two vast epics; the *Harivaṃśa* (about Kṛṣṇa); the *Purāṇas*, and the oral traditions of the various regions of the subcontinent.

Philosophies
Behind the stories were erected the philosophies, above all those systems of belief known as Vedānta, which contains several great variations. There is the

doctrine of the aphoristic scripture known as the *Brahmasūtra*, which sets forth Vedānta, "The End or Final Part of the Veda." Its doctrine is probably a version of that system known as Bhedābhedavāda or "Difference-in-Nondifference": Brahman is both different from and not different from the world and souls. The most influential in modern times has been the Advaita, or Nondualistic Vedānta, of Śankara (eighth century C.E.) and his later followers, which sets forth the identity of the soul and Brahman, and the illusoriness, therefore, of the world as multiplicity. There was in the eleventh century the *bhakti*-oriented theism of Rāmānuja's Viśiṣṭādvaita or Qualified Nondualism, which sees the world and souls as God's body and instruments of his will. In the thirteenth century there was Madhva's Dvaita or Dualism, in which an eternal difference between soul and soul, soul and world, soul and Brahman, the world and Brahman is affirmed, again a kind of theism. These philosophies underpinned spiritual practice: Śankara could only assign *bhakti* to second place, as something fit for the unenlightened person still mired in the world of magical illusion (*māyā*). Mystical intuition of identity with the One is the fruit of the higher path.

The mythic dimension: an 8th-century Pala bronze of Viṣṇu.

Commonly these philosophies are held to conduce to liberation or *mokṣa*, which was the last of the four ends of life laid down in classical Hinduism – the others being *kāma*, pleasure (sex being the most intense of the pleasures, the word also stands for this as in the famous *Kāmasūtra*), *artha* or economic gain, and *dharma*, virtue or action in accord with the Dharma. This last was summed up in the law books of Manu, which set down the varieties of duties of Hindus within the structure of the caste system.

Social Existence in the Classical Period

In the early classical period it was thought necessary to fight the challenge posed to orthodoxy by Buddhism and the other śramanic movements. There was evolved the theory of the four stages of life or *varṇāśramadharma*: student, householder, parent of adult son, ascetic; and Hinduism developed its own monastic orders, one of which was founded by Śankara.

Classical Hinduism saw the increasing articulation of the caste system. Caste groups married within each group, and ate only with that group. These practices of endogamy and commensality were the framework for various castes based upon occupation, traditional god, region, and history. The framework of the four *varṇas* was filled in with a vast mosaic of more refined distinctions, in a social hierarchy topped by the Brahmins and undergirded by the "fifth class" or untouchables, whose occupations were specially polluting (leather work, butchering, brewing, cleaning latrines, fishing, etc.).

And so during the Gupta period, a most florid episode in Indian history, from the fourth to the sixth centuries C.E., we can imagine the glories and complexities of classical Hinduism – the temples, the great rivers, the pilgrims, the parades of gods, the recitations of the epics, the fervor of *bhakti*, the wandering *sannyasins*, the yogins in meditation, the pandits exploring metaphysics, the elaboration of caste, the sacrifices for princes and emperors, the chanting of vastly ancient verses, the household rites, the pomp of weddings, the countless villages, the wandering of sacred cows, the smell of cowdung burning, the hovels of untouchables, the pride of Brahmins, the rites of the Goddess, the lingam of Śiva, the tales of Kṛṣṇa – a great amalgam which yet through the Brahmins had a loose orthodoxy. Hinduism by now had a loose federal existence through the idea that those who accepted the *śruti*, whatever else they did not accept – God, Viṣṇu, *karma*, rebirth, virtue – accepted the primordial authority of the Veda, coeval with time.

And in our mental picture of the times we should recall too, mingled in with the Hindu conglomeration, the shaven-headed monks and nuns of the Buddhists, the various ascetics, the angular temples of the Jaina tradition, the *stūpas* and Bo trees of Buddhist compounds, the cells of monks, the flags of unorthodox festivities, the Buddha statues and the Jātaka tales, the moral discourses, the huge scriptures, the *bhakti* to Amitābha, the giving of protective spells, wives who followed the wise teachings of the Buddha, households of Jains gentle toward animals and insects – in short the whole mingling of the unorthodox traditions with the religion where the Brahmins held sway. India then was a glorious jumble of customs and beliefs, as indeed it is to a lesser extent today.

The Goddess and Hindu Tantra

Though the roots of the worship of the Goddess go right back to the Indus Valley civilization, it was in the late classical and medieval periods that it achieved a central importance in the Indian tradition. It was especially important in the northeast, in Bengal and Assam; but everywhere in India, scattered through villages and in domestic rites, there were varieties of goddesses, who came to be seen as diverse manifestations of one Goddess, who represents the creative power or *śakti* of the Ultimate. There is of course no reason in doctrine why we should think of God as female or as male, since she/he is neither, strictly. It is only human imagery that needs to make the decision. But there are powerful connections with the idea of the Supreme Female, with the earth as being our Mother, with fertility, with motherly love, with falling in love. A devotee could see the Goddess under so many disguises, as provider of food, as great creatrix of the world, as object of affection and devotion, as lover of my soul, as all-devouring Time or Death, as bringer of smallpox and cholera, and so on.

Śaktism could be connected in practice with Hindu Tantra. The main ideas behind this magico-spiritual outlook have been in part touched upon in regard to Buddhist Tantra: but in the Hindu context it especially is expressed through the idea of harnessing magical and spiritual energy – the *śakti* which the female both personifies and wields. Another motif is secrecy, mimicking the restrictions which apply to Vedic knowledge, but here devoted to keeping apart the techniques and initiations of those adept in harnessing the energy. Like a number of other religious movements, Tantrism broke down caste barriers, as it indeed could violate other taboos.

The ritual and mythic dimension: the personification of the River Ganga, a notable object of pilgrimage and personification.

Regional Movements

In examining the varieties of Hinduism in the medieval epoch I shall be necessarily selective, and shall choose four from differing regions: Śrī Vaiṣṇavism from Tamil Nadu; the Lingayats of south central India; Kashmiri Śaivism from the far north; and the Caitanya tradition from the northeast.

Śrī Vaiṣṇavism and Tamil Poetry

The greatest thinker in the Vaiṣṇava tradition was undoubtedly Rāmānuja, who lived around 1000 C.E. His great synthesis reconciled the Tamil Vaiṣṇava and Vedānta traditions. His motives were not primarily philosophical but religious. He found the Nondualism (Advaita) of Śankara to be a great danger, mainly because with its theory of levels of truth and reality it assigned the Lord, and the worship of the Lord, on the lower level, below the mystical intuition of Oneness. It cut at the root of devotional religion. It also cut at the root of sacrifical Brahmin practice; but that was less serious. Rāmānuja wished to express a fervid devotion to the Lord which at the same time could be seen as a good interpretation of the *śruti* or revealed truth of the Hindu faith, notably as expressed in the Upanishads and the *Brahmasūtra*, and as shown forth in the *Gītā*, which was the jewel of *smṛti* or holy memory.

57

For five centuries the great poets of Tamil Nadu had been composing sacred songs to both Viṣṇu and Śiva. These poets were known as the Ālvārs (Vaiṣṇavas) and the Nayanars (Śaivas). Twelve Ālvār poets are found in the tenth-century collection known as "The Four Thousand Divine Verses." The works of the sixty-three Nayanars, of whom the most important was Mānik-kavāsahar, were incorporated in the Śaiva canon (*Āgamas*) which provided an alternative to the Veda (sometimes it was called a fifth Veda) for the followers of the Tamil movement known as Śaiva Siddhānta.

After Rāmānuja, Śrī Vaiṣṇavism became a very powerful force in the south, splitting into two schools, based on Sanskrit and Tamil scriptures and sources respectively, and holding different views on the subject of God's grace. Both stressed that salvation from the ocean of rebirth flows from God's love; the debate centered on the interpretation of this – whether the devotee has to do nothing, like the kitten being transported by the scruff of its neck by its mother, or to reach out, as the little monkey uses its arms to cling to its mother – but the essence of the faith was loving devotion to and reliance upon the Lord. The Lord's mythic deeds and goodness were to be celebrated in song, in the rites of clothing and feeding him (present in his image), and in pilgrimage to the sacred sites commemorating his glory. Socially, Śrī Vaiṣṇa-vism was egalitarian before the Lord. Since it is not by works that you are saved, your status – arrived at through *karma* – does not matter. Thus, as elsewhere, *bhakti* could be a protest against the hierarchical nature of Indian society. The *bhaktas* or devotees of south India picked up some of the ethos of Buddhism and Jainism which they had done so much, by their fervid missionary spirit, to phase out.

Rāmānuja thought of the cosmos and the souls which transmigrated within it as being God's body. By "body" he meant that which subserves a soul. God, being perfect, perfectly controls his body; we do so with ours only imperfectly. He guides us also from within each individual soul as the *antaryā-min* or "inner controller." *Karma* is merely the working out of God's will; and if we call on God in faith we shall be rewarded by being born in God's glorious heaven, close to him. By the metaphor of the body Rāmānuja preserves the sense of intimate unity between God and the world, as expressed in the Upanishads themselves.

The Lingāyata Contrast

Lingāyata was founded in the twelfth century by an intellectual and reformer called Bāsava. Its other name is Vīraśaiva or heroic Śaivism. It has a certain austerity, deriving ultimately from the Jain tradition. The Lingāyats are called "*lingam*-carriers," the meaning of their name, because each person is supposed to carry a small phallic symbol in a tube fastened round the neck or to the arm, and this is virtually the sole icon in their faith. It is useless to go on pilgrimage or worship in temples or perform any other ritual actions, and for the major part of life the sole practice enjoined by Bāsava was the reverencing of the *lingam*, symbol of Śiva, twice a day. Some other rites and the use of holy water, ashes, rosaries, and so on also came into Lingāyata practice, which concentrates in other respects on the paying of homage to Śiva, through the formula *Namaḥ Śivāya*, and the inner recollection of the God.

Striking features of Lingāyata are its rejection of the caste system, its condemnation of child marriage, and its proclamation of the equality of the sexes. Though it has a hereditary priesthood of its own, it avoids all the ritual of the Brahmins, and in some respects seems a protest against Brahmin domination. Though it rejected caste at the outset, the inevitable of course happened: it was itself treated by the other castes as a caste. There is little escaping the embracing arms of the system in Hindu India. The ethics of Lingayata are those of equality and humility, as befits those who follow the great God. Honesty and hard work in one's daily occupation were deemed important; and in some ways the group seems like a Hindu counterpart of Protestant Christianity.

Kashmiri Śaivism: a Synthesis

Very different in emphasis from the two regional movements we have looked at is the so-called Trika (Triad) Śaivism of Kashmir, which started as a Tantric movement directed at absorbing and utilizing the energy of a three-

Śiva and his Śakti: a concrete illustration of God and his (female) creative power. Their ritual act of intercourse is considered as a means of attaining the highest state of interior knowledge and a union between the exterior and interior worlds.

59

The mythic dimension: a statue of Kṛṣṇa in the Belur Temple, Mysore State. Kṛṣṇa is most often shown drawing humans towards the Divine Principle through the power of love, symbolized by the power of his flute.

some or triad of goddesses, later seen as three manifestations of Śiva's powerful consort Kālī (probably the most potent of all Indian representations of the Goddess). The movement had its base primarily in Kashmir; and its chief exponent and theologian was the philosopher Abhinavagupta (975?–1035?). He wrote important works on aesthetics, partly because the rites of this kind of Śaivism emphasized dance, song, and poetry. Abhinavagupta argued against various positions, though he was sympathetic to their general sense, such as Śaiva Siddhānta (the theology of south Indian Śaivism), the Yogācāra school of Buddhism, and Advaita Vedānta. In combining elements from the orthodox tradition of Śankara and the unorthodox Tantric Śaivism, which involved sexual intercourse as a means of attaining the highest state of interior bliss and knowledge, he claimed to teach the most catholic of Śaiva doctrines and practices. He saw the world as a triadic unity between the individual, the divine Śakti or Goddess, and Śiva as the underlying being behind the Goddess. This "new triad" was intended to give a positive view of the notion of nondualism: the nondual experience could be had in ecstatic participation in the world, and not (as with Śankara) by some kind of withdrawal to a higher level of Truth.

Kṛṣṇa Devotion and Caitanya

Late in the premodern period of Hinduism, in the sixteenth century, we have in Bengal and elsewhere in the northeast (Orissa and Assam) the revival of an intense form of Kṛṣṇa devotion and Vaiṣṇava *bhakti* through the life and work of Caitanya. At the age of twenty-two, while on pilgrimage to Bodh-Gaya to perform rites for the death of his first wife, Caitanya had an intense conversion to loyalty and love toward Kṛṣṇa. He changed his name to Kṛṣṇa-Caitanya ("he whose consciousness is Kṛṣṇa" – hence his modern followers refer to their movement as "Krishna Consciousness"). The chief practice of devotees, whether they be mendicants or householders – and the movement made powerful headway among the middle classes – was the utterance of Kṛṣṇa's name, calling on him for divine mercy. Love of Kṛṣṇa was often modeled after the loves that Kṛṣṇa himself had with the milkmaids of Brindavan or with his divine mistress Rādhā. Separation from him was pain, and the individual *bhakta* clung to Kṛṣṇa with passion. Persons were, as elsewhere in the main Hindu tradition, caught up in a cycle of rebirth; but by God's grace and mercy they would be delivered and restored to communion with Viṣṇu, from whom, like sparks, they had originally emanated. In this latter age, the Kaliyuga, it is not easy at all for people to undertake religious duties: it is fortunate that God in his love makes salvation available to those who throw themselves upon him in faith and love.

CHAPTER THREE

Modern Hinduism

The Modern Period

In this chapter we take the story of Hinduism onward beyond medieval times, through the momentous events of European conquest and the successful struggle for independence, culminating in the establishment of the Republic of India in 1947 and the evolution of a powerful Indian presence in the dynamics of South Asia. The whole period saw the renaissance of Hinduism into a much more unified and self-conscious religion than it had been. Important expressions of the new spirit also intertwined with the growth of Indian nationalism. The material culture of the region was heavily influenced, through the extensive railway system built during the late nineteenth century and in various other ways, by British domination.

This major conquest was foreshadowed by earlier operations of the Portuguese, Dutch, and French. It was the aftermath of the Seven Years War (1756–63) – when the British defeated France – that brought British domination of Ceylon [Sri Lanka: since "Ceylon" was the name most used during the colonial period, and until 1972, I shall use it in discussing the developments of this period] and India [again, at this time the term covered the whole subcontinent, and this is how we shall use it for events up to 1947]. It was a novel experience, historically speaking, for India, which had hitherto always been invaded from the northwest. It was also novel because the nation that came to conquer was already undergoing various industrial, social, and political changes which were to have their echoes in India and Ceylon. How could these old civilizations respond to the challenges of an emerging modern world? The matter was complicated by the very heterogeneous character of India and Ceylon themselves at this time.

The Islamic impact on India had been great, but by the time of the major British advances it was in severe decline. It was said that the power of the great Mughal, whose seat was in Delhi, only reached as far as Palam, where Delhi airport now stands. In the latter part of the eighteenth century there

61

were various powers in India – the Maratha Confederacy dominating central India, the state of Mysore and a number of smaller kingdoms in the south, the remains of the Mughal empire, the rising Sikhs in the Punjab, and many other principalities. It was not yet a unified land. Differences of language, religion, and interest left it largely divided as the British extended their control. By 1805 the Mughal emperor had come formally under the control and protection of the conquering power. Much of the Ganges river area was under the British, who ruled out of Calcutta. The east coast was conquered, and so was a large part of the south. The British had taken the island of Ceylon from the Dutch, except for the kingdom of Kandy in the central mountains (it fell in 1815). The various areas controlled by the British, however, still displayed great religious variety. In many areas Islam was the dominant religion; in most of the rest, that undeveloped federation of rituals and beliefs which we now know as Hinduism; and in Ceylon Buddhism predominated. Christianity was beginning to capitalize on colonial rule. The Sikhs were breaking away to form a new political power and, in effect, a separate religion.

British Influences

With the defeat of the Sikhs in 1849 and the occupation of Sind, the mosaic of British rule in India was complete. However, in 1857 a rebellion by Indian soldiers, disturbed at rumors that the grease used for gun cartridges contained beef and pork fat, offending religious susceptibilities, spread into a wider revolt. This in a sense was an early war of liberation, though rather blind, since there were no clear ideological goals. It was fiercely crushed, and in 1858 the old administration by the East India Company – originally a purely commercial enterprise – ended. In 1871 the empire of India, with the Queen as empress, was instituted.

This system was a kind of unity, and brought the whole of India under an aegis that was interested in modernizing and unifying the country. Under the East India Company, missionaries were long excluded from Company territory, since commercial interests did not like the prospect of upsetting the inhabitants. But from 1820 onward mission activity in British territories began. Before that – apart from the old Catholic missions under such workers as the highly original Roberto de Nobili (1610–56 in India), who adopted Brahmin ways and Indian philosophical concepts in expounding the Christian religion – there had been the highly successful work of establishing a college and missionary center in Serampore, which was a Danish enclave, and in one or two other places.

In the early British mission period the evangelical Christian critique of Hindu customs was strong, and led to the government's suppressing suttee, namely the practice wherein a widow followed her husband on the funeral pyre. It was partly because of such incursions on tradition, and out of a desire to restore the old order, that the Indian Mutiny, so called by the British, occurred. But after 1858 there were plenty of modernizations and critiques of tradition – railways, a whole system of higher education, new commerce, agricultural changes, English as the language of government, and so on. It was these changes which led to various responses on the part of the Indian religious traditions.

The forces which the British Rāj brought with it can be systematized as follows, particularly as they bore upon the developing Indian middle class which was at the interface between the cultures.

First, there was mainly evangelical Christianity, confident in the superiority of Western culture, and often believing that modernization and Christianity would go together. It was critical of what it saw as Islam's social backwardness and Hindu idolatry and harmful customs (e.g. child marriage, caste, and temple prostitution).

Second, there was the more secular ethos of imperial administrators, heavily influenced by the utilitarianism of Jeremy Bentham (1748–1832) and John Stuart Mill (1806–73), which held that the rational basis of ethics and law is the maximizing of happiness and the minimizing of suffering. Such administrators did not shrink from social and administrative reform.

Third, there was the force of capitalism, which demanded a railway network (a major creation), but also ruined indigenous industries such as cloth-making in favor of the cotton mills of Lancashire: but it was a force which, with imperialism, was creating a global system of economics, and from that no country could escape.

Fourth, there was the force of nationalism, which in Britain's case held to the superiority of Western Christian civilization and in particular that of Britain: it was self-righteous and confident, and epitomized in the attitude of the historian Lord Macaulay (1800–59), who advised higher education for India because then the follies of Asian thinking would be left behind. But of course nationalism is generated by an opposing nationalism, and for the first time, from the 1860s onward, India began to experience a sense of India as a people.

Fifth, there was the force through which many of these others were to be conveyed and implemented: education, and in particular higher education, whereby a new English-speaking elite was fashioned was to be the main impetus toward change. Colleges and universities were set up in various centers: Bombay, Madras, Calcutta, Delhi, and the princely states. Education was encouraged by missionaries, many of whom devoted their lives to it, feeling that by some osmosis Christianity would rub off on the new elite.

Sixth, lying behind education was the force and prestige of science. It could be seen that a new scientific worldview had contributed to the technical powers of British and Western civilization, which had such important economic and military effects.

First Stirrings of Hindu Response: the Brahmo Samāj

Bengal was the center of the East India Company's power, and it was there that the first consciously reforming movement within the Hindu framework started, led by Ram Mohan Roy (1772–1833). He had been educated in the

Muslim center at Patna on the Ganges, and had then undertaken Sanskrit studies. He then learned English, and gained a job with the Company in 1803. In 1804 he published a book in Persian, which criticized the polytheistic aspects of the Hindu tradition. His exposure to Islam here allied itself to his attraction to eighteenth-century rationalism. His translations of five main Upanishads into English were designed to show that the Hindu tradition had as its true focus the one Reality, Brahman. He published, too, in 1820 a book called *The Precepts of Jesus* which argued that Jesus taught a vigorous ethical way of life, which need not be overlaid by the complexities of myth and doctrine which the Christians had added to the original message. In brief, he expounded a Hindu unitarianism, espousing belief in one God, and was iconoclastic about the many images and rites presided over by the priesthood.

Roy founded the Brahmo Samāj or Divine Society, which carried forward, through other leaders such as Debendranath Tagore (1817–1905) and Keshab Chandra Sen (1838–84), the message of social reform from a Hindu perspective. He also played a part in the agitation which led to the abolition of suttee in 1829. He was influenced by Unitarian missionaries in Calcutta, but was keen to express what he himself could take to be an essentially Hindu worldview. This he found in his unitarian interpretation of the Upanishads. Smitten by a disease when visiting England, he died in Bristol in 1833.

His movement was of profound importance in pioneering a new view of the Hindu tradition from the perspective of a class of upwardly mobile caste Hindus. These were not of the upper echelons of the Brahmins, whose concern was too much with ritual purity, but lower-class Brahmins, merchants, landowners, and others, who stood to benefit by the replacement of Muslim power and culture by the British. The ultimate problem for the Brahmo Samāj was that its "rationality" and purism in belief would cut it off from the mass of Hindus.

There is of course more than a hint in Ram Mohan Roy of the transcendent unity of universalist traditions (Muslim, Hindu, and Christian), and this cross-religious unity was ultimately destined to be a most vital factor in the formation of a modern Hindu ideology. As far as the forces sketched above are concerned, the Brahmo worldview could cope well. It was able to make a reply to evangelical Christianity in its purity and even faithfulness to the original message of Jesus (naturally such a "reduction" of Christianity greatly infuriated the missionaries in Calcutta). It was adapted to social reform and a new economics. It was compatible with the new English education. It had not yet developed a nationalism, which was yet to come: it was early days for Indians to think of themselves as unified. But it appealed to Bengalis, who had their own national sentiments.

Dayānanda Sarasvatī and Hindu Fundamentalism
Brahmo Samāj also had some influence on a Gujarati guru whose movement was to have wider influence: Dayānanda Sarasvatī (1824–83), founder of the Ārya Samāj ("The Noble Society" or "Aryan Society"). His reform ideas

went even further back than the Upanishads, to the rishis (*ṛṣis*) of the Vedic hymns.

Born in Kathiawar in western India, Dayānanda left home to become a wandering recluse: into this mode of life as a *sannyāsin* he was ordained in 1847. For a while he studied with a famous grammarian of the old style in Mathura in north India. The pundit held that the only true texts were the ancient ones of the seers, and that much later Hindu philosophy and theology was false and sectarian. Dayānanda came to attack Hindu image worship: but it was not until he visited the Brahmo Samāj that he saw the value of modern methods of propagating his message. Debating in Sanskrit was not the way.

In 1875 he founded the Ārya Samāj, and two years later the movement took off when he gained the support of merchants and others who wanted arguments to stave off Christian attacks on the Hindu tradition. The message was radical, in that so much of the Hindu tradition, including the rights of Brahmins, was renounced. Dayānanda held that the only true scriptures were the Vedic hymns: even the Brāhmaṇas and Upanishads were to be abandoned as later accretions. The germ of modern science was to be found in the Vedic hymns (such items as atomic theory), and their main teaching was pure monotheism.

The rituals of the Ārya Samāj – their worship of the one God – were open to all, and could be conducted by anyone; women and outcastes could study the scriptures. It was thus a radically egalitarian movement, with some feeling of nationalism, not yet however fully developed. It happens that the Ārya Samāj made great headway among overseas Hindus of the Indian diaspora, in such places as South Africa and Fiji, where Indian laborers had been transported on contracts known as indentures (so that they were called "indentured laborers," after the abolition of the slave trade) to work mainly in the sugar plantations.

But because the Ārya Samāj was so strong a reforming movement it became rather cut off from the mainstream of the Hindu tradition. It became, if you like, a sect within the wider confederacy of Hindu religions. In response to Christianity and to the dominance of Western civilization, something more forceful was needed, which would mobilize and reform the Hindu way of life. It would have to make sense of the mass of Hindu practice and at the same time provide new growing points in the intellectual and nationalistic life. For one thing, the Ārya Samāj's extreme scriptural fundamentalism excised too much of Hindu learning; for another its iconoclasm was unacceptable to a great many Hindus, fond of their myths and festivals, and less in revolt against the Brahmins than against too much foreign influence.

It may, however, be useful to pause here to consider the strategies of response to foreign criticism and reform. If you want to remain somehow true to your tradition, and yet you wish to or need to effect reforms within it, you can base your reform on some element in the past, for instance you can reach back right to what you conceive to be the very beginning of your tradition. Such a reaching back to foundations is better called "neofoundationalism" than "fundamentalism," and can, while appearing to be very conservative, be remarkably radical. In the case of the Ārya Samāj, virtually everything was changed – ritual, ethics, doctrine, myth, social organization, material focus.

There can, though, be other models. You may wish to repudiate some features of your tradition in the name of establishing some golden past that may be later than the scriptures. If it be the classical age of your culture, you could call such a reforming move "neoclassicism." It was this reaching into the classical past, and then interpreting it in modern terms, that turned out to be the most successful way of coping with the challenge of the West, in both India and Sri Lanka. In these various ways to hold on to tradition while making the adaptations necessary to survive vigorously in the modern world, part of the question was how much of the existing tradition it was necessary to sacrifice. The more one can retain, the more satisfactory the adjustment will seem.

In fact the Ārya Samāj, though using more up-to-date methods of evangelism, still did not come to terms fully with modern science and education. Modern scholarship had already turned its attention, of course, to India's past, including its scriptures. The neofoundationalist approach of the Ārya Samāj had less appeal to those who knew something of liberal scholarship. Its position about the Vedic hymns was not easy to sustain. Moreover, Dayānanda Sarasvatī, through no fault of his own, did not understand well the nature of modern scientific method. To hold that the scriptures contain the gist of modern scientific knowledge is to miss the point of the dialectical, critical character of the development of science. Nevertheless, his movement was about to continue and to expand because he devolved responsibility to branches, and gave expression to practical democracy.

There was another factor at work, which militated rather against the hard line of the Ārya Samāj. That factor was the coexistence of different religions in India. From the perspective of Indian nationalism, now growing with greater self-consciousness, some view of Hinduism which could make sense of the other religious traditions could be important and attractive.

Ramakrishna, Vivekānanda, and the Modern Hindu Ideology

It was indeed such a pluralist perspective which made itself felt through the life of Ramakrishna (1834–86) and the missionary work of Swami Vivekānanda (1863–1902). Vivekānanda can be said to be the chief spokesperson for the modern Hindu ideology. This drew on the resources of the classical age in the shape of the Vedāntin philosopher and religious reformer Śankara, and through a modern interpretation of his thought presented a picture of the Hindu tradition that seemed to make marvelous sense of it, and also of the other religions. It also made wonderful sense of the great sweep of Indian culture, and offered a potential framework for expressing Indian nationalism.

A statue of Ramakrishna in a Ramakrishna Vedanta temple.

It was, moreover, an ideology well able to cope with the various forces mentioned earlier. It could also help to resolve a question of the times: whether the only way forward was violent revolution, as some held; or whether there could be some evolution which would allow India to develop its own form of democracy. The issue of violence was taken up, of course, by Gandhi, and the democratic impulse was developed further by his great political ally, Jawaharlal Nehru. To these figures we shall of course return.

The alliance between the sainthood of Ramakrishna and the sophisticated teachings of Vivekananda gave a kind of dual status to the new ideology – it could appeal both to the masses, for whom the figure of the Kālī-worshiping guru was familiar, and the middle classes, to whom the English-educated Vivekānanda could write appealingly. It paralleled the later alliance of the archetypal Gandhi and the sophisticated Nehru.

Ramakrishna (his religious name: he was born Gadadhar Chatterji) came from a Brahmin Vaiṣṇava family in rural Bengal. After the death of his father, he went to Calcutta to assist his brother, who was running a new temple to Kālī, which also had shrines to Śiva and to Rādhā and Kṛṣṇa: it thus effectively contained the main strands of Bengali and Indian *bhakti*. After his brother's death, Ramakrishna became priest of the Mother (Kālī) and became absorbed in ecstasies relating to her. He felt himself mad with Kālī, but a wandering ascetic woman, skilled in Tantra, came to the temple and put him through a long course of Tantra which moderated his *bhakti* and turned his ecstatic experiences into more playful and manageable forms. Still later an Advaita Vedāntin ascetic came there, one Totapuri. Ramakrishna took up the practice of nondual meditation and achieved the highest state, regarded as liberating, in which even the Mother and God as personal entities disappeared. Ramakrishna also experimented with meditating on Allah and Christ, and claimed that his intense visions of God in following these paths were of like character to his Hindu experiences. This convinced him of the ultimate unity of all religions.

Despite all this inwardness, Ramakrishna was a teacher of some popular appeal, speaking in vivid images and stories and parables. He attracted attention among the middle classes of Calcutta too, and among those who were toying with Western religion in order to "modernize." Ramakrishna recalled some of the strength of the Hindu heritage, especially its experiential dimension. Among these folk coming to the half-mad religious genius of the Kālī temple in Dakshineshvar was young Narendranath Datta, of the *kāyastha* caste (originally *śudra*, but upwardly mobile and part of the gentlefolk, or *bhadraloka*, of Bengal). This young man was impressed enough himself to become a renunciant, under the name of Vivekānanda, but only after completing college and after his father's death. Ramakrishna saw in him a person of great power and destiny.

It happened that Vivekānanda was a member of the Brahmo Samāj, and he found Ramakrishna's image-laden earthiness a problem, but he held him as his guru and prepared himself spiritually up to the time of Ramakrishna's death, after which he helped to continue Ramakrishna's message. During an extensive pilgrimage which he made through the length and breadth of India he came to evolve the main tenor of his philosophy. This was to have a profound impact because he was able to visit Chicago for the World Parliament of Religions in 1893, where he made his reputation and eventually returned to India a famous man. In 1895 he founded the Vedānta Society in New York, now seeing his mission as worldwide, and in India in 1897 he started the Ramakrishna Mission, with an order of monks as a modern group to teach social reform, perform works of education and social service, and preach a universal Hinduism.

Basically Vivekānanda's views were as follows. The Divine exists at two levels. At the higher level it is without qualities; it is not to be described. But in the nondual meditative experience it can be known: indeed, one knows the Divine from within, for one is divine. This realization dispels any illusions we may have about the world. But at a lower level God has qualities and takes on form: she is Kālī or he is Śiva or Viṣṇu . . . or Ramakrishna. Humans experience God in these various images, and they become the recipients of devotion or *bhakti*. All the religions have the divine at the core, but they present God in differing images. The Hindu heritage is the one which has seen most clearly that the various names of the Real are just that, different labels. World religions could work together if only they took this positive path of seeing the different myths and doctrines as providing the guidelines for paths which all lead to the One. Within each one of us there resides the divine, since we can achieve nondual union with it. So humanity is itself divine. Once we see the divine in one another, it will promote an ethic of love and social concern.

This ideology presented Hinduism not as a backward religion but at the forefront. It was the rather benighted Christian who tended to ascribe absolute truth to his or her own faith and complete error to alternatives. It was the forward-looking Hindu who saw his or her own pluralistic faith as a foreshadowing of the emerging World Religion. Vivekānanda's neo-Vedānta also made sense of Hinduism for perhaps the first time. Now Hindus could explain the unity of their own baffling, diverse religion or religions. It could be said that now Hinduism truly came into existence, or at least into self-conscious integrity. This was why Vivekānanda's message became so immediately popular with the English-speaking elite. And it did so without taking a superior line about the imagery and icons of village and popular Hinduism. It might be that the person who venerates a snake has a rather limited view of the divine, but he is on his way, and may in due course rise to the heights of nondual awareness where all differences are put on one side. So Vivekānanda first of all dealt effectively with the Christian challenge.

Next, as to utilitarianism and social reform, he could claim, too, to be a humanist concerned about human happiness: but happiness has to be seen in depth. It is not enough to equate it with fun and pleasure. You must be true to human nature, and human nature is divine. And of course we need to take seriously the needs of individuals, and it is for this reason that the Ramakrishna Mission engaged itself in social action. As for the new global awareness brought on by the capitalist system, Vivekānanda himself was living testimony to it by going to the World Fair in Chicago; and what he preached there was a religion for the whole of humanity, a new global religion but at the same time a very ancient one. From the gleaming insights of the rishis you could draw light for the modern and future world. As for nationalism, Vivekānanda's ideology was perfect for India: it could unite all Indians, Muslims, Jains, Parsees, Christians, as well as Hindus. It expressed pride in India, for its vast cultural achievements, and it could do all this in ways that were not necessarily chauvinist. With Vivekānanda, Indian national self-consciousness came of age.

The ideology also fitted higher education. The philosophy which was taught in colleges in his day was neo-Hegelianism, following some of the British developments of Hegel's ideas. It was very similar to the philosophy of Śankara, and so it was easy to combine the two. The logical positivist and empiricist revolution was yet to come. It was therefore not difficult to harmonize the thought of East and West. Moreover, it was clear to those who went into these matters that Indian philosophy itself was highly sophisticated, and had much to offer those who wished to have greater understanding of the relation of science and religion. As for science, the scientifically educated person should have no great problem with Vivekānanda's philosophy. There could not be any clash between physics and biology on the one hand and belief in God on the other, since the Divine in itself was inexpressible, utterly transcending thought but not experience. The experience of religion was also empirical. It was not just uncritically accepted dogma. Moreover, the Hindu tradition was not plagued, as was Biblical Christianity, with the problem of evolution: Sāṃkhya philosophy, indeed, laid out an evolutionary scheme. Not only this, but historical enquiries into the sacred texts did not invalidate their central meaning. They were like fingers pointing to the moon, and the moon is the nondual experience of the Divine Being.

Though Śankara's philosophy provided the underpinning, it was in fact adapted by Vivekānanda, and also by later exponents of the modern Hindu ideology. The main problem with the original Advaita Vedānta philosophy was that it stated that this world – indeed everything other than Brahman, the indescribable Absolute – is an illusion (*māyā*). This doctrine was scarcely designed to stimulate social and political action. The teaching about *māyā* was therefore played down – with some justification, in the sense that Śankara's reason for taking this world as illusion was that it was not eternal. Nothing which is not eternal is fully real, from a spiritual point of view. But it is not of course literally the case that what is impermanent is unreal. Anyway, the new prophets of Indian nationalism and of the unity of religions took a positive view of this world. From this they could indeed turn to the teachings of the *Gītā*, and the notion that one should serve the Divine through the path or discipline of works or action (*karmayoga*). This stress on *karmayoga* was something which Gandhi would also draw from his beloved scripture.

Although Vivekānanda's own message and mission were channeled through the Ramakrishna movement which he founded, his appeal was much wider, and the general kind of position which he expressed became the regular middle-class view about Hinduism and religions. The dividing line between piety and patriotism could easily be blurred. The national hymn became *Bande Mataram*, a Bengali hymn addressed to the Mother (Kālī); and India itself was figured as a Mother. The geographical limits of India were more consciously in people's minds, too. Vivekānanda, among other things, had initiated the building of a temple on a tiny island just off the coast at Cape Comorin (Kanyakumārin) at the tip of India. It was a recognition of the unity of India: this was not – as earlier Bengali pilgrims might have thought – a foreign country (Kerala, speaking Malayalam). Others before had made similar journeys; but the temple expresses national sentiment, not just piety. So later leaders, while not accepting all or part of Vivekānanda's teachings – men such as Nehru, who was an agnostic – were still impressed with his position. And modern ideas of Hinduism flow as much from him as from any other interpreter in relatively recent times.

Hinduism as a single all-India system had been invented: and not just the Hinduism of the sacred books and philosophies (for the Upanishads were fairly far removed from ordinary practice), but a Hinduism that embraced all its florid aspects – images, processions, pilgrimages, temples, fasts, holy men, bathing, ashes, caste, and all: for Vivekānanda had struck upon a fine way of justifying the whole ritual dimension of Hinduism, save perhaps those aspects which tied in with social discriminations. All rituals were imperfect responses to an only fragmentarily seen divine Reality.

The Dimensions of Modern Hinduism

If we look to the middle-class expression of the Hindu tradition in this century, what does it look like from the perspective of the various dimensions?

The Doctrinal Dimension

First, in doctrine, we have noted that a predominant place has been given to Śankara's philosophy: equally important ones such as that of Rāmānuja have been comparatively neglected, at least in public rhetoric. They were supposed to have been taken care of under the synthesizing umbrella of nondualism. The doctrines of rebirth and *karma* as the working out of the effects of your actions in other lives were still affirmed; but small problems were beginning to arise about how such a belief blended with modern biology, e.g. genetics. If I owe my characteristics to my two parents, how is there a place for a third force (the effects of previous actions)? The most canvassed response was: my soul homes in on my parents in order to have the proper effect of previous lives. A good soul will home in on holy and prosperous parents, a bad one on disaster-prone parents. So it turns out in India that, though there is little problem about belief in God, there may be growing doubts about rebirth.

The Mythical Dimension

In regard to the mythic or narrative dimension, much that was there simply stays in place in the modern ideology. Stories of the gods, especially of the great incarnations of Viṣṇu, are edifying. It was noted that the importance of sexual themes contrasts with the very inhibited views of nineteenth- and twentieth-century Britons. However, a new puritanism had spread, especially among the educated elite. Stricter emotional controls on sex were more important as higher education stretched beyond youth into early womanhood and early manhood, particularly in a country where marriages tended to be dictated by families and within the framework of the caste system. Indians tend to defend such a system as producing better relationships than the unstable Western ethos of love-marriages.

As Indian contributions to civilization and modern thought became more openly expressed on the world scene, so there was a recognition of some kind of destiny in history which India had: perhaps to teach the materialist West some of the spiritual ideas and techniques and values which she could draw from her long history. Among the heroes of this new destiny was Vivekānanda: but there were to be others, notably Mahātma Gandhi.

The Ethical Dimension

As to ethics and social life, Vivekānanda appreciated the need for change and modernization of attitudes. Caste was a sensitive issue: mostly it was defended as a system for the division of labor which had alas been turned into a hereditary affair, and hedged round by unnecessary religious scruples. It was Gandhi who was to do most on this front. Already some changes had come about socially. The most pure castes, who worried most about contamination and pollution from others, did not do so well as others under the new system, where contact with the British and with other castes in offices and on railways became closer. But the hardest aspect to change was in regard to intermarriage.

The Ritual Dimension

Regarding ritual life, the modern era has produced changes, but largely through nonideological forces. The railway and then the bus network has greatly increased pilgrimages and put heavy pressure on centers such as Banaras. But the general principle of the modern Hindu ideology was to leave as much in place as possible.

The Emotional and Experiential Dimension

Regarding emotion and experience, the modern period saw the growth of national sentiment, as we have seen. Sometimes such feelings found outlets in extreme political pro-Hindu organizations which interpreted the Hindu tradition in a much less pacifist sense than Vivekānanda, Gandhi, and others: for instance the R. S. S. (Rastriya Svayamsevak Sangh), founded in Maharashtra by Dr. K. B. Hedgewar (1889–1940), which combines revived Hinduism with military exercises (Sanskrit and arms drill) and has a dedicated celibate leadership with wide influence in youth organizations.

However, Vivekānanda and others have stressed the importance of inner spiritual experience, which has always been more important ultimately than patriotic feelings, and which realizes a person's true divinity. This aspect of modern universalist Hinduism was taken up by a number of Western writers, notably Aldous Huxley. The wide diffusion of Śankara's ideas in the West tends to cause more emphasis to be placed on this liberating experience than the actualities of Hindu life would dictate, for in India *bhakti* and the adoration of a personal God mythologized in various ways is much more dominant. Still, Hindu yoga was new to the West, and it was something which India could offer as central to its culture, to which the Indians, both Hindus and Buddhists, had devoted much effort in the past, and which might be illuminating for the West. This sometimes reinforced an often expressed opinion among modern Hindus that India has an essentially spiritual culture, while the West has slipped into a crass materialism.

The Social Dimension

From the point of view of social organization, the modern period has seen some erosion of the position of Brahmins. This was partly because it became common to translate Hindu scriptures and to preserve them in books rather than to rely on the sacred memory of trained Brahmins and the haunting tones of chanted sounds. The new middle class might itself importantly contain Brahmins, but many others besides, and the new knowledge was

The material dimension: the contemporary Hindu artist Venkapathy uses themes from Hindu mythology in a modern idiom. Here the traditional threefold form of Siva (Trimurti) is shown trampling on an enemy, the demon of ignorance.

from a foreign source and different from the traditional authoritative sources of Hindu sacred knowledge. Also, some of the revivalist movements were anti-Brahmin. In the old days it was maybe the Brahmins with their Sanskrit knowledge who had cast a net of cultural unity over the subcontinent; but now there were stronger bonds – the railways, the British Rāj, the English language. Indeed, the whole status of Sanskrit was in doubt. What part would it play in a modern India? The fact was that the influential books written in India in the late nineteenth and early twentieth centuries were all in English. For these reasons there was some disturbance of the social hierarchy. But caste has remained a powerful force, hard to deal with, for any revolt against caste still simply produces a new one.

The Material Dimension

As to the material side of Hindu life, there is not much to say in regard to the modern Hindu revival. Craftsmanship of the old kind in fashioning temples and statues is doubtless on the decline. But there has been no absence of pious people to put up temples and monuments that help to celebrate the new India. We have noted for instance Vivekānanda's temple at Cape Comorin. After his time we would have to note developments such as the mythological movie – long translations into film form of the great epics – and new styles of the printing of holy pictures and so on. But the material things that the new ideology celebrated were the great shrines and carvings of the past, which testified to the grandeur and strength of Indian society.

The Early Twentieth Century

Gandhi: a New Force in Hindu Response

If there was a criticism that could be made of the modern Hindu ideology it was that it could be left at the theoretical level. But with M. K. (Mahātma) Gandhi (1869–1948) we meet someone who solidly combined practical and theoretical ideas. He was raised in Kathiawar, and had close contacts with both Hindus and non-Hindus. His mother's religion was a kind of evangelical devotionalism, within the *bhakti* tradition, somewhat influenced by Islam. The area he came from was one of the main Jain regions, and he was influenced by the Jain ideal of nonviolence.

At the age of nineteen he went to London to study law, and there came into contact with the Theosophical movement, which combined Eastern motifs with a concern for comparative religion. Annie Besant (1847–1933), a leading Theosophist, was to play a notable part in Indian nationalist politics. He also was in touch with followers of Tolstoy. After his return to India he practiced law unsuccessfully in Bombay before being offered a job in Durban, Natal, South Africa. He went there in 1893 (a significant year, since it was also the date of Vivekānanda's trip to Chicago).

Gandhi worked for twenty-one years in South Africa, until 1915. It was in South Africa that he worked out the methods of nonviolent political resistance which he was to use to good effect against the British in India. It was in South Africa too that he took on the garb and mien of a saintly holy man. But he was not a recluse: he was always in the thick of events. What he did in effect was to give the old Jain and Indian idea of *ahiṃsā* (nonviolence) a political context and meaning. He also gave the notion of renunciation a new social context. The main point of his practices of austerity and simplification of life was to prepare himself spiritually for the struggle against oppression and injustice. The most important single thing that he taught was that our motives in such struggle must be pure. It is no use being outwardly nonviolent if you hate your enemy in your heart. In this he was influenced by the Christianity of the Gospels: "Love your enemies" became for him a prime precept.

In principle the line which he took on religion and religions was very like that of Vivekānanda, but it was stated imprecisely. He made much use of the word Truth (*satyam* in Sanskrit), and for him Truth was God and God was Truth. His method of passive resistance he called *satyagraham*, or holding fast to truth.

In his prayer meetings, Gandhi used devotional prayers and hymns, including Christian ones. Thus in *practice* he held to some view about the unity of religions; but he did not wish to spell out a highly systemized philosophy or

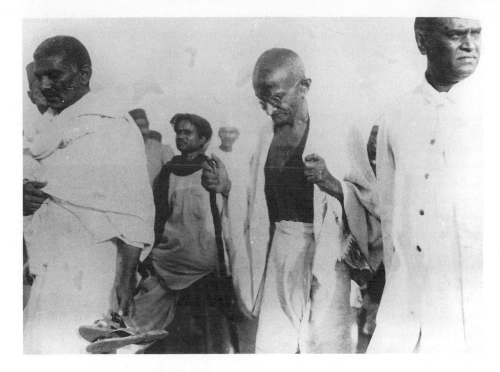

The ethical dimension: Mahatma Gandhi gave a new ethical and political value to the principle of non-violence, characteristic of the Jain, Buddhist and, to some extent the Hindu traditions.

set of *doctrines*. Nor did he make much of the *narrative* and *ritual* dimensions of religion. Yet he was very observant of his own rules of abstinence, in order to train himself better. The main locus of his action was at the *ethical* and *social* level, and he was less interested in the formalities of religion. But he was undoubtedly influenced by the monastic ideal, both Indian and Christian (in South Africa he was in touch with Trappists). His ashrams or communities were a creative adaptation of the Indian model to the purposes of the modern struggle. Round him he gathered dedicated followers who helped him organize his boycotts and strikes and other forms of action.

He struggled initially for the rights of Indian workers in South Africa. These workers had been brought mainly to work the sugar plantations, being reckoned more amenable to that kind of work than the local Africans. Gandhi set up two ashrams, one called Phoenix near Durban, the other Tolstoy Farm near Johannesburg.

Because of the publicity from his leadership of the Indians in South Africa he was already famous when he got back to India in 1915, where he joined the nationalist movement now burgeoning during World War I. It was in 1919, after the war in which Indian troops had loyally fought, that a most dis-illusioning event occurred for those who counted on British gratitude. In the Jallianwalla Bagh in Amritsar, in the Punjab, a British general fired on a crowd causing great bloodshed. An official enquiry was held, but General Dyer went unpunished. The Rāj was nervous. This helped to spark Gandhi's first great noncooperation campaign, a year later. At this time Gandhi was cooperating with the Islamic *khilafat* movement, arguing that Muslims should get autonomy because they owed allegiance to the Caliph in Istanbul. However, the Caliphate was abolished by the Turks in 1924. The Muslims of India were to follow a different vision.

Gandhi, in and out of jail between the wars, conducting fasts, marching to the sea against the Salt Tax, meeting with viceroys, managing to be the leading voice in the Congress movement, was a major factor in the struggle for independence, which ended – successfully in one way, and unsuccessfully in another – in 1947. A socialist government in London had decreed the end of the Indian empire. But the Muslim alternative vision meant that India was to be divided, and it was a division that sparked massacres by Muslims of Hindus and by Hindus of Muslims, along the troubled borderlands of the new states and far beyond. The population, the heat, the poverty, the multiplication of rumours – these things make India volatile at the best of times.

This end to the national struggle deeply upset Gandhi, who, however, immediately set about trying to bring peace to the troubled areas. It was his concern that Hindus should respect Muslims that attracted criticism from fiercer nationalists, one of whom gunned him down at a prayer meeting in Delhi in 1948. But Gandhi with his spiritual power, his wiliness, his humor, and his kindliness was to influence many others, including Martin Luther King. There are many Christians who look to his example (maybe asking themselves the question of how it came to be that the best "Christian" in this century, as some think, had to be a Hindu). He represents the practical poise of the new Hindu ideology.

India since Partition: Some Trends

The principles of pluralism were built into the Republic of India's constitution. India became a secular state, in the sense that there was a separation between religions and the state (the only exception being a clause about cow-protection among its guiding principles). It was important to achieve some kind of political balance, so a Muslim and a Sikh as well as Hindus have been president (a largely ceremonial office, but important symbolically).

One of the presidents, in office from 1962 to 1967, was Sarvepalli Radhakrishnan (1888–1975), who had been at the forefront of popularizing Indian philosophy in the West, and in working out a coherent account of what I have called the modern Hindu ideology. He stressed the importance of work in the world, and criticized the view that an idealist view of life is detached from the processes of this world. In this he modified some versions of Advaita Vedānta. He was also influenced by south Indian Vaiṣṇavism. He was critical of Western scientific materialism in so far as it left no space for the intuitions and experiences of religion.

Independent India reformed women's law in the traditional Hindu context, but was less bold in relating to Muslim law. There were other social changes, including the attempt to moderate the impact of untouchability by using various forms of what in the United States came to be called "affirmative

श्रीरामजानकीरथ

श्रीराम जन्मभूमि मुक्तियज्ञ

Hindu political revivalism: an estimated 100,000 Hindus marched in Lucknow, capital of Uttar Pradesh state, in 1984, and staged a rally to demand the return of a temple converted to a mosque 400 years ago.

action." The impact of rapid modernization in various sectors was to expand the Indian middle classes, and some of the religious movements which began to have an impact in the West had their impact too among Indians. It was, from the 1960s on, a favorable period for the export of Indian gurus, yoga, and objects of devotion. With the spread of a greater prosperity through the Green Revolution, industrialization, and other factors (though poverty was desperate too), access to travel increased the popularity of a whole number of pilgrimage centers and intensified religious worship throughout India.

While the Vivekānanda-Radhakrishnan style of modern Hindu ideology stayed important, some of the non-Advaitin schools of Vedānta, plus some of the regional schools, such as Śaiva Siddhanta in Tamil Nadu and Sri Lanka,

made their public voices heard. Publications drew attention to these various strands in Indian theology and philosophy. A richer perspective on the Hindu tradition could be had. There was also the development in Indian politics of a more conservative kind of Hindu attitude, which looked more to the founding of what was seen as a genuinely Hindu state, rather than the pluralistic version which came into being in 1947. But India is such a tinderbox of ethnic, communal, and linguistic tensions that the pluralistic alternative has so far proved to be necessary. The Republic moreover carved itself up into states built primarily on a linguistic basis, and this helped to stimulate indigenous poetic and religious traditions in the various regions. It also brought the Punjab to be divided fairly evenly between Sikhs and Hindus, and this led one faction of the Sikhs to agitate in the 1970s and 1980s for a separate state.

Conclusion

The Indians were fortunate in having in their heritage the materials for forming a sophisticated ideology which did not alienate the masses but was able to harness their religious feelings to political ends (above all through the charismatic figure of Gandhi). They were thus not forced, in the interests of national independence, to change so drastically that many of their traditions had to be jettisoned. They reached back into their tradition, reshaped it, and gave it modern force.

Part of this new Hinduism was the self-confident claim that after all Hindu ideas have universal application, and Hindu practices have much to show the world. In the 1960s and 1970s, particularly, this was demonstrated by the fact that elements of Hinduism were taken up in the West. There were first and foremost the gurus. There was the whole complex of yogic practices, sometimes simplified, as in Transcendental Meditation (popularized in part by the Beatles). There were *bhakti* movements, such as ISKCON (International Society for Krishna Consciousness). The general theory of Hinduism in this modern form – that all religions point somehow to the same truth – is attractive to many in the West, and there has certainly been an increase in ecumenism and friendship between liberal religious leaders. So a sort of neo-Hindu ideology may itself become more widely accepted in the future. All these developments mean that the Hindu tradition is a universal religion in the world today, with its own positive message. It is not just a religion for those born within the caste structure of the Indian subcontinent.

We may note, too, that from the last century onward there has grown up an increasing Hindu diaspora beyond India – in East Africa, South Africa, Fiji, Mauritius, the Seychelles, Guyana, the West Indies, Malaysia, Singapore, and elsewhere – largely as a result of the export of labor to plantations. More recently a middle-class wave of doctors, scientists, and other specialists has reached the Western world, as for example in Los Angeles (in Malibu Canyon a lovely recreation of a south Indian temple has

(*opposite*) The importance of the female: a temple dedicated to the Goddess Kālī in Nepal. In northern areas of the Indian subcontinent Kālī is worshipped in her dual aspect as creator and destroyer, the embodiment of an all-powerful female energy.

79

A woman sadhu venerating the goddess Sarasvati, at Puri in Orissa.

been built by the subscriptions of well-to-do Indians in southern California). This diaspora Hinduism has tended away from the stricter requirements of caste, and toward a greater concern with such movements as the Ārya Samāj, the Divine Light Movement, and the Ramakrishna Vedānta Mission. These Hindus have also been prone to move into Pentecostalist and other emotionally charged forms of Protestantism, which supply some of the feel of *bhakti* religion. But they will constitute a more and more important part of the voice of modern Hinduism, and will probably reinforce the message of the Hindu tradition as a universal faith.

In brief, the Republic of India, and Indian culture more widely, has been able to make a good use of its resources, selectively of course, in order to create a Hinduism which makes sense both of pluralism and of unity, and to have something which is both ancient and modern. At the same time the smaller religions in India have been able to make their way in the new India, thanks in part to the pluralism implicit in the secular constitution. Hinduism has entered on the world stage.

CHAPTER FOUR

The Jain Tradition

Jain Origins

Ancient India contained within it a number of religious groups. Among these was an array of ascetics with diverse theories about the world, who lived alongside, and sometimes in rivalry with, the Brahmins who came to dominate the emerging synthesis known as Hinduism. One of the major revivers and formulators of the ascetic outlook was the Buddha's contemporary, Mahāvīra. He is often considered to be the founder of Jainism – though Jains would claim that he merely restored an ancient faith and did not originate it. It has a more severe character than Buddhism, and its central virtue is *ahiṃsā* or non-injury to living beings, practiced in a very comprehensive way. Monks should tread the ground softly for fear of squashing insects and smaller forms of life. They should sweep the terrain with peacock feathers to clear away such beings. They should strain their drinking water, wear masks, and so on, to prevent the accidental taking of life. For such actions, even when not intended, bring bad karmic consequences. The monks, nuns, and dedicated lay followers practice severe austerity, or *tapas*. It is a religion which involves mental training; but physical austerities lie at its heart. The noblest ideal is for the saint, when he is ready, to starve himself to death.

Vardhamāna, or Mahāvīra ("Great Hero"), was born, according to Jain tradition, in 599 B.C.E. – but some scholars put his date fifty or more years after this – in a village near Vaiśālī in what is now the state of Bihar. At the age of thirty he, like the Buddha, renounced the world, and plucked out all his hair, to lead the life of the wandering holy man. After twelve years of fasting and penances he gained release and the sense of omniscience. He went on to gather disciples and refounded in a fuller form the religion of his predecessor, Pārśva, the previous Tīrthaṃkara (or "Fordmaker," i.e. person who shows the crossing to the other shore of existence), who may have lived in the eighth century B.C.E. At seventy-two Mahāvīra gained a final *nirvāṇa*.

He was thought to be the last of twenty-four Fordmakers. The Jain religion came to be quite influential in medieval times, but its numbers now in India are less than three million. Because followers could not take up agriculture and other death-dealing professions, they entered the merchant and artisan classes and are a relatively prosperous community. They feel that the religion, as we get away from Mahāvīra's time, and as history goes on in a downward direction, is in decline. They are divided into two denominations, the chief difference between them being that one demands that monks and nuns be unclothed and the other that they wear robes. The one is called the Digambaras or "Sky-Clad" and the other the Śvetambaras or "White-Clad."

Jainism has no doctrine of a creator. The universe is roughly in the shape of a huge person, with the earth situated at the waist. Above are various heavens and below are hells. The liberated *jīva* or soul rises, free of the weight of its depressing *karma*, to the top of the universe where it remains, free from pain and motionless. Every soul is in itself omniscient, but due to defilement it loses this knowledge; through emancipation its original omniscience is regained.

These beliefs, seemingly archaic, have provided the framework for the practice of a religion which through the centuries has had important influences on Indian civilization as a whole. In the Buddhist texts it emerges, with the Brahmins, as the chief rival to Buddhism.

We shall later analyze the chief beliefs and practices of the Jains in more detail, but meanwhile let us look a little more closely at the history of the religion.

Jain History

In order to preserve and collate the sacred texts a council was held in the late fourth century B.C.E., about two hundred years after Mahāvīra's decease, at Pataliputra on the Ganges (today's Patna). Prominent in this congregation was Bhadrabāhu, who has been seen by subsequent Jain traditions, whether Śvetambara or Digambara, as the last person who knew and could recite the original canon. Nevertheless, the Śvetambaras claim canonical status for their own *āgama* or traditional authoritative collection, even if the original version of the sacred texts has been lost. This collection was written down in the fifth century C.E. The Digambaras hold that some of the original material was incorporated in some of their treatises. Through the centuries a vast number of commentarial and expository works was composed.

The Śvetambaras were successful in establishing themselves in western India, especially in Gujarat and Rajasthan. In the twelfth century the famous Jain leader Hemachandra (1089–1172) served as chief minister in the Calukya kingdom and influenced society in the direction of Jain norms. The arrival of Muslim rule diminished Jain power, but the architectural monuments to Jain prosperity are evident throughout the region, and especially at the sanctuary of Mount Abu in Rajasthan. From the fifth century Digambara Jainism was important in south India, especially in Karnataka. There too are some famous

Jainism some key terms

Ahiṃsā Nonviolence toward all living beings, a virtue central to Jainism, and important in aspects of Hinduism and in Buddhism, as well as in Gandhi's thought.

Ajīva Non-living matter, including human and other bodies: everything which is not *jīva* (soul).

Anekāntavāda Perspectivism or non-one-sidedness: the doctrine that no one perspective gives you the whole truth.

Angas The earliest texts in the Jain tradition.

Digambara Sky-clad ones, that is, Jains who keep to the rule of nudity for monks, as a sign of ultimate lack of possessions.

Jina Victor or conqueror, the main title of the great Jain teachers, notably Mahāvīra: from it is derived the name *Jaina* or follower of the Jina.

Kevala State of liberation in which the *jīva* exists motionless at the summit of the universe, pictured as a colossal human.

Mahāvrata Great vow taken by a monk or nun, pledging to practice *ahiṃsā*, and to avoid lying, sex, stealing, or owning anything.

Śvetambara White-clad ones: those Jains belonging to the group which does not practice monastic nudity. Each monk or nun has three pieces of white cloth to wear.

Tapas Austerity, widely practiced in India, but especially by Jains.

Tīrthaṃkara Fordmaker, that is, a great leader such as Mahāvīra who makes a way across the stream of life to salvation.

shrines, above all the striking temple at Sravana Belgola (where the Maurya emperor Candragupta is supposed to have starved himself to death in pursuance of the Jain ideal for the wise man in leaving this life). In the twelfth century Tamil Śaivism eclipsed Jainism. But there can be little doubt of the great influence and importance of Jainism in early medieval India. However, in accordance with its own predictions the religion is in decline. Nevertheless, the modern period has seen a revival of Jain scholarship, partly under Western stimulus, and editions of many crucial works have been published, as well as some fine systematic studies of the doctrines, practices, and iconography of the community. Because the Jains have a strict ban on taking life – indeed their rigorous non-injury or *ahiṃsa* has proved influential on the Indian tradition as a whole – the lay people naturally gravitate toward business. Since they are *nāstika* they are not themselves Brahmins, though they may employ them for some rites; and farming involves of necessity the destruction of animal, bird, and insect life. As businesspeople they have always been influential out of all proportion to their numbers. Moreover, the monastic community, both male and female, earns wide respect among the general population.

Let us now turn to the analysis of the Jain religion in terms of the seven dimensions.

The Dimensions of Jainism

The Mythic Dimension

Central to the Jain understanding of history is the notion of the Fordmakers or Tīrthaṃkaras, who are supreme leaders who create the ford which can convey their followers across the waters of suffering and rebirth to the other shore, namely salvation or *mokṣa*. A Tīrthaṃkara arises after innumerable births and vast and strenuous effort. The teachings of the Tīrthaṃkaras renew the Jain order of recluses and lay persons, which always tends to decline during the periods when there is no Tīrthaṃkara. In the present cycle of existence the last is Vardhamāna, known as Mahāvīra, whose life followed the typical pattern of a Fordmaker. The previous one was Pārśva, supposedly born in Banaras 250 years before Mahāvīra: some scholars think he may have been an historical figure. At any rate this hypothesis may remind us that according to the Jains their religion was not founded by Mahāvīra but merely renewed by him.

Mahāvīra was counted the twenty-fourth Fordmaker, whose line stretched back into the deepest antiquity. Like his predecessors he was born of a princely family, his mother Triśāla being of royal lineage. While still in the womb he followed the spirit of non-injury, causing his mother no pain. He married, say the Śvetambaras, though the Digambaras deny this. He waited till his parents died before renouncing the world, and then only after asking permission from his elder brother. He followed the severe life of a recluse, adhering to the five great Jain vows (including giving up sex and possessions). By performing tremendous penances which eliminated bad *karma* he eventually, after a little more than twelve and a half years, gained omniscience and the assurance that he would not be reborn. He then preached the

---

Non-Injury and the Path: Sūtrakṛtāṅga

This is the quintessence of wisdom: not to kill anything. Know this to be the legitimate conclusion from the principle of the reciprocity with regard to non-killing.

He could cease to injure living beings whether they move or not, on high, below, and on earth. For this has been called the *nirvāṇa*, which consists in peace.

Master of his senses and avoiding wrong,

he should do no harm to anybody, either by thoughts, or words, or acts.

A wise man who restrains his senses and possesses great knowledge should accept such things as are freely given him, being always circumspect with regard to the accepting of alms, and abstaining from what he is forbidden to accept.

मह ...

final and true teachings, and created, with eleven disciples who headed companies or groups of followers, the Jain community. Finally, in 527 B.C.E. according to traditional dating and some fifty or sixty years later according to Western scholars, he starved himself to death. He thus became a perfected soul, rising to the summit of the cosmos, where, like others of the perfected, he remains motionless and inaccessible, in a condition of painless omniscience. As Fordmaker for this age Mahāvīra is the most important focus of pious aspiration, but Jains also revere all the other great figures. Because such souls are perfectly immobile, however, there can be no transactions between them and humans: revering them does not mean entering into relationship with them, so, like Buddhas too in the Theravāda, they cannot help people, save by their example and the teachings they have left behind, to gain liberation.

Jaina cosmology: the cosmos is seen in this Jaina manuscript as a huge human. Liberated souls eventually rise to the top of the universe and stay motionless forever.

The Doctrinal Dimension

The cosmos is imagined in Jainism as being like a human figure of truly immense proportions. We on earth are at the waist. The world below this disk-like area consists of seven layers of purgatories where the most evil beings suffer. Immediately above the earth are various heavenly bodies, also belonging to the middle world, inhabited by various gods, and above this in the upper world the heavens become more rarefied, culminating in the area corresponding to the top of the cosmic person's head, where dwell the perfected souls. The Jains do not deny the gods, but assign them inferior status. Sometimes Jains worship the guardian spirits of the Tīrthaṃkaras, and other Hindu figures, for minor boons.

Reality is divided between *jīvas* or life-monads, some of the minutest size and others corresponding to the dimensions of bodies (thus the human life-monad fills the human body), and *ajīva* or non-living matter. Damaging living things is a serious affair, having bad karmic consequences. Like Buddhism, and later Hinduism Jainism believes in reincarnation. *Karma* is seen as a sort of material substance which weighs down the life-monad. When *karma* is annihilated through ascetic practice, the soul becomes buoyant and ascends to the top of the cosmos. Intrinsically a human *jīva* is omniscient: lack of knowledge comes through the contamination of the soul.

Jainism at the philosophical level subscribes to belief in relative pluralism or *anekāntavāda*. An object, according to this doctrine, can be viewed from a number of perspectives – without distinguishing its specific and generic properties; as exhibiting its generic properties; as exhibiting its individual characteristics; as a contemporary phenomenon; and so on. Also Jainism holds to the so-called *syādvāda* or "maybe-ism." This expresses an anti-dogmatic attitude, and also emphasizes ways in which the nature of an object may be in part inexpressible. This is an interesting idea: though Jainism is highly conservative and very rigorous in practice it has a soft outer stance, resisting dogmatic certainty.

The Ethical Dimension

The central ethical virtue of Jainism is *ahiṃsā* or non-injury. Through this it has had a lasting effect on Indian thought, and most notably in this century because of its influence on Mahātma Gandhi, who gave the idea a new political interpretation, stressing the importance of nonviolent resistance toward unjust authority. Lay Jains are expected to adhere to five lesser vows, including non-injury, truth and honesty in business affairs, refraining from wrong sexual conduct, not stealing, and renunciation of attachment to material wealth. They are expected to be strictly vegetarian and not to consume alcohol and other drugs. Monks have a severer set of duties: for instance they should sweep the path before them and wear masks and filter water, to avoid crushing or swallowing insects and minuter forms of life. They live by begging, and should have no possessions (the Digambaras going to the extent of nudity, though this is not so often practiced in public today). They should meditate to purify the mind and to reinforce the sense of the transitoriness of the world. Ideally they should starve themselves to death, to protect living beings and as a culmination of the austerity which annihilates *karma*.

Lay people naturally have to support the monks and nuns, not to mention the increasingly rich and elaborate temples and ceremonies. So *dāna* or giving is an important duty. In many ways Jain ethics parallel those of the Buddhists.

The Emotional and Experiential Dimension

A great deal of emphasis in Jainism is put upon the existential realization of the fundamental features of the world. It is not enough to believe in some superficial way that life-monads and matter are different: it has to be felt. So Jains are supposed to cultivate a deep sense of the impermanence of things, the difference between souls and bodies, the impurity of bodies, the presence of *karma*, individual responsibility for one's own salvation, and so on. But in another respect the emotional dimension of life needs to be eliminated in the sense that the Jain aims at complete dispassion and indifference. The use of

The ethical dimension: Jain ascetics wear masks so that they do not inadvertently inhale insects. This is part of their non-violent practice.

meditation may induce a sense of internal serenity and emptiness. Some rituals also help lay persons to have a pleasurable attitude toward the ultimate goal of complete austerity.

The Ritual Dimension

The monks' and nuns' days and nights are divided into periods for meditation, study, begging, and sleep. Monastic dwellings near temples house the recluses during the rainy season for four months each year. During this period an annual eight- to ten-day sequence of confession occurs, and in general much importance is attached to regular confession, as a means of helping the individual along his or her lonely and arduous path. The erection of temples helped to focus lay piety, and the reverence paid to often colossal statues of the Fordmakers helps to reinforce people's dedication to the Path. Offerings are symbolic, in the sense that, as we have seen, there can be no transaction between a Tīrthaṃkara and the faithful. But the ritual life of the householder reflects his or her commitment to the three jewels of right

viewpoint, right knowledge, and right conduct. The life of the monk or nun is, of course, much more minutely prescribed.

The Institutional Dimension

It seems that Mahāvīra organized the Sangha most effectively, since it has persisted till today, and, though divided primarily into two main denominations, it is not much divided as to teaching and practice beyond the disagreement over the importance of nudity. Within the order there are differing ranks and functions – for instance there are the intellectual teachers who supervise the inculcation of scriptural and commentarial learning. In parallel there are *ācāryas* or spiritual teachers who look after the meditational and other practices of the recluses. On entry to the order there is a relatively short period of novitiate, some four months. The nuns have a slightly secondary status to the monks, but a life of equal severity. Part of the Sangha is the lay wing, and beyond that a penumbra of folk who may not formally belong to the religion but respect and give to the monks and nuns on their rounds of begging. In many respects, moreover, Jainism is integrated into the wider structure of Hinduism. Where castes are endogamous, that is marrying within the caste, it is obvious that those groups excluded from the structure become paradoxically included. By being excluded from the caste structure and intermarrying among themselves, Jains automatically become (from the Hindu point of view) a caste. Since, too, the religion is monastic rather than priestly, it is not surprising if Jain laity make use of Brahmins, for instance to perform weddings. It is difficult to escape the warm, octopus-like embrace of the Hindu system, even while purporting to be *nāstika* or unorthodox, that is not recognizing the Hindu scriptural tradition.

In more recent times, since the consolidation of British rule in India, Jains have become increasingly aware of modern scholarship and have set up institutes in western India, at Ahmedabad and elsewhere, for the publication of Jaina texts and research into the Jain past.

The Material Dimension

Perhaps the most significant and resonant of all Jain sites is the temple at Sravana Belgola in the region of Mysore in south India, where there is a vast stone figure on a hill rising above the plain representing Bahubali, son of the first Fordmaker of the present downgoing period. This stupendous figure, 57 feet (17.4 m) high, is naked, and stands there, feet slightly apart, with creepers growing up them, signifying how long he stood immobile, a wonderful and serene representation of self-abnegation. Every twelve years there is a huge ceremony there when his head is anointed with milk and honey. The site attracts large numbers of pilgrims. Another important place is Mount Abu in Rajasthan, where the temple complex dates from the eleventh century, and where a number of the buildings are in fine white marble. But there are rich shrines in a number of other centers in India, sometimes matching famous Hindu shrines.

(*opposite*) The ritual dimension: a small boy makes an offering in the Jain Temple in Bombay to Rsabha, the first Tīrthaṃkara or Jaina liberator.

The material dimension: the Jain saint Bahubali is honored by a colossal 57 feet (17.4 m) high statue. The second son of the first Tīrthaṃkara, Bahubali (or Gommatesvara as he is more usually known) renounced fighting and stood in rigid penance for untold ages.

Yet at the other extreme is the symbolic simplicity of the monk or nun, equipped with a simple cloth, a napkin, a brush for sweeping the ground, and a begging bowl.

Conclusion

Jainism, like Buddhism, demotes the gods. Its central idea is the Tīrthaṃkara, who stays motionless at the summit of the anthropomorphic cosmos. There is no God. Beyond the universe lies fathomless and infinite space. Suspended therein, the cosmos is everlasting, unmade. Both Jainism and the Theravāda are clear testaments to the possibility of non-theistic religion. It seems that before the Upanishads and the rich unfolding of the Hindu tradition the ancient śramaṇas had no need of a God nor even of the magical power of Brahman. But unlike Buddhism, Jainism never made much progress overseas, and remains as an inset into the wider Indian Hindu environment. But it is a fascinating and indeed heroic faith, pessimistic about its future, but able to command loyalty to its severe principles.

CHAPTER FIVE

The Buddhist Tradition

The Background of the Rise of Buddhism in India

By the sixth century B.C.E. in north India, especially in the Gangetic plain where Buddhism had its rise, a mercantile and farming society had achieved a fair degree of prosperity. Traditional priests, Brahmins, shared the respect of lay folk with *śramaṇas* or wandering recluses, often practicing strict austerities and begging for their living. The Brahmins preserved the texts of the Vedic hymns and presided over rituals, from elaborate horse sacrifices for princes to humbler rain-making and other rites. Certain ideas such as that of reincarnation or rebirth, through which living beings circulated through vast ages as animals or humans or demons or insects or gods or ghosts in accord with the merit of their deeds or *karma*, were common among the *śramaṇas* and were beginning to penetrate Brahmin thinking. In the mixture of beliefs of the period, the one which came to be spectacularly successful in the broader history of Asia and the world was Buddhism. The ferment of ideas occurred above all in the region around the cities along the Ganges such as Banaras and Patna (Pataliputra). Because of new political and economic forces, including the emergence of strong kingdoms and republics, a new mercantile class was becoming more important, and this was attracted to some of the new movements that were springing up, especially that created by the Buddha.

All dates in early Indian history are the subject of scholarly debate. But it was probably in the sixth century B.C.E. that the Buddha was born and various other major figures flourished. Some scholars date such events later, but we shall stay with a more traditional scheme.

The Buddha's story is legendary: onto some historical facts were glued some wondrous stories. This fact means that it is hard for us to get to what may be called the "historical Buddha." But the legendary account of the Buddha's life is important, for it is that on which the remembrance and piety of Buddhists through the ages has fastened. Moreover, it has served as a kind of model for analogous lives, such as that of his supposed contemporary Mahāvīra, who founded or refounded the Jain tradition.

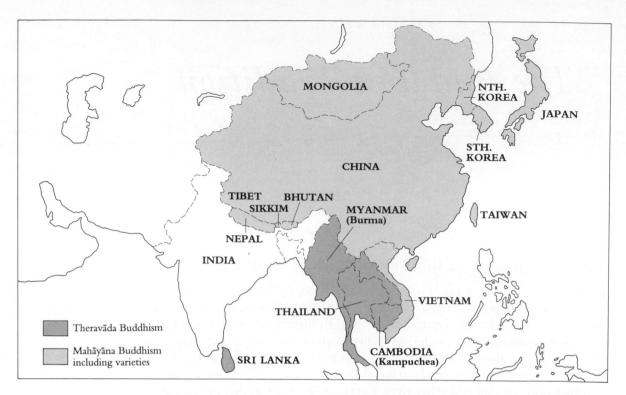

Theravāda Buddhism

Mahāyāna Buddhism including varieties

MONGOLIA

NTH. KOREA

JAPAN

STH. KOREA

CHINA

TIBET

BHUTAN

SIKKIM

MYANMAR (Burma)

TAIWAN

NEPAL

INDIA

VIETNAM

THAILAND

CAMBODIA (Kampuchea)

SRI LANKA

Map showing the approximate distribution of Theravāda and Mahāyāna Buddhism in Southeast Asia today.

Later Buddhists were to have the creed: "I take refuge in the Buddha; I take refuge in the Dharma; I take refuge in the Sangha." We can translate this as "I take refuge in the Enlightened One; I take refuge in the Teaching; I take refuge in the Order" (that is, of monks and nuns). This summary of loyalty pinpoints the three most vital ingredients in the Buddhist tradition: the narrative of the Buddha; the doctrinal or philosophical worldview presented; and the institution that carried on the practical path to liberation, namely the body of dedicated followers of the Buddha. Beyond this simple credo Buddhism was to take many forms, and it is useful here to give a small sketch of that history of divergence.

The History of Buddhism in Brief

There are four main periods of development in the history of Buddhism – preclassical, classical, medieval, and modern. First, there is the preclassical period, in which the Buddha lived and the teachings and practice were consolidated. This period can be said to last from about 500 B.C.E. down to the first century C.E., by which time the canon of scriptures was already written down in Pali, in Sri Lanka, and was taking a fixed form in the shape of what is known as Theravāda or the Doctrine of the Elders. This form of Buddhism is still practiced in Sri Lanka and Southeast Asia, though not without admixture from the other great branch, the Mahāyāna or Greater

92

(*left*) A sandstone Buddha from Katra, early 1st century C.E. Seated in the typical Mathura style with wheel marks on the soles of his feet, he holds up his hand to banish fear.

(*below*) Gold coin with figure of standing Buddha from the Greek influenced northwest of India, c. 169–191 C.E.

Vehicle. The Mahāyāna, which had roots parallel to those of the Theravāda in early Buddhism, emerged in India in about the third century B.C.E.

Second, from the first century C.E. onward, Buddhism spread into China and eventually into Korea and Japan. Both in Indian Mahāyāna and in the Theravāda, Buddhism achieved high articulation, and we can call this the classical period.

Third, from the seventh century C.E., there developed a form of Buddhism, sometimes called the Vajrayāna (Diamond Vehicle) and sometimes the Mantrayāna (Vehicle of Sacred Utterance), with a strong emphasis upon magical and sacramental rites, in which spiritual consequences were thought to flow from the recitation of *mantras* or sacred formulae. This was gradually assimilated into the Hindu practices of the era, and was one reason for the ultimate virtual disappearance of Buddhism from subcontinental India. On the other hand it became the dominant form of Buddhism in Nepal and Tibet, where the religion spread during this period. We may call the era from the seventh century C.E. till the eighteenth century the medieval period.

Fourth, there came the modern period, which eventually affected Buddhism not only in South Asia but in the rest of Asia. The impact of colonialism will be discussed later on page 127.

All these periods apply primarily to Buddhism in South Asia, and differing periodization will be used in regard to East Asia and elsewhere.

In sketching Buddhist roots, I shall deal with its different dimensions as follows. First, the *narrative* dimension, telling the story of the Buddha and the world out of which he came. Second, the *doctrines* he taught: these philosophical ideas are geared to the practical life, but are especially important in the Buddhist tradition, which has a strong emphasis – for reasons which will become clear – upon analysis of the world and of human nature. Third, the ritual or *practical* dimension, so central in the question for liberation. With this we shall connect the *ethical* dimension. Then we shall look to the inward *experiences* of both the Buddha and his followers. We shall move on to sketch the *social* organization of the religion. Finally we shall look at the *material* dimension of early Buddhism.

The Dimensions of Buddhism

The Narrative Dimension

Where indeed should one begin to tell the story of the man who came to be called the Buddha? His life as an individual never really began, for, like us all, he was, in the Buddhist view, a beginningless wayfarer in the round of *saṃsāra*. There are many wondrous and edifying tales told of him in the scriptures about how he was a snake, or a hare, or a king, or whatever, in previous births. These so-called Jātaka tales were a great source of instruction in social life and compassion for the peoples who came to follow the Buddha. Immediately before his birth in this world as a human and more-than-human teacher and liberator, the Buddha-to-be, or Bodhisattva, resided for millions of years in a heaven, called Tuṣita, enjoying great happiness like a god. But he had to give this up to help living beings to relieve and ultimately to get rid of their sufferings.

It was possibly in 586 B.C.E. (but probably much later, more like a hundred years later) that he was born into this world as Siddhartha Gautama, on the periphery of the new civilization emerging along the river Ganges. He was born into a people known as the Śākyas, and came to be known as Śākyamuni, the sage of the Śākyas. They were under the general suzerainty of the kingdom of Kosala. His father Śuddhodana was a ruler, and his mother was Mahāmāyā. It was predicted at his birth that he was destined to become a world ruler, but it was uncertain whether this was to be in a political or a spiritual sense. The birth itself was miraculous, according to legend. His mother dreamed that the Buddha-to-be took the form of a white elephant and entered her womb, and she ceased to have any wish for sex. So though she was not a virgin, having borne other children, it was in a loose sense a virgin birth; and it occurred at the time of the full moon in May at a park called Lumbini.

The young Siddhartha grew up in some luxury, but eventually, after he had married and become father of a son, he was impelled to leave the worldly life, and to take up that of the wandering recluse. He had been struck by the four sights of a very old man, a sick person, a corpse being taken to the burning-ground, and finally a holy beggar. He left his wife and baby and lived a nomadic life of severe austerity and reflection. He studied and prac-

---

Buddhism some key terms

Bodhisattva Buddha-to-be who puts off his final liberation to work tirelessly for the sake of other living beings. The most famous Bodhisattva figure is Avalokiteśvara who became Kuan-yin in China and Kannon in Japan.

Buddha An enlightened being who has seen the truth of Dharma.

Dhyāna Meditation: usually in eight stages of ascending purity of consciousness.

Nirvāṇa Final liberation when the saint will no longer be reborn.

Prajñā Insight or wisdom concerning the nature of the cosmos.

Pratītyasamutpāda Codependent orgination of events, the law which links together all the events of the world in sequences of *saṃsāra*.

Saṃsāra The living flux of existence in which individuals are involved in the process of rebirth.

Sangha The order of monks and nuns founded by the Buddha to carry on the teaching of the Dharma.

Śīla Virtue or a precept encouraging a virtue, such as the five precepts summing up Buddhist morality.

Stūpa A mound for containing relics, formalized into the central feature of temples and pagodas.

Śūnyatā Emptiness, the pervading characteristic of all events, in that they are empty of self-subsistence and are relative.

Tantra A ritual text or method in the so-called Vajrayāna form of Buddhism (chiefly now in Tibet) for acquiring sacramental power, usually through the instruction of a guru.

---

ticed for a while with a group of six fellow *śramaṇas*. Eventually, on his own, and at a place now called Bodh Gaya, under a sacred fig tree or pipal, he attained full insight into the nature of the world and of the way to overcome suffering and tribulation. As Enlightened One, he was henceforth to be called the Buddha.

He returned to Banaras, to a deer park outside the city at a place called Sarnath, where he had left his companions, and delivered to them his first sermon in which he expounded his insight. It was referred to as the Sermon of the Turning of the Wheel, in which he set the wheel of Dharma in motion. They became his first disciples and the core of the new order of Sangha. Thereafter, for forty-five years until he was eighty, he traveled about, teaching and consolidating the organization of the Sangha. He visited the great new cities of the region – Banaras, Uruvela, Rajagriha, Vaisali, Sravasti, Kausambi, and his own town Kapilavastu. According to Sri Lankan chron-

The grief of his
followers at the
passing of the Buddha
– he had told them,
however, that all
compound things are
impermanent and that
the Teaching would
remain.

icles, the Buddha made three journeys to the island in his lifetime, one being
to the peak of Sumanakata, later called Adam's Peak, where he left a huge
footprint which became the focus of the island's most important pilgrimage.
He consorted with princes and kings, courtesans and smiths. He preached his
saving doctrine of the Way to Liberation.

At last, he died of a digestive complaint. As with other major events in his
life, there were heavenly and earthly portents – earthquakes and showers of
flowers. His decease was one of insight and peace: all compound things are
impermanent and sooner or later the death of the physical Gautama Buddha
had to take place. He had fought off more than once the wiles of Mara the
Tempter, who would have liked the Buddha not to have gained insight, and
not to have kept on in the world to deliver his message. He had overcome the
forces of death, and now he would be no more reborn. He came to be called
the Tathāgata, or Thus-Gone, and his final state was mysterious. He would

not be reborn, but it was wrong to think of him as either existing or not existing, or both or neither. His followers cremated his body, and his relics were installed under cairns in various places.

This was the life of the most recent in the line of Buddhas. In the Pali canon, various others are listed, such as the Buddhas Vipassi, Sikhi, Vessabhu, Kakusandha, Konagamana, and Kassapa. It is not thought that the Buddha founded the faith, but restored it.

The Doctrinal Dimension

The Buddha's doctrines belonged to the general pattern of śramanic religion of the time, but he gave that a radical new interpretation. The primary questions turned round the problem of rebirth and how to gain liberation from an unsatisfactory world. Like the contemporary Jain and Ājīvika groups, he was attracted to the practice of austerity; but in the end he found mere austerity too negative. He learned from others the arts of yoga, and evolved a system of meditation; but he thought that meditation without understanding was blind, and understanding without meditation was without fruits. You had to combine the two, and for this a right orientation to philosophical questions was vital.

Small stupa in Varanasi, c. 3rd–4th century C.E. A reliquary monument to the Buddha, the stupa is worshipped as a representation of his death and attainment of Nirvāṇa.

His central insight was of the impermanence and interdependence of everything. He sought the causes of every event, and especially those which directly concern the human being: we need to train ourselves in self-awareness to perceive the nature of events taking place inside us and their conditions. But he rejected determinism (as preached by the Ājīvikas, for instance). We are free to reshape our destinies, even though we inherit from previous lives tendencies which, if unchecked, will lead to other existences, each one impregnated with *dukkha* or illfare (usually translated as "suffering"). Indeed, in the popular view of the nature of the universe which Buddhism adapted and reshaped, there are many heavens – though even in these the good life must come to an end – and many purgatories of a horrifying kind, while humans could become ghosts, or worms, or any other kind of living being, in accordance with their deeds.

Because nothing in the universe is permanent, no satisfaction can last for ever; and its disappearance is painful. All life therefore is permeated by suffering. This was the first of the Four Noble Truths which the Buddha proclaimed. The second is that the cause of suffering is craving or thirst for existence (Pali: *taṇhā*). The third is that this cause can be eliminated. And the fourth is that the mode of doing this is by treading the Noble Eightfold Path.

This path has eight aspects, and is an expansion of a more fundamental idea, that there are three elements in the Way (or Path), namely trust, ethical conduct, and meditation. The first two aspects of the Path concern trust: they are Right Belief and Right Attitude. The next three are to do with ethical conduct: Right Speech, Right Bodily Action, and Right Livelihood (that is, not engaging in an occupation which would necessarily cause the infringement of the Buddhist ethic, such as butchering). The last three, to do with yoga or self-training, are: Right Effort, Right Self-Awareness, and Right Meditation.

The Path was thought of by the Buddha as "Middle," that is, as centered between extremes: between the extremes of self-indulgence and self-mortification, and between the extremes of thinking that the soul is eternal and that it is cut off at death. It is in various other ways a moderate faith.

One aspect of the Buddha's teaching which was highly original was the analysis of the individual human as consisting of five groups of events or *khandhas* (Sanskrit: *skandhas*). One of these is bodily events. Another is perceptions. A third is feelings. A fourth is dispositions or impulses. Finally there are the states of consciousness which help to illuminate the perceptions. These events are mutually connected, since the body forms the locus of the sense-organs which give rise to perceptions. These perceptions in turn generate feelings, since so many of the things we perceive give rise to feelings of pleasure or aversion. Feelings form the basis for dispositions to act; to grasp for that which gives us pleasure. These dispositions if unchecked give rise to future lives, and maintain our states of consciousness. So it is that the interconnections between the different groups which make up the individual are a vital part of that whole chain of dependence or *paṭiccasamuppāda* (page 104).

The Path leads to a condition in this life of complete insight and serenity, such as the Buddha himself achieved at his Enlightenment; on death the saint disappears like a flame going out or a spark disappearing in the darkness. It is not extinction, but it is not continued individual existence either. So the Tathāgata was seen as having no further relations with this world. The best

Dependence and the Middle Path: Saṃyutta Nikāya

On ignorance depends *karma*;
On *karma* depends consciousness;
On consciousness depend name and form;
On name and form depend the six organs of sense;
On the six organs of sense depends contact;
On contact depends sensation;
On sensation depends desire;
On desire depends attachment;
On attachment depends existence;
On existence depends birth;
On birth depend old age and death, sorrow, lamentation, misery, grief, and despair. Thus does this entire aggregation of misery arise.

But on the complete fading out and cessation of ignorance ceases *karma*;
On the cessation of *karma* ceases consciousness;
On the cessation of consciousness cease name and form;
On the cessation of name and form cease the six organs of sense;
On the cessation of the six organs of sense ceases contact;
On the cessation of contact ceases sensation;
On the cessation of sensation ceases desire;
On the cessation of desire ceases attachment;
On the cessation of attachment ceases existence;
On the cessation of existence ceases birth;
On the cessation of birth cease old age and death, sorrow, lamentation, misery, grief, and despair. Thus does this entire aggregation of misery cease.

way to point to his transcendent condition is by silence.

The best way to go for salvation is to become a nun or a monk. Such a life of spiritual community, with periods of solitude, is best for meditation. Lay followers not yet ready for the relative severity of the Sangha might, through ethical living and by giving to the order, attain a future in some better or heavenly state, and might thereafter come back to earth ready to assume the ocher robe.

The idea of impermanence, the rejection too of a permanent soul in the individual, the concept of universal causation, and the goal of an ineffable ultimate state – *nirvāṇa* – are the bare bones of the Buddha's message. We shall see later how these notions came to be developed. Underpinning the world-view was the thought of rebirth and the pervasive power of *karma*. It was original in its substance and presentation and had a strong appeal in the areas where the Buddha taught.

It rejected the appeal to revelation, and in particular Brahmin claims for the Vedas. The Buddha had directly experienced the truths he taught, and the Brahmins (he argued) relied on mere tradition and authority. They had not seen the gods they called upon. The true Brahmin was not the one born into a priestly class, but the person who followed virtue and self-control.

The Practical Dimension

The most important practice invoked in the Buddha's teachings is that of yoga, in which an individual, seated in some serene spot, tries to control his mind, and is eventually able to climb up through the various stages of *dhyāna* (Pali: *jhāna*). He might begin with some simple object such as a blue flower and learn to see it just as a patch of blue. Then he might discard such a device and ascend through various levels of increasing purity of consciousness. The adept does not by such exercises alone attain to *nirvāṇa* and sainthood; but they form an integral part of the earliest pictures we have of Buddhism. It is above all a faith of meditation and self-training.

The structure of the Sangha prevents, however, too great an individualism, since the Buddha envisaged his followers as living together according to the rule or *vinaya*. At each phase of the moon, they would make a mutual public confession of faults; and at the end of the rainy season there would be a larger and more formal occasion for such confession and mutual forgiveness.

Another important aspect of early life was that like other śramanic groups Buddhist monks and nuns would get their food by begging. It was an exchange: they received food, the lay folk got merit. This giving (*dāna*) was the primary lay duty toward the order. Early on, the important sites of the Buddha's life may have been thought worth visiting to gain merit: where he was born, where he gained his Vision, where he preached the first sermon, and where he died; at Lumbini, Bodh-Gaya, Sarnath, and Kusinagara. In the treatment of Gautama's relics, at his death, lay the germs of later devotion and indeed worship (though in a sense the Tathāgata was "not there" to worship: only his memory served as a spur to good deeds and self-salvation).

The Ethical Dimension

As a Middle Path, the Way emphasized that intentions count, rather than a literal application of the rules. Our actions should be controlled by the Five Precepts (*pañcaśīla* in Sanskrit and *pañcasīla* in Pali). One should refrain from taking life, from taking what is not given, from wrong sex, from wrong speech, and from drugs (substances which obstruct self-awareness). To these basic rules was added a set for controlling more narrowly the life of the nun or monk: such rules about not using a high bed, or money, and following the conditions of the order. Such morality was to be suffused by certain great virtues, such as compassion. This was one of the Four Divine Dwelling Places in which the good person should reside – friendliness, compassion, sympathy, and equanimity.

The Experiential Dimension

What kind of inner experiences did earliest Buddhism aim for? We can learn something from the accounts of yogic practice. The supreme point in the ascending scale of purifying consciousness is a kind of tranquil bliss, from which height the adept looks down, when he comes out of trance, at ordinary experience as being mundane and yet itself, in tranquility, suffused by a kind of joy and assurance.

Such illuminated consciousness is sometimes referred to as mystical experience. However, in the Buddhist case there is no question of seeing it as a union with the Ultimate, such as a personal God. Buddhism does not deny the gods, even the great God Brahmā, creator of the world according to Brahmins (though not according to the Buddha: he is merely the first god to come into existence at the beginning of a new cycle in the universe's existence). But the gods too, however splendid, are impermanent. So the supreme bliss and insight of *nirvāṇa* are beyond all words and all ideas of being united with Anyone.

This seems the central experience of the Buddha and of his saintly followers – that is, those who attained *nirvāṇa*. But such high consciousness is accompanied by an intellectual realization that all things are impermanent. Such a realization could occur in a flash, in a moment of understanding. We have accounts of such moments in some of the autobiographical poems of the early monks and nuns which were incorporated into the Pali canon. It took time for a more fervent devotional religion aimed at celestial Buddhas to come about. But there is plenty of recognition in the early canon of the keen appreciation of nature and the poignancy of life, and such sentiments form a fine counterpoint to the depths and glories of Buddhist meditation.

The Social Dimension

The Sangha was at first perhaps much more loosely brought together than it later became. Many monks and nuns were hermits over much of the year, camping in caves and by river banks in huts, save for the wet season when they would congregate and live in some of the centers given by rich laity in and around the cities and larger villages. Though the Buddha acted as monarch of the Sangha in his lifetime, thus being a spiritual world-conqueror and imperial figure, he made no provision for a successor. He preferred the republican model of some of the peoples now being absorbed into the kingdoms burgeoning along the valley of the Ganges. The new leader would be the Dharma, the Teaching. After I am gone, said the Buddha, there will remain the Teaching.

Similarly organized were some of the other śramanic movements, notably those of the Jains and Ājīvikas, led by Mahāvīra Vardhamāna and Makkhali Gosāla respectively. So we can see the Buddhist Sangha alongside its rivals, and surrounded at the periphery by a miscellaneous population of wandering recluses, some shaven, some naked, some with matted hair, some weird and frightening, others gentle. It was also a rival to the hereditary priests or Brahmins. The civilization was mixed, and the Brahmins, recluses, and monks of the various traditions had to live together. Buddhism had plenty of rich support, from kings and merchants. It was modernizing and subtle, and gave opportunities for lay people to use their wealth and clean living in ways which promised better things for the future, and possibly heaven.

It was also a period of political change. Some of the tribal republics were being absorbed into the kingdoms which dominated the region. The Sangha offered an alternative life at a time of great social change.

The Material Dimension

The relics of the Buddha were distributed at his death. They were installed in cairns, which were the precursors of the great mound or *stūpa* of the classical Buddhist temple. Such concern with relics was to prefigure much else. But it was some time before Buddhist monasteries, with all their accompanying art, were to be created. Only later was there to be the wonderful development of statuary and paintings which made Buddhist art one of the glories of human civilization. In the beginning, there was perhaps a strong sense that by the doctrines taught by the Buddha there was "nothing there" to portray. The Teacher was trackless, like a rhinoceros or a bird in the sky.

Theravāda Buddhism

The Mauryan Empire and Aśoka

Of the states arising in the Ganges region in the period of the Buddha the most vital was Magadha, which eventually became the basis for the Mauryan empire, named after Candragupta Maurya, who came to the throne in 326 B.C.E. He expanded the empire to cover most of north India, defeating the Greek successor of Alexander, Seleucus, in the process and acquiring large swaths of territory in the northwest. Of those who followed him the most important was Aśoka, who came to the throne probably in 268 B.C.E. A few years later he conquered Kalinga, a troublesome eastern kingdom. The massacres and miseries consequent upon this action afflicted his conscience, and

The sacred Bo-tree in Sri Lanka. The Buddha was beneath the Bo-tree (or Bodhi tree) when he attained enlightenment.

he became a lay follower of Buddhism. The rock edicts he inscribed in various parts of his dominions testify to his concern for religious tolerance and the values of the Dharma. The Dharma was drawn from the full Buddhist teaching, but it enjoined virtue and discouraged practices such as meat-eating. The moderating effects of Buddhist values were brought into Aśoka's practice of statecraft. In 258 B.C.E. he celebrated a great festival of Buddhism in his vast capital of Pataliputra on the Ganges (the largest city of its time in the world), and began to send out missionaries and ambassadors to distant regions, including Greece and the successor states to Alexander's empire. Partly thanks to his energy, Buddhism spread into Central Asia, whence in due course it was to be taken along the Silk Route into China. Aśoka gave an example of the virtuous king, which was to remain an important ideal in both Hindu and Buddhist traditions.

One of his most lasting achievements was the spread of Buddhism to Sri Lanka, carried there by his son (or nephew), Mahinda. It was in Sri Lanka that the Pali scriptures were written down, and there a major form of Buddhism, Theravāda, rose to its height in the civilization which flowered first and most strikingly in Anuradhapura.

Classical and Medieval Theravāda

The coming of Mahinda, and the importance of Aśoka in the legendary past of Buddhism, added to the belief that the Buddha had set foot in Sri Lanka during his lifetime. For the Sinhalese people, who spoke a language derived from north India, it seemed as if their blessed isle was singularly favored to carry on the Dharma of the Buddha. It was a rich place, especially because of the development of irrigation in the dry north-central region. In the capital, as Buddhism came to be firmly established as the royal religion, there arose the great monastic settlement known as the Mahāvihāra, with its huge relic mound or *stūpa*, known as the Ruanväli. Later another monastic settlement known as the Abhayagiri was established, which was more hospitable than the conservative Mahāvihāra to non-Theravādin forms of Buddhism. In the third century C.E. the infiltration of too many unorthodox elements (as the rebels saw it) brought the hiving off of a third great settlement, the Jetavana.

Though some Mahāyāna and Hindu elements in the end were incorporated into the fabric of orthodox Theravāda – such as the use of Buddha statues (which for obscure reasons were not favored in early Buddhism) and the building of shrines to the gods inside temple complexes – Theravāda remained remarkably unchanged in the long period from King Dutthagamini in the first century B.C.E. until the advent of the British. It became a civilizational region, both forming and being formed by the culture of the island. A solid bond related monarchy to the Sangha. The king was to keep an eye on the monastic community, in case moral and spiritual abuses became too widespread. The Sangha ensured the prosperity and order of the kingdom. Monarchy contributed in a worldly way to the spiritual health of religion, and religion in a spiritual way to the wordly health of monarchy. Such a pattern was to be followed in Thailand and other Buddhist societies of South and Southeast Asia. Theravāda of course also flourished over a long period in India itself; but it is convenient for us to trace its shape through the living tradition of an Indic civilization outside of mainland India proper. Let us look to its various dimensions.

The Dimensions of Theravāda Buddhism

The Ritual and Practical Dimension

We have seen that meditation was a central part of early Buddhism. In theory this was a main occupation of monks and nuns. Also increasingly important, as the Pali canon of scriptures came to be written down, was study, with a growing body of commentaries. The complexities of Buddhist analysis were considerable: there were analyses of the material and psychological constituents of the individual, from blood, pus, and semen to mental dispositions and states of consciousness; and of forms of perception; and of rules of conduct; and so on. There was, then, fertile ground for commentarial work. Monks also had a duty to preach to the laity and instruct them in the values of social life. Then, as time went on there were increasingly elaborate public festivals, for instance at Vesak, the full moon in May, celebrating the birth, Enlightenment, and final decease of the Buddha. The clergy were also in demand to perform rites for the sick, and to protect households, and the like. In theory nuns and monks got their food by begging, but modern excavation has revealed arrangements for serving the monastic inhabitants with large quantities of food, doubtless ultimately supplied by the king and other laity. At the end of Vassa, the rainy season of retreat, lay folk presented new robes to the monks, and this was an occasion of joyful ceremonial.

What made the great monasteries possible was high income from food-growing, and orderly government to control a society which had to maintain large irrigation works. Naturally, over the centuries there were attempts at reform of a religion which risked becoming self-satisfied in a very rich environment. There were those who became *araññika* or forest-monks, and who revived the custom of the hermit life, dwelling alone in caves and huts in the jungle, and practicing strict meditation. They were important to outlying village life, for their reputation for merit made the villagers' offerings especially potent.

Theravāda Buddhism some key terms

Anattā The doctrine that nothing and no one has a permanent self.

Arhant A saintly monk who has attained *nibbāna* and serenely awaits his final liberation.

Buddha An enlightened being who has attained *bodhi* (enlightenment) and has seen the truth of Dhamma.

Dhamma The teaching of the Buddha which leads to liberation.

Dukkha Often translated "suffering": the lack of welfare or satisfaction in anything and a fundamental characteristic of life in the world.

Jhāna Meditation or a stage of meditation (usually there are reckoned to be eight or nine such stages).

Kamma Action and the effects of action in determining your situation in the round of rebirth.

Nibbāna The state of a saint, in which his craving has been "blown out," as with a flame.

Paññā Insight or wisdom concerning the nature of reality.

Paṭiccasamuppāda The law of codependent origination which links together the events of the world.

Saṃsāra The flux of existence and the round of rebirth.

Sangha The order of monks, nuns, and lay disciples founded by the Buddha to carry on the tradition.

For the laity, various works of piety were the norm: feeding the monks and nuns, sending a son or daughter into the order, going to the monasteries to circumambulate the *stūpa* or relic-mound, often huge and white, its plaster surface shining against the greens of the tropical landscape. There were gifts which the poorest and the richest might give to the Sangha. All such deeds brought merit which might help an individual to attain heaven next time, or at least a more favorable station in life. For the laity perhaps heaven was the dominant hope; but, as still today, they were able to distinguish between the desire for enjoyment, of which rebirth in one of the many heavens would be the greatest example, and spiritual growth, of which *nibbāna* (*nirvāṇa*) would be the culminating point. In their lives the monks and nuns stood as constant reminders of the ideal of "giving up" and looking to a goal beyond all ordinary goals.

Largely under outside (Mahāyāna) influence, there came to be shrines at the temples which included Buddha statues, some of enormous size. These became objects of piety, and again merit and mental purification could be had by making offerings to the Buddha. And surrounding Buddhist practice and mingling with it were the various gods and spirits, to whom the villagers still turned for help with harvest, possession, sickness, and other concerns. This interface with ordinary culture has been characteristic of Buddhism throughout its spread.

The Ethical Dimension

Theravādin ethics pointed to the importance of intentions. Ultimately it was the psychological state of the actor which determined the impact of *karma*. Underlying the Five Precepts, which enjoined people to avoid killing, taking what is not given, wrong sexual activity, wrong speech, and taking intoxicants, were the great duties of cultivating compassion, sympathy, benevolence, and equanimity. The pious lay person and the monk or nun alike were encouraged to practice self-awareness, noting their own impulses and motivations, with a view to purifying intentions. If, as we have noted, lay persons were often motivated by the thought of acquiring merit and so gaining a better life in the future, this was in effect a popular encouragement to virtue. Morality was also encouraged by the Jātaka stories, being tales of the Buddha in previous lives, manifested as an animal or a human in each account. The stories often underlined ideas such as self-sacrifice. They helped also to hold up the example of the Bodhisattva or Buddha-to-be which was due to undergo powerful development in the Great Vehicle.

The Experiential Dimension

One of the reasons why the classical Theravāda is so important in the history of religions is that it is the prime example of mysticism without God, and even without some all-pervading Absolute such as Brahman. The monk, nun, or pious lay person who follows the prescriptions of one of the famous manuals, for instance Buddhaghosa's *Visuddhimagga* (*Path of Purity*, fourth-fifth century C.E.), is doing something very like those Sufis and Christian contemplatives who empty their minds to make way for a divine vision. But here the ultimate experience is seen as realizing or (so to speak) touching *nibbāna*: coming in contact with that unborn, transcendental state which for the Buddha is the Ultimate. The training of one who takes this path to the Highest includes much besides the purification of consciousness – it involves moral improvement, for instance – but at its heart is the practice of the *jhāna* (Sanskrit: *dhyāna*), to which we referred earlier (see page 99). But since the Buddha did not believe in anything Beyond in the form of God or Absolute, mysticism in the Theravāda tradition does not involve any kind of sense of union.

Though the Theravāda has no place for a Supreme Being, its practice has tended to invest its ceremonies and artifacts with something of that sense of the sacred. So the lay person might feel awe at a Buddha statue, as well as with the lesser deities of daily life. In popular cults, too, there were aspects of shamanism in the healing ceremonies for those possessed by demons. But the gods and spirits were outside the Sangha's realm of organization. For the spiritual path itself, emphasis was laid upon purity of life and self-training through meditation. It was through this that holy monks and nuns showed a strange power.

The Narrative Dimension

It became a commonplace that the story of the Buddha's life could be traced through many generations. His previous lives were edifying; and after his decease his influence still lived. For monks and laity alike in Sri Lanka this tale was continued in the various chronicles, which saw the island as creating a fine Buddhist civilization and as battling (against Tamil Hindu dynasties, for instance) for the preservation of this spiritual heritage. This was reinforced by the pilgrimage to Adam's Peak, which emphasized a sense of the holy presence of the Buddha in the island. There was also the shrine at Mihintale, recalling Mahinda's coming at the behest of the legendary great emperor, Aśoka. In these ways, the story of the Buddha was extended to history, giving the assurance of the central place of Sri Lanka, blessed island, in the whole story of liberation.

The Doctrinal Dimension

Though there was plenty of the miraculous in the scriptural accounts of the Buddha, Theravāda saw him primarily as a great human being who, however, in attaining a full understanding of the Dhamma, came to embody it. So there was a transcendental side to his nature. But believers adhered to the view that it was unwise to go beyond what the Buddha had said, so that though analysis could be elaborated, no large-scale development of doctrine was possible. Little could be said as to the nature of *nibbāna*, except that it was Beyond the perishable events of this world. They stuck to the fourfold negation expressed by the Buddha. On the question of whether a Tathāgata

Adam's Peak, Sri Lanka.

existed after death, he said: "It is not correct to say that he does, or does not, or both does and does not, or neither does nor does not." Such comprehensive denial suggested that the question was wrongly put: *nibbāna* as a condition escapes our ordinary language.

Great emphasis was placed on the *anattā* or nonself doctrine. Individuals transmigrate, but there is no permanent soul. What use is an unchanging soul? It can achieve nothing by the very fact that it is unchanging: there can be no development without change. It merely stands as a symbol for the possibility of salvation, and that was sufficiently taken care of by use of the concept of *nibbāna*.

The world of the Theravāda is vast: there are many world systems apart from ours, and each "galaxy" has its own heavens and hells and earth, its own gods, including Brahmā, and its own Satan, Mara, the death-dealing Tempter. The universe is virtually unending and beginningless, and exists in vast dimensions of space and time. The individual transmigrates through this vast system, now going to heaven, now assuming human, animal, or ghostly form, now suffering torments in one of the hells, now rising to the insect class, and so on and so on, till hopefully he may be reborn as a monk and approach final liberation: *nibbāna*. Then he will no longer be reborn. Pure selflessness in spirit will ensure that he will not regret the final disappearance of his individuality.

The Buddhist analysis of persons was designed to reinforce this sense of "selflessness": a person was made up of five types of events – bodily events, perceptions, feelings, dispositions, and states of consciousness. These five groups of events were dispersed at death and reassembled because of the continued impulses contained in the dispositions. So if you still have a craving for this or that you will be reborn. What holds one part of your life together with another is just a complex chain of causes; similarly with what holds one life together with another. The person, then, is a temporary putting together of five kinds of impermanent events.

Much of the close doctrinal analysis in the Theravāda is in the third portion of the Tripitaka, that is, the threefold canon of scriptures. This, known as the *Abhidhamma* portion (the name means "Analysis of the Dhamma": Sanskrit *Abhidharma*), was the last to be assembled, after the two other portions, the *Sutta* (supposed discourses or *sūtras* of the Buddha) and *Vinaya* (Rule).

The Institutional and Material Dimension

The Vinaya rules control in great detail the daily life of the monk and nun. They can in theory be altered by majority vote, since the Sangha is constitutionally based on a republican form of government extant in the Buddha's time. But on the whole the conservative tendencies of the Theravāda have held the system fairly tight. The scriptures are shared, of course, by other Theravādin communities in other countries, such as Burma and Thailand, and there has been much interaction over the centuries between the Theravādin countries.

The brilliant capital of Anuradhapura came to be replaced by the glories of Polonnaruwa to the east, the center of a renewed irrigation-based civilization in the eleventh and twelfth centuries C.E. At this period there was greater integration between Buddhist and Hindu rites, and shrines to the gods were brought inside the temple complexes. We find, then, in Theravādin Sri Lanka a rich Indic civilization, which had a strong feeling of its glorious destiny in the spiritual life of the human race. Its central values were expressed in the marvelous Buddha-statues, some of which still survive.

Mahāyāna Buddhism

The Rise of the Mahāyāna

In parallel with the full formation of the Theravādin tradition there came into existence a type of Buddhism which regarded itself as a Mahāyāna, a Greater Vehicle toward salvation than the more narrowly conceived Theravāda and other "Lesser Vehicle" schools. Its roots relate to the ethical, ritual, and philosophical dimensions. At the ethical level, there was felt to be an increasing strain in the conventional interpretation of Buddhism: if a person strove through the practice of *dhyāna* and the like to better himself or herself and ultimately to attain *nirvāṇa*, was not this essentially selfish and ego-oriented? The ideal of the serene *arhant* or Theravādin saint was in the final analysis as egoistic as the pursuits of the wealth-gaining merchant. The problem was the tension between insight and compassion, and was resolved, said the proponents of these ideas, in the ideal of the Bodhisattva, or Buddha-to-be, who out of compassion puts off his own final salvation till all are saved. This was a development of ideas implicit in the Jātaka stories and in the career of the Buddha himself, who was tempted to leave the world but stayed to preach the liberating, but subtle and difficult, Dharma.

In the ritual dimension, there was a growth in northwest India, from about the second century B.C.E., of the use of Buddha statues. It was not a long step from this to the idea that Buddhas continue to be present to us and so can be worshiped. This generated a type of Buddhism in which *bhakti* (warm devotion) came to supplement and even displace the austerer form of self-training, and mysticism. Out of this arose mythological innovations: stories about great Bodhisattvas such as Avalokiteśvara, the Lord Who Looks Down (with compassion), and Amitābha, the Buddha of Infinite Light. Already about the third century B.C.E, a group known as the Mahāsanghikas had begun to break away from the Sthaviravādin (Theravādin) tradition in India, arguing for a more open community, and for a less rigid adherence to the words of the historical Buddha. They regarded the Buddhas as *lokottara*, beyond the world and transcendent, and yet somehow still present. All these tendencies came together from the first century B.C.E. onward in the worship of a multiplicity of Buddha and Bodhisattva figures. This gave Buddhism a rich *bhakti* dimension. It also developed ideas of merit, so that the laity, and indeed monks and nuns, could gain merit by *pūjā*, the worship of these semidivine beings; and this in turn paved the way for a doctrine of grace, that is, salvation granted from above.

In some ways the philosophical changes were even more dramatic, though they are not always easy to grasp. Parallel developments occurred in the writings known as *Prajñāpāramitā Sūtras*, or *sūtras* of the Perfection of Wisdom, and in the writings of the philosopher Nāgārjuna of the early second century C.E. It may be noted that scriptures (*sūtras*) of various kinds were being composed in this period in Sanskrit or what is called Buddhist Hybrid Sanskrit. The writings are not cryptic and secretive, like Hindu parallels (their *sūtras* cannot be understood without a teacher or commentary); Buddhist writings are generally long and open, to the point of being repetitive. But the fact that new scriptures were being composed was important: it was a period when writing was becoming more universal, and something of the mystique which writing possesses for those who are still being weaned from oral traditions rubbed off on such literature. Texts were even to be put in *stūpas* and so reverenced like relics. The words describe the Truth and participate in the Truth; so in reverencing texts you reverence the Truth, and in doing this you reverence the Buddha, whose body is Truth. Naturally the

Theravāda resisted the introduction of what it regarded as new and unwarranted "scriptures" into the canon. But the composers of the new texts thought of themselves as drawing out the essence of the Buddha's message, and so the writings could be ascribed to the Buddha himself.

The fundamental teaching of the Perfection of Wisdom is that all things in the world are relative to one another. They are mutually conditioned. Nothing has its own nature in itself. Intrinsically all things are "empty." If there is any ultimate truth it is this: the truth of emptiness, which is ineffable and can only be realized through direct experience – the mystical experience of the Buddhas.

Nāgārjuna's Mādhyamika or "Middle" philosophy is very similar and is argued in a more explicitly philosophical manner, refuting alternative theories. It can be shown, according to Nāgārjuna, that certain fundamental concepts which pervade all our thinking and talking, such as the idea of cause, are contradictory. If causes are short-lived events, then they go out of existence before their effects arrive; and this implies that the existent is caused by the nonexistent, which is absurd. And so on with all theories. If our fundamental ideas are vitiated by contradictions, so then are all accounts of the world. At best our language is a convenience, but it cannot "get at" the nature of reality, which is relative, empty, unspeakable. So we follow the Buddha, for he pointed the way through the contradiction, to the experience of liberation which can replace all philosophy, including the Buddha's own. This approach of Nāgārjuna's implies a two-level theory of truth: a distinction between ordinary pragmatic truth and ultimate, experienceable, Truth.

These notions from the Perfection of Wisdom and the Mādhyamika combined with religious ones. In attaining Truth we in effect become Buddhas, just as at the ethical level in treading the path of the Bodhisattva we are indeed Buddhas-to-be, and the Buddha nature resides in each one of us. In worshiping Buddhas and Bodhisattvas we are still at the lower level and, as it were, worshiping our future state. The whole apparatus of celestial Buddhas and belief in the earthly Buddha eventually can be discarded when we enter the Beyond, in indescribable enlightenment.

There was another twist to the tale. If you recognize with Nāgārjuna that our usual conceptual distinctions between one thing and another are merely provisional, then so is our conventional distinction between *nirvāṇa* and *saṃsāra*. In other words, we already are in the realm of *nirvāṇa*, but do not know it until we have the "higher" point of view. All this fitted together with a new role for the lay person, who could as well tread the Bodhisattva path in the ordinary life of *saṃsāra*.

The Mahāyāna Pure Land
Three centuries or more after Nāgārjuna's work, the brothers Asanga and Vasubandhu propounded the so-called Vijñānavāda or Consciousness school. It is often thought to teach the unreality of the world and its origin in the mind. So it is in the philosophical sense "idealist." But more strictly it teaches

The doctrinal or philosophical dimension: Nāgārjuna, the greatest philosopher in India after the Buddha.

that everything which we claim as the truth or knowledge is qualified by consciousness: that is, it is reality as interpreted by consciousness and language. It is always seen through the lens of the subject–object structure of consciousness. In itself, however, reality does not have this subject–object character. We can seek to obtain a unitive consciousness through the higher experience of Buddhism.

More important in the life of ordinary people was the Sukhāvatī or Pure Land school, which arose about the time of Nāgārjuna; it holds that the Buddha Amitābha has constructed a Pure Land far to the west, full of splendors and joys, such as deep and warm rivers and trees made of jewels. This place is highly conducive to the ultimate attainment of *nirvāṇa*; but its glories tended to dominate the imagination and it became for many an end in itself, like the Christian or Islamic Paradise. Just by calling on the name of Amitābha, the faithful were assured of translation at death to the Pure Land.

We shall return to these forms of the Mahāyāna when we are dealing with Chinese and Japanese experience in Chapter 9, for there they had their fullest expression. These and many other schools of Buddhism flourished in India during the first millennium C.E. They flourished in such study centers as Nalanda in the north and Nagarjunikonda in the south; and were interwoven with the fabric of growing Hinduism. There still remains one more phase of the life of Buddhism in South Asia, before the modern period; and that is its journey into Tibet and life there. This is tied in with those developments known as Tantra.

Buddhism Spreads North: the Tibetan Experience

The cultural region which stretches from Ladakh and Nepal up over the mountains into Tibet, and east beyond today's Tibet into western China, can conveniently be called the Tibetan region. It came gradually to absorb influences from both China and India, but in the end Indian, and in particular Buddhist, influence was predominant. The area assumed a special significance, for the destruction of Buddhist centers in north India by Turkish Muslim pillagers left Tibet as the great repository of Mahāyāna texts, as well as of a whole assemblage of esoteric or secret Tantric texts. The form of Buddhism which had developed in northern Bihar, Bengal, and Kashmir was naturally accessible to Tibet. And it included what is often referred to as the Vajrayāna or "Diamond Vehicle," sometimes also called the Mantrayāna or "Sacred Formula Vehicle." The reason for this last name was because of the particular emphasis put on the use of ritual utterances in this form of Buddhism.

The Vajrayāna was concerned with new ways of transforming consciousness, typically in conjunction with the guidance of a guru, through the practice of relating both to sacred formulae and to the visualized figures of various Buddhas and deities. Equations between the different aspects of individual life, the cosmos, and the deities led to a fusion of inner and outer magical and psychological methods. Sometimes Tantric initiates used forbidden practices, such as meat-eating and sexual intercourse, to help them to rise "beyond morality" and so beyond the world. Such methods, by the use of secret rituals and the breaking of taboos in a ritual context, were pioneered also in the Hindu environment of north India. But though they were an element in the kind of Buddhism which came to be established in Tibet, Tibetan Buddhism could also more broadly be defined as Mahāyāna. The texts that they studied, much of the yoga they practiced, and much of the spirit of Tibet could be said to be "Greater Vehicle" in character.

The "Diamond" of the name of the Vajrayāna refers to the eternal Buddhahood resident in all beings, unsplittable, and achieved through the cutting edge of wisdom (*prajñā*). The spiritual exercises of Tantra aimed at identification with this Buddhahood here and now, and conceived of the individual as being of the same nature as the universe. So by self-purification, usually using earlier Buddhist methods of meditation, an adept could visualize his chosen deity or Buddha-figure and thus attain unity with him. The use of magical diagrams or *maṇḍalas* combined the elements of sacred formulae and the internal use of the visual imagination. Various equations occurred: the five *skandhas* or groups of events which make up the individual (bodily events, perceptions, feelings, dispositions, and states of consciousness) were equated with five Buddhas – Vairocana, Akṣobhya, Ratnasambhava, Amitābha, and Amoghasiddhi (their names mean: Illuminator, Imperturbable, Jewel-Born, Boundless Light, and Infallible Success). These in turn correspond to the five directions of the cosmos (center, east, south, west, and north), and to five kinds of evil and five kinds of wisdom. By imagining

vividly your deity, you gain unity with him and he with you. This nondual unification is often symbolized by the sexual bond, where two bodies become fused into one.

Female deities took on great importance as consorts or *śaktis* of Buddhas; the greatest of them, Tārā, the Savioress, is the consort of the great Bodhisattva Avalokiteśvara. Though gentler in nature and purer in appearance than the somewhat fierce representation of the Goddess in the Hindu tradition, the Goddess here is part of a very old stream of sentiment going back to the beginnings of Indic civilization, but here translated to Tibet. Avalokiteśvara and Tārā, incidentally, are thought to have procreated monkeys who transformed themselves over generations into the Tibetan people. (No emotional problems here over the theory of evolution!)

The first monastery in Tibet was founded near the end of the eighth century C.E. There was some resistance to the new religion from the indigenous religion, commonly referred to as Bön (see below). It was in the eleventh century that there was a second and more vigorous diffusion of Buddhism. It was in this period that the great teacher Atiṣa, who had been to Sumatra to advise the court there, came to Tibet at the insistence of the Buddhist rulers of west Tibet. One of his disciples founded the religious order of bKa'-gdams-pa. In the same century, in consequence of the teaching of Marpa, a famous Tibetan monk who had studied at one of the great north

(*above left*) In the Himalayan Region, as in Sikkim, the Vajrayāna or Diamond Vehicle predominates: this thin old Buddhist woman uses a prayer wheel to express her piety.
(*above right*) A Tibetan painting of Avalokiteśvara as a meditation Buddha to be.

A mandala or ritual diagram displaying Aksobhya, the Eastern Buddha, one of the Buddhas of the five directions (North, South, East, West, and Center).

Indian universities, the Sa-skya order was started. A third order, the Bka'-rgyud-pa, was host to Tibet's most beloved religious teacher, Mi-la-ras-pa (or Milarepa, 1079–1153).

On the whole the reason for the importation of Buddhism into Tibet by its secular rulers seems to have been political, to provide a "modern" ideology of rule and to open up to Tibet the advantages of literacy and philosophy. In the ensuing centuries it became more important due to the conversion of many Mongols, especially the emperor of China, Kublai Khan. The grand lamas of the Sa-skya order were nominated in effect as viceroys, under Mongol suzerainty; eventually, after political conflict, sometimes armed (so we have the spectacle of Buddhist orders fighting one another as monks of war, but overwhelmingly for political and not ideological reasons), the chief rule passed in the seventeenth century C.E. to the head of the reformed Dge-lugs-pa order, which had been founded by the great Tson-kha-pa in the fourteenth century. The succession of the Dalai Lamas, as they are still called, is by a process of identifying a reincarnation of a deceased Dalai Lama. This was a method of succession which had been used by other orders in Tibet since the twelfth century.

Thus we have established in Tibet a kind of theocracy or mingling of deities into one personality. (One could call it a Buddhocracy.) Though the country was thoroughly infused with varieties of the Vajrayāna, it also contained something of its own native Bön tradition. But this too had undergone a transformation over the years as a result of Buddhist influence. Ascribing its founding to the legendary Gśen-rab, from a country far to the west, who was a fully enlightened being at birth and spent his life as a prince propagating the Bön religion, the religion had its own corpus of scriptures corresponding to those of the Buddhists. Just as the Tibetan Buddhists believe that the scriptures in their corpus, the Tanjur, were expounded by the Buddha Śākyamuni himself, so the Bön-po think of *their* Tanjur as having been uttered by Gsenrab himself. Also like the Buddhists, they have a body of commentaries and other works known as the Kanjur. The Bön-po have their own monasteries, order, *stūpas*, and so on: they have produced a sort of mirror image of Buddhism. They circumambulate their *stūpas* and other holy objects counter-clockwise, and likewise spin their prayer wheels; but they teach that the Buddha was a fraud, and that the coming of Buddhism to Tibet was a great disaster, the cause of evil *karma*. Even so, their aims and methods and popular piety are much the same as those of Buddhism, and the two religions live side by side amicably enough.

The Dimensions of Mahāyāna Buddhism

In many ways there were affinities between the Great Vehicle and the Theravāda. But generally the Great Vehicle extended ideas and practices present in the latter. Thus its *ritual* dimension added worship to the central practice of meditation. This was encouraged by developments in the *material* dimension, in the cult of Buddha statues and representations of Bodhisattvas in the increasingly elaborate temples. These were in turn imported into the Theravāda over the centuries. As to the *philosophical* dimension the notion of Emptiness was a way of reinterpreting the notions of impermanence and momentariness, although the equation of *nirvāṇa* and *saṃsāra* was a more radical departure from the Lesser Vehicle's dualism between life in the round of rebirth and the state of liberation. The *narrative* dimension emphasized the idea of the Bodhisattva, and tended toward the exaltation of celestial Buddhas. The *ethical* dimension gave a much stronger place to the ideals of self-sacrifice and compassion, as people were encouraged to take the view of the Bodhisattva and devote themselves to the service of all living beings. In the main life of the Mahāyāna in South Asia, the *institutional* dimension stayed much the same, with the celibate Sangha playing a central role. In the *experiential* dimension meditation remained central, save that in the Pure Land school devotionalism became ever more prominent, with numinous and loving experience of the god-like Buddhas such as Amitābha often replacing the inner light of meditation. Other motifs can be pointed to in later Indian developments, such as Tantric Buddhism, where ritual, sexual, and other means were employed to achieve enlightenment. Sexual coupling has long been thought symbolic of the union of the mystic with the divine. For the inner higher experience is supposed to overcome the normal contrast between subject and object, as the meditator achieves an objectless experience.

Mahāyāna Buddhism dies out in India

In some ways the shape of Buddhism by the eleventh century C.E. had approximated too closely to the Hinduism of the period. Becoming thus spiritually superfluous, its influence on Indian culture was greatly weakened. Moreover, at this time there were serious inroads made into north India by Islamic powers from Central Asia. They were horrified at the use of images in both Buddhist and Hindu institutions. Being less tied to monasticism, the Hindu way of life found it easier to survive: but many famous Buddhist institutions, including the university at Nālandā, were destroyed. Except for the area close to the Himalayas and in parts of Bengal, Buddhism largely died out in the subcontinent. But the Mahāyāna in particular was highly successful in its life beyond India, in the Far East. In Sri Lanka the Theravādin tradition continued. It was admittedly in severe decline in the period leading up to the final British takeover of the island in 1815. However, it remained vigorous in Southeast Asia.

CHAPTER SIX

Buddhism in Southeast Asia

Buddhism in Southeast Asia

Southeast Asia comprises the states known as Burma (now Myanmar), Thailand, Malaysia, Brunei, Singapore, Indonesia, the Philippines, Kampuchea (now Cambodia), Laos, and Vietnam. All of these areas except for the Philippines came heavily under Indian influence – or, in the case of Vietnam, Chinese influence, which itself contained Indic elements in the shape of Buddhism. The patterns of the past, which included Hindu kingdoms, as in Kampuchea, have been largely overlaid by Theravāda Buddhism and Islam: the former is the predominant religion of Burma, Thailand, Kampuchea, and Laos, while Islam is predominant in Malaysia, Brunei, and Indonesia. Singapore is basically Chinese in culture, and the Vietnamese tradition has been greatly under Chinese influence and has similar religious characteristics. The Philippines are largely Catholic. The Chinese populations of Southeast Asia postdate the colonial era, having resulted from the importation of Chinese labor into Malaysia and Singapore under the British, and into Indonesia under the Dutch.

Indian influences began to penetrate Southeast Asia from the second and third centuries C.E. Because roughly speaking India had a mixed Buddhist and Hindu culture, there was a Hindu–Buddhist mix of ideas and institutions ready to take root in Southeast Asian soil. The main period of the importation of Indian influences was from the seventh century C.E. onward, and the next six centuries saw the establishment of, and interplay between, a number of important cultures. From the thirteenth century, over much of mainland Southeast Asia, there was a consolidation of Theravāda Buddhism after the Sinhalese (Sri Lankan) model. This was also the period when Muslim power began to penetrate the area. The empire of Malacca, strong in the Malay peninsula and Sumatra, adopted Islam, and became a center for the spread of Islam into many of the Indonesian islands and into the southern Philippines. Meanwhile the north Vietnamese state of Dai Viet had fought off Chinese invasions, designed to reclaim it for the Chinese empire to which it had at one

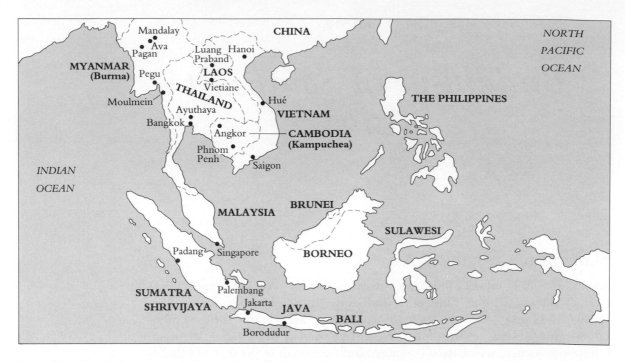

Map of Southeast Asia and Indonesia.

time belonged, and expanded southward to take over the kingdom of Champa, forming an empire roughly the same as modern Vietnam. In addition to the major faiths to be found in the area, various smaller-scale religions belong to the various tribal groups existing right across the region.

It must be emphasized that, despite Indian influences and the fact that some Indian Brahmins, merchants, and Buddhist monks must have migrated and settled in the region, the cultural importation of Indian and Chinese elements was just that: it was convenient to borrow the Indian ideology of kingship, for instance, or to use Buddhist ideas in justifying political rule. The substratum of peoples upon which such a culture was grafted was a mixture, but neither Indian nor Chinese in the proper sense. So the imported great religions lived in balance with home-grown popular religions.

It is convenient to look upon the period up to the seventh century C.E. as the early period; the time from the seventh century C.E. to the shaping of Theravādin orthodoxy and the substantial presence of Islam – i.e. to the thirteenth century – as the preclassical period; and the thirteenth through sixteenth centuries as the classical period. Thereafter we are in the modern period and witnessing the varied responses of the region to the impact of the colonial times.

The Origins of Indian Influence

There have been differing theories as to why Indian cultural influences, both Buddhist and Hindu, crossed the Bay of Bengal and established themselves in Burma and other regions of the area. Whence ultimately came those vast monuments at Angkor Wat in Kampuchea and Borobodur in Java? Was it a matter of trade, or conquest, or religion, or what? There might have been elements of all three. But the evidence seems to have moved against what may be called the *vaiśya* and *kṣatriya* theories, that is, those views which look to the merchant and warrior castes, respectively, as the most important in the transmission of Indian cultural forms. The fact is that already there were kingdoms forming themselves in Southeast Asia, of an indigenous kind. But contact with south India (which must have involved some measure of trade) presented these smaller kingdoms, on their way to the creation of empires, with a model of ideology and theory of rule which were highly attractive. The agents of Indianization were similar to those which saw the spread of north Indian ideas and practices into south India: the Brahmins and the *śramanas* – Brahmins and recluses – many of the latter being organized into Buddhist and Jain orders. Holy persons were the bearers of a new civilization and theory of government. Not only that, but Brahmins, who had long acted as skilled advisers, could transmit the theories of government and of architecture. It seems then most likely that the "conversion" of much of Southeast Asia was a religious and ideological one, in which a new theory of rule was deliberately imported to consolidate the power of local princes and empires. All this was superimposed on a basis of the mingled agricultural religious practices of the varied indigenous peoples, who were now being organized by political means into more formidable wealth-producing units through the creation of irrigation schemes to enhance wet rice cultivation on a grander scale.

Kingdoms and Empires

An early empire mentioned by the Chinese was that of Fu-nan, which is probably a representation of the Khmer (Cambodian) word Phnom, meaning "mountain." No doubt, even as early as the second century C.E., its rulers adopted the title (reflecting practice in south India) of "king of the mountain." This was part of a mythic theory. The capital was built in the shape of a *mandala*, in which the central feature was a stone representation of the sacred mountain at the center of the world on which dwelt the God. The king's palace was a representation of the sacred center, and he was seen as divine representative on earth. It was he who, through his organizational power, did the earthly work of creation, bringing order out of chaos and ensuring the fertility of the realm. So in a way, as far as the people were concerned, there was a fair exchange. In exchange for the rice and other agricultural products and artifacts which served as taxes on the population they were given civil order and richness of harvests. A similar ideology was probably used in the kingdom to the east of Fu-nan, namely the state of Champa in the southern part of what is now Vietnam. The northern part of Vietnam was ruled as a Chinese province down to about 900 C.E. In distinction from the rest of Southeast Asia this part was subject to Chinese, rather than mostly Indian, cultural influences.

Apsaras or singers, whose heavenly music and dance give pleasure to men and gods, carved on a main building of the Angkor Thom complex at Angkor in Cambodia, built by King Jayavarman VII about 1200 C.E.

Eventually, in place of the old state of Fu-nan, a Khmer empire was established, especially under the ruler King Jayavarman II in the ninth century. Its capital, Angkor, came to be a wonderful repository of great buildings; the most important was the Viṣṇu sanctuary of King Suryavarman II (1113–50), known as Angkor Wat. It was later overgrown by the jungle, to be discovered and restored in modern times. The chief sacred focus of the Khmer kingly cult was Śiva: the *stūpa* or sacred mountain is in many cases surmounted by the *lingam*. In such a setting it was important to have Brahmins to perform the essential rites.

Meanwhile, with the decline of Fu-nan, there rose the power of the extensive maritime kingdom of Srivijaya, which probably developed from Indian trading settlements in southern Sumatra, and flourished because of its control of the convenient sea routes between India and China. Its capital was at Palembang, and it ruled over much of Sumatra, parts of Borneo, and the Malay peninsula. There were also Buddhist states to the east, in Java, especially remembered through the vast and beautiful temple complex at Borobodur, a *stūpa* complex fashioned like a *maṇḍala*. Up to the thirteenth century, Srivijaya, united to the Sailendra kingdom of Java, was undoubtedly the dominant power in Southeast Asia, and showed the effectiveness of a sea-based empire. It was long an important center of Mahāyāna Buddhist Sanskrit learning.

During the eleventh and twelfth centuries there arose a powerful state in Burma, based on the holy city of Pagan. Its power was destroyed by Mongol invasions, but to some degree it profited from the Islamic conquest of north India, which led many learned refugee monks from the Buddhist university city of Nālandā to flee to Pagan.

The Theravāda and the Classical Period

What we have termed the "classical period" of Southeast Asian culture overlaps with colonialism. But though toward the end of the period, in the sixteenth century, Portuguese and other powers from Europe were making their presence felt in the region, this was also the time of the flowering of a Theravādin civilization which has left its imprint on modern societies in the region. Burma, Thailand, Kampuchea, and Laos became predominantly Theravādin, and maintained a continuity of trade and scholarly exchange with Sri Lanka.

In Burma the way to a thoroughly Theravādin model of monarchy and civilization had been prepared by the conversion of King Anawrahta (Pali: Aniruddha), who came to the throne in 1044. His conversion to Theravāda by a famous monk, Shin Arahan, led to the wide influence of the religion, especially under his successor Kyanzittha, who caused the erection of the vast Schwezigon Pagoda in the city of Pagan. Anawrahta had sent for a Buddha relic from Sri Lanka, which was installed there, and a copy of the scriptures, the Tripitaka, to check out against scriptures that had been gained from the conquered Mon people. These contacts with Sri Lanka are significant and heralded much closer ties later on. Hitherto a prevalent variety of Buddhism was Tantra, which Anawrahta set out to replace.

The Burmese and others in Southeast Asia acquired the theory of kingship partly from the Sinhalese, whose Buddhist civilization had its heyday in the twelfth century under King Parakramabahu and after. According to this theory the king follows the myth of Aśoka Maurya, the ideal Buddhist emperor. A monarch might have to use evil means in coming to the throne or in expanding his empire, as did Aśoka, but ultimately he is a good king and pious Buddhist, who promotes vegetarianism, brings about justice, and encourages the spread of good religion. Such an ideal also sees the king as *cakkavattin*, the "Wheel-turner" (Sanskrit: *cakravartin*), the worldly counter-

The Buddha reflected in a pool at Maha That in Thailand.

part to the spiritual role assumed by the Buddha Śākyamuni. He is seen too as a *bodhisatta* (*bodhisattva*) or Buddha-to-be, and this links up with the myth of the future Buddha, Metteyya (Maitreya). The king incarnates the future Buddha, and thus links past to future, as well as the spiritual to the worldly life. This ideology was a useful one: it assigned parallel roles to political power and to the spiritual force wielded by the Sangha, in a new synthesis which tried to ensure both material prosperity and moral virtue in the state.

This model was perhaps at its most successful in the Southeast Asian mainland nations. In the fifteenth century Burma was ruled from Pegu, in the lower part of the country, by King Dhammaceti (reigned 1472–92), who sought to unify the Sangha; monks from Burma itself and surrounding countries such as Kampuchea and Thailand came to receive ordination. There were missions to Sri Lanka, and Sinhalese monks visited the center at Pegu. This period was represented as being the golden age of the Theravāda political system in the Burmese context.

Thai culture owed something to Kublai Khan's extension of Chinese boundaries and the forcing of many Thai-speakers southward to conquer areas that had been under Mon and Khmer dominance. They learned from these cultures and, under able monarchs, established Theravādin polities in differing parts of what is now Thailand, at Chiangmai in the north and at Ayuthia in the south, which dominated much of central Thailand. Buddhism continued to flourish, and to maintain links with the Sinhalese.

Widespread Thai influence in Laos and Kampuchea was one factor in ensuring that the "Theravādin revolution" spread to these kingdoms. In the case of Kampuchea, the older Hindu polity was undermined both politically and spiritually. The Theravādin monastic ideal kept the monks and nuns in close

The That Lang Temple in Vietiane, capital of Laos, with the monument to King Setthathirat, who built the temple in 1566.

relationship with the people, and their life of relative poverty was impressive. Moreover, it was possible, as throughout the region, to blend local cults of spirits relevant to the agricultural life with orthodox Theravāda, so that a happy symbiosis could be effected.

In those various Theravādin countries there is a similar worldview, but with some divergences of atmosphere and the contents of local religion where it is integrated into the Buddhist structure (there are also tribal cultures which lie partly outside the patterns of Theravāda influence). In the cosmology, the king is seen as a central figure, whose task is to protect the Dhamma (Dharma), assure the prosperity of his people, and encourage the ethical life. The round of rebirth is a generous one, for it includes heavenly possibilities of existence for the faithful lay person who gives generously to the Sangha. The monks and nuns are kept to their role of meditation and learning, as well as preaching to the people and assisting at ceremonies to ward off evil and the like. The capital city itself may become an important center of pilgrimage due to the building of splendid temples and the importation of prestigious relics from Sri Lanka and elsewhere. The local area will have its temples too, and they will incorporate shrines to local spirits, such as the *nats* in Burma.

Religion in Vietnam: the Chinese Influence

Unlike the other regions of mainland Southeast Asia, Vietnam was mostly under the influence of China, having indeed been part of the Chinese empire for a thousand years after its annexation in 111 B.C.E. by the Han dynasty. Subsequently, except for a short time in the early fifteenth century C.E., when it was again under Chinese control, it had its own independent existence; but as the kingdom of Dai Viet it mirrored the Chinese system. Confucianism

123

was the ideology of the court and the basis of the examination system; Taoism and Mahāyāna Buddhism were woven into the triple worldview. It was probably the Taoist element in this mix which was most closely integrated into indigenous folk motifs, partly through mediums, both male and female, who exercised shamanistic powers of healing, and partly through local and national tutelary deities who would preside over the affairs of each village or larger community. But Mahāyāna Buddhism, too, was firmly rooted in the soil of Vietnam, and though there remained some Theravādin monasteries, it was chiefly Chinese-affiliated Mahāyāna that predominated in the country. Thus we have a marked divergence in official religion between the Vietnamese and the rest of mainland Southeast Asia, especially in the classical period, just before the advent of the West.

Buddhism in Ceylon: a New Modernism

Meanwhile a somewhat special evolution of events had occurred to the south, in the administratively separate island of Ceylon (now Sri Lanka). The British had taken the central kingdom of Kandy in 1815, and for a while, according to the terms of the treaty settling the war, were obliged to support the Buddhist establishment of the Sangha. But the interpolation of Christian missions led to other pressures, and for a while Buddhist morale was depressed. In the latter half of the century a number of public debates between Christian missionaries and Buddhist monks revived interest in the defense of the faith, and Buddhists were satisfied of the greater rationality of their traditional religion.

Also important from the angle of reinvigorating Sinhalese self-esteem was the visit by an American, Colonel Henry S. Olcott (1832–1907). He had been involved originally in the formation of the Theosophical Society in 1875, with the charismatic Russian H. P. Blavatsky (1831–91), in New York. Olcott became a Buddhist, and the Theosophical Society always had Buddhist leanings, though its headquarters were established in Adyar, Madras. His support of Westerners who saw deep value in Eastern spirituality was of incalculable encouragement to Sinhalese Buddhists. And Olcott himself was very vigorous. He and the Theosophical Society helped to found Ananda College, the leading Buddhist school in Ceylon, and he prepared the way for the renewal of Buddhist scholarship, though himself not a scholar.

There is some analogy to Olcott's effect in Ceylon with that of Annie Besant (1847–1933), another Theosophist, and feminist. A brilliant speaker and organizer, her work in India included being so involved with the Indian Congress movement that she was elected its first woman President in 1917, and the foundation of the institution which grew into Banaras Hindu University, one of India's foremost universities and enshrining Hindu values. Interestingly, she adopted a gifted Hindu boy, Krishnamurti (1895–1986), who was expected to be a Theosophical World Teacher. After Besant's death he struck out very much on his own, and in fact taught ideas very similar to those of Mādhyamika and Zen Buddhism, on the inability of concepts to capture the real world.

At the turn of the century, Westerners like Olcott and Besant performed a valuable service in helping the people of South Asia to see, in a period of cultural arrogance on the part of the British and other Westerners, the vital meaning and importance of the indigenous religious traditions. Also important was the work of editing and publishing the Pali texts. This was in large measure due to the impetus of the British scholar T. W. Rhys Davids (1843–1922), who founded the Pali Text Society. This helped to give Ceylon Buddhists a clear view of their own basic heritage.

The introduction of Western-style education into Ceylon had similar effects to those in India. But the transition to independence was much gentler in Ceylon than in India. The cosmopolitanism of the Sinhalese found Western democracy congenial, and home rule was already partially established before World War II.

Two major forms of Buddhist modernism arose in this context. One was neofoundationalist, treating the Buddhism of the Pali canon as the norm – or rather seeing the Pali canon when suitably censored as being the norm. It was thought that rather a lot of the matter in the canon, about gods and spirits and so on, was the result of mythologizing the Buddha's original message, which had been purely rational and spiritual. Shorn of these supposed accretions, the canon was seen philosophically as generally in line with modern science (which sees the world as evanescent atoms in motion) and philosophy (for was the Buddha's teaching not empirical?). The difference from some Western forms of rationalism was that Buddhism admitted the importance of paranormal, illuminating experiences. If there was room for doubt it might be over the doctrine of rebirth, but that too could be accommodated with modern thinking provided we did not think about it naively. Naturally, this slimmed-down Buddhism was not the religion of the masses: for them color and myth were more important than philosophy. But Buddhism had the merit of teaching an ethical path, which could be conveyed to the masses. Such a Buddhism of course was quite attractive to an English-speaking elite: and for Europeans this Buddhism gave one the possibility of spirituality without having to believe in God (a belief which many Westerners had come to find incredible and even tiresome, with what they saw as its tendency to childish anthropomorphism).

Among other signs of revival and modernism was the work of the reformer Anagarika Dharmapāla (1864–1933), who did much in Buddhist education, and who worked to restore the Buddhist pilgrimage sites of India, especially Bodh-Gaya, the site of the Buddha's Enlightenment. In 1891, he founded the Mahabodhi Society, which received support from Buddhists in other parts of Asia and was a factor in the rise of ecumenical Buddhism, issuing in the creation of organizations such as the World Fellowship of Buddhists.

Though nationalism was a powerful ingredient in the Buddhist revival in Ceylon, its impact was muted by the relatively easy transition which the country made to independence. It was mostly after independence, achieved in

The Pious layman:
here a Sinhalese does
homage at the feet of a
vast Buddha statue in
Sri Lanka.

February 1948, that the strongest period of national resurgence came among the Sinhalese. This was expressed in the election campaign of 1956, when many Buddhist monks were involved on the side of the newly formed Sri Lanka Freedom Party. What it wanted was a reestablishment of something like classical Sinhala Buddhism, from the great days of Parakrama Bahu the Great and the high tide of Buddhist civilization. Its aim was now not so much modernist, philosophical Buddhism but a new arrangement in which Sangha and state would once again have a close relationship.

For a major problem in Theravādin countries – not only Ceylon – was how to reconstruct the world once the king had been removed by conquerors. In the old days there had been a reciprocal relationship between king and Sangha, with mutually defined roles. In a democratic age with modern institutions (and moving from under a foreign monarchy), what was the system to be? The ideal of Sinhala as the only official language (the main slogan of the 1956 campaign) reinforced the concept of a Sinhala Buddhist culture. Of course there were Sinhalese who were not Buddhists, mainly Christians, and their position was not easy. But the vast majority were Buddhist. Sri Lanka (it changed its name in 1972 with a new constitution) embarked on a period of neoclassical Sinhalese revival, in which the Buddhism of the chronicles was more stressed, and money was poured into reviving the architectural glories of Anuradhapura and Polonnaruwa and in fostering Buddhist schools and universities.

All this caused unrest among the Tamils, mainly Hindus of the Śaiva Siddhānta school, whose ancestors had been brought in as laborers in the nineteenth century. It was a conflict that ultimately led to the civil war of the 1980s. The Buddhist revival in Ceylon did not generate a clear ideology of toleration, such as that created by modern Hinduism, despite the generally tolerant character of the Buddhist tradition. The majority Sinhalese moreover felt themselves really to be a minority, because of the large number, over 50 million, of mainland Tamils in the Indian state of Tamil Nadu.

Despite these problems, the period after independence was one of great cultural vigor. Buddhist philosophy, especially, flourished through the writings of such vital figures as G. P. Malalasekara (1911–68) and K. N. Jayatilleke. A new parliament building in traditional Sinhalese style near the place of the old capital at Koṭṭe was created, and the fostering of Buddhist arts saw a considerable revival of the material dimension of the tradition. Buddhist monks traveled abroad, and the influence of Sri Lankan Theravāda on world spirituality has been great, in part because of a vital renewal of the practices of meditation. At the same time Buddhism has involved itself in social work. In this it has been influenced by Christian organizations, which are also reflected in such institutions as the Young Men's Buddhist Association.

Southeast Asia and the Colonial Period

The impact of the colonial powers in Southeast Asia was rather piecemeal. Early on, the Dutch and Portuguese, especially, penetrated the Straits of Malacca, and in due course the Dutch created a wide-ranging empire in the East Indies (Indonesia). The British came to be interested, also for trading reasons, in Singapore, which they virtually founded, and Malaya, with parts of Borneo left for dispute between the two European powers. The British also in the nineteenth century acquired lower and then upper Burma, as an adjunct to their Indian empire. The French, rather late in the colonial scramble, had an interest in Vietnam, and eventually annexed virtually all of Indochina, including North and South Vietnam, Laos and Cambodia (Kampuchea). The United States, after its war with Spain in 1898, rewarded itself with the turbulent Philippines. The only nation not to be administered by foreign powers was Thailand.

Burma and most of mainland Indochina were Theravādin in religion, and Vietnam also had a strong Buddhist presence. To the south, Malaya and Indonesia were predominantly Islamic (see Chapter 7). The Philippines is the only predominantly Christian, in this case Catholic, country in Asia.

The effect of colonial rule on the Buddhist countries was partly to sever the bond between the Sangha and the government, by removing the existing monarchies. It also dramatically injected into these societies the educational systems and fruits of Western culture, forcing some reappraisal of the traditions.

The colonial period did not last all that long, however. World War II brought the Japanese into the area, at first hailed as Asian liberators from European rule. Although the Vietnam War (which was a continuation of the anti-French struggle resumed after the expulsion of the Japanese in 1945) did not end till the 1970s, substantially it was the 1950s that marked the main boundary between the colonial and the postcolonial eras.

The region came to evolve, in response to the colonial era, along very different lines. The Philippines' modernization came in effect through its conversion to Catholicism and occupation by Spain and the United States. The restoration of its Constitution after the Japanese occupation was not sufficient to prevent the slide into military dictatorship and the persistence of Marxist and Islamic rebellions. In many ways the country followed the pattern of Latin American countries, since the existence of large landowners has given point to communistic ideas among the poor peasantry.

In the rest of the region there are some interesting variations. Thus, ultimately, a rather old-fashioned line in Marxism prevailed in Vietnam after many years of anticolonial and civil war. There were other, rejected options: a rather right-wing dictatorship based on Catholic and conservative Confucian support; and a Buddhist neutralism which was a significant factor in the Vietnam War. In Laos and Cambodia there were fruitless attempts to restore the stability of the old-style kingship with Sangha support in the face of revolutionary movements. That movement in Cambodia was the "Red Khmer," or "Khmer Rouge," a movement with its own ideology, which we shall call for the sake of analysis "post-Buddhist quasi-Marxism," which had devastating effects on the country, and has been replaced essentially by orthodox Marxism under the occupation forces of Vietnam.

In Thailand – which managed to escape occupation – a modernized Buddhism stayed on as the ideology of the state, despite some Marxist and Islamic rebellions. Alliance with the United States kept it importantly in the capitalist domain. Burma, on the other hand, had been affected by socialist values, which it saw as a means of preserving the organic identity of the society, and most of the period of independence after World War II has been devoted to the practice of isolation. It has what may be thought of as a Buddhist autarkism or self-sufficiency as its aim: this ideal has some resemblance to the Khmer Rouge ideology. Finally, in the other predominantly non-Muslim regime of the region, namely Singapore, this island republic has undertaken a rapid modernization through welfare capitalism under a vaguely Confucian paternalistic regime.

In the whole region some complications follow from the embedding within the larger ethnic groups of smaller nations or tribes, such as the

Hmong in Laos and the Kachin and Karen in Burma, who have played an independent part in events – being for instance in perpetual civil war with the Burmese government and under non–Buddhist, mainly Christian, leadership.

Buddhism in Thailand: the Process of Modernization

The survival of Thailand as an independent state in the 1840s and beyond, when European traders were becoming active in the area, was largely the work of two reforming kings. The first, Mongkut (1804–68), had a remarkable career. He happened (somewhat in the Thai fashion) to be in a monastery when he was passed over for succession to the throne in favor of an uncle, and he stayed on as a monk until his accession quite a time later, in 1851. During this period he became a fine Pali scholar and questioned many of the existing practices in Thai monasticism – which led him to accept reordination, together with a number of followers, in the Mon lineage (the Mon being a minority ethnic group), and in effect found a new branch of the Sangha, which was called the Dhammayuttika Nikāya or "Branch of Those Adhering to the Dhamma" – or, in Thai, Thammayut. It gained considerable prestige among the Thai elite, both in towns and in the countryside, and attracted the patronage of influential lay persons, both men and women.

Later, when Mongkut became king, he had to patronize the whole order, including of course the majority, the validity of whose ordination and practice he questioned. But it was the Dhammayuttika branch which still attracted his special favor, and it became an arm in his concern for the modernization of his country. His attitudes were not only spiritual and directed to the deepening and reforming of the life of Buddhist monks and nuns, and restoring Pali studies. Doctrinally he was a neofoundationalist, going back as he saw it to the canonical foundations of the faith. Like others, later, in the West, he saw the Buddhist canon as essentially rationalist and empirical. It was from this point of view that he came to reject the old model of the universe which was used to justify the role of kings in the medieval period.

According to this model the king exists at a focal cosmological point. The universe is conceived as being at three levels. Above is the ascending scale of heavens, to which you have access through meditation; different gods of varying bliss and longevity exist at this level. To be reborn in such a heaven is the reward for especially meritorious work. Below the earthly realm there is the world of ghosts and demons and purgatories, where those who have sinned greatly are reborn, and where they undergo grisly fates. In the middle realm, which is where Buddhas appear, there are various sorts and conditions of living beings, and one's height in the scale of beings is again determined by merit. At the heart of this earthly realm is the *cakkavattin* or universal monarch (literally "Wheel-turner" – a title for the Buddha who began the turning of the wheel of the Dhamma or Teaching, but assigned also to the figure of the ideal ruler). The ideal is usually identified with the emperor Aśoka, who became a template for Southeast Asian monarchy. The king has a crucial role in the scheme of things, because in maintaining order and the Sangha, and in promoting virtue, he increases merit and gives humans greater opportunity to ascend in the scale of life and to attain heavenly as well as earthly welfare.

It was a noble picture, but it was presented in an antique way. It involved, as did Christian and other traditional cosmologies, a three-decker universe, infested too in this case with gods and spirits permitting fanciful explanations of natural phenomena. It was this kind of picture which Mongkut demythologized. He saw the universe as essentially moral and the role of Buddhism as promoting ethical and spiritual welfare. He had his foreign minister and close associate write a book setting forth this more empiricist account. In it, heaven and hell became not so much places as states of mind and useful pedagogical devices. Scorn was lavished on the older explanations of natural phenomena in terms of gods. Religion was thoroughly spiritualized. It was an early and courageous version of Buddhist modernism and was suffused with the spirit of naturalism.

The program of reform was carried on by Mongkut's son, Chulalongkorn (reigned 1868–1910), who further centralized the Sangha under government supervision, and set up Buddhist academies for the better training of the clergy. Buddhists in Thailand, and elsewhere in Southeast Asia, came to see Buddhism as compatible with or even prefiguring modern science, and the law of dependent origination was seen as a way of stating the fundamental principle underlying the universe. It is true that there are many naturalistic elements in the Pali canon, and the rationality and intellectualism of the Buddha are evident in the texts. So the neofoundationalist style of modern Thai education of the clergy lent itself to the interpretation of the faith in a modern manner.

The ritual dimension: people light incense sticks at the Lak Muang Shrine, where Bangkok was founded in 1782.

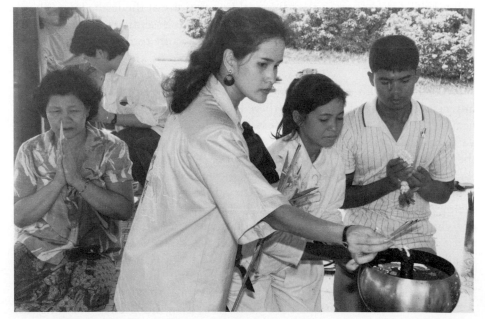

130

At the same time, however, nationalism was intensified, in accordance with the spirit of the age, but also as a means of unifying the country. This made Buddhism into the national religion in a more intense way, and led to some chauvinist formulations of Thai Buddhism in the 1970s. But the spiritual improvement of the Sangha has led to a dialectic between official religion and the spirituality of outstanding and saintly men who have attained advanced states of meditation and to whom the laity often ascribe miraculous powers. They often operate at the periphery of political life, but still such saints have a role in reminding the laity that the Sangha is a vehicle of spirituality and not just an organization for maintaining social and national values.

The retention of the monarchy in Thailand has given the polity a certain stability through a variety of military coups and changes of regime since World War II. There remain problems here as elsewhere about the status of minority religions, particularly Islam in the south of the country, under a Buddhist establishment. It is a problem not effectively solved, either, in Burma, the other Buddhist state in the area.

One may see the Thai model as an effective realization, primarily through the genius and farsightedness of Mongkut and Chulalongkorn, of a modernist transition without the severe political disruption caused by foreign conquest, and one where the monarchy was retained, so that it could play a modernist role in the emerging national polity. But in other countries, though monarchies were kept on, it was under foreign control, as in Laos, Cambodia, and Vietnam, under the French. In due course these monarchies were swept aside in the establishment of Vietnamese communist domination in 1975. Though there had been lay movements and Sangha reforms in Laos and Cambodia, they were not at a very developed level, because of the slow emergence of higher education. But Cambodia had benefited from Thai reforms in that the Dhammayuttika branch of the Sangha was brought in there.

Buddhism in Burma: Withdrawal from the World

Burma was absorbed into Britain's Indian empire through three nineteenth century wars. Through the war of 1826 Britain took the coastal states of Arakan and Tenasserim, with Assam (which remained part of India after Burma was administratively separated in 1935). Through the war of 1852 Britain got lower Burma. Through the war of 1885 it gained upper Burma, right up to the Chinese frontier in Yunnan. In 1890, it added the Shan States, wedged between China and Thailand. The country as a whole never fully settled down under British rule, there being a succession of rebellions, some under Buddhist leadership. For instance, in the Saya San rebellion in 1930–1, put down with some hardship by the British army, a former monk was proclaimed king and gained support from members of various nationalist societies formed in the 1920s.

This attempt to go back to the model of kingship was not, as it happened,

131

The organizational dimension: the charismatic King Mindon of Burma (1853–78) made it his aim to be the pattern of a Buddhist ideal monarch. The King as world ruler matches the ideal of the Buddha as spiritual ruler of the cosmos.

very attractive to the emerging intelligentsia, who were more attracted by socialism. The attempt was made to blend Buddhist and socialist values, especially in the thought and practice of U Nu (b. 1907). He sought to establish a Buddhist socialist regime in Burma, before being eventually removed in a coup by General Ne Win in 1962. Though the new regime did not so explicitly work toward his goals, in effect they followed the same ideology, and until the end of the 1970s Burma was largely cut off from foreign influences, travel being banned or severely restricted. A constant campaign had to be fought against secessionist forces from among the Christianized, non-Buddhist ethnic groups.

Though Ne Win repealed U Nu's ordinance making Buddhism the state religion, Buddhism remains predominant, and there is a strand in Buddhist thinking which favors Burma's isolationism. In 1956 the Burmese Sangha had gained prestige by the holding there of a Great Council of Buddhism to celebrate the 2,500th anniversary of the Buddha's decease and attainment of final *nirvāṇa*. Burmese Buddhist methods of meditation also became influential in Sri Lanka and the West in the years after World War II.

The isolationism of Burma can be explained, perhaps, by the collectivist

A crowd of over 200 youths of Burma's Anti-Fascist Peoples' Freedom League assemble at the Shwedagon Pagoda in Rangoon in 1963 to pray for the release of the League's leaders who have been detained by the government of Ne Win.

transposition of ancient individual ideals. The notion of the hermit or forest-dwelling monk is vital in the Buddhist tradition: in Burma, it is as if a whole nation has wished to withdraw from the wider world. The ideal is that Burmese values will thus remain pure and uncontaminated, either by the destructive forces of Marxism which have done so much harm to Buddhism over so much of Asia, or by the corroding influences of Western materialism and capitalism. Buddhism in Burma will remain thus free, perhaps a bit mixed up with the religion of the spirits, the *nats*, but within the framework of the Dhamma. We note that not only in Burma but also in Sri Lanka and in Kampuchea there are similar ideas of withdrawal from the capitalist world, but in these cases the ideals are more secularized and politicized.

Cambodia and the Purification of Kampuchea

In 1887 Cambodia became part of the French Union Indochinoise, after the suppression of a major rebellion. Cambodian troops fought for the French during World War I, and as a reward higher education and administrative opportunities for native Cambodians were somewhat expanded. But throughout Indochina the French somewhat alienated the intelligentsia by

The social dimension: against a background of glittering golden stupas in the Shwedagon Pagoda in Rangoon, an initiation procession winds its way with a little boy, dressed in ornate robes, being carried by his father. The boy will become a novice in a Buddhist order.

their insistence on purely French education, based on the assumption of the great superiority of French culture.

Though Laos and Cambodia became independent under their own monarchies in 1954, after the First Vietnamese War had ended in French defeat at Dien Bien Phu, they came to be sucked up in the general armed struggle of the region in the 1960s and 1970s. In 1975 the Cambodian capital, Phnom Penh, fell to insurgents of the Khmer Rouge under the political control of Pol Pot, who ruled till 1979. Then Vietnamese intervention brought in an orthodox Marxist regime under Vietnam's control; but not before there had been great changes and massacres.

These were carried out in the name of an ideology which had been sketched out first by Khieu Sampan (b. 1925) and articulated by him in a doctoral thesis he wrote for the Sorbonne in Paris. In that work he analyzed the condition of Cambodia, which he saw at that time under colonial and neocolonial domination. In order to get true economic independence, he argued that it was necessary to isolate Cambodia completely and to go back to an agricultural and self-sufficient economy. It was a bold vision, which he thought out with clarity to its bitter end. Though he thought in Marxist terms, the direction was un-Marxist, for it looked backward to an agrarian past rather than forward through the smoke of the industrial revolution. As a British academic, sympathetic to the regime, put it wittily after a visit there: "I have seen the past, and it works."

134

In addition to the strictly economic vision of Khieu Sampan there were notions of national purity at work too. Kampuchea (the name was changed under Pol Pot) was to be rid of the impurities brought by colonialism and capitalism. One of these impurities was education, another urban living. Shortly after taking the swollen capital, the Khmer Rouge ordered everyone out. People went, thinking it a temporary measure, even if they had to rumble along in hospital beds. But it was permanent: the Khmer Rouge simply abolished Phnom Penh as a functioning city. Educated people were everywhere executed: and among these were counted the members of the Sangha. About a third of the population perished, many of them by hunger. A new, intolerant religion had taken over, what I have called a "post-Buddhist quasi-Marxism." It still persists as a minority faction in the continuing civil war that has followed on from the effective takeover by Vietnam, which retains an army of occupation both there and in Laos and has tightly curbed Buddhism.

Victorious Khmer Rouge soldiers are cheerful in their final success, but the regime they ushered in proved disastrous both to Cambodian culture and to the people, since they tried to purge the country brutally of dissent and education.

In the Khmer Rouge ideology, Kampuchea saw the application of a secularist hermitism, a more brutal and greatly less traditional version of Burmese isolationism. And yet the logic of it all was in the last analysis nationalist: it was done in the name of the Khmer people, in the context of Khmer independence and "freedom." Ideology was ultimately at the service of the most powerful secular value of them all – the power of national feeling and the national idea.

Vietnam and the Long Struggle Against Foreign Domination

As we have said, the French did much to alienate the intelligentsia of the region, especially in Vietnam, with its strong infusion of Confucian thought, which was scarcely ready to admit the superiority of French ideas. The diverse tendencies in Vietnam rose to the surface during and after World War II, when Japanese rule gave way first to the proclamation of independence by the most organized of the wartime resistance movements, the communists under Ho Chi Minh (1890–1969), and then the attempt by the French to regain their former possessions. That struggle led to the French withdrawal and the division of the country into North and South. But this did not prevent the fight from slowly resuming, by guerrilla means in the South; and so eventually, for fear of communism, the United States got sucked in, sending troops in 1965.

It was during the following decade that the religious tensions in the South were manifest. The population was mixed. Though there was a strong Buddhist Sangha, there were also many Catholics: Vietnam was by far the most Catholic country in Asia, after the Philippines. Many Catholics had fled from the North and swollen the numbers in the South. But the ideology of Catholics tended simply to be negative: anti-communist. There were also in the South some new religions, like the Buddhist-inspired Hao Hoa and more importantly the syncretistic Cao Dai. There was a growing lobby of Buddhists who took a neutralist stance, wanting neither Marxism nor Western materialism (as it was often perceived: and certainly the Americans fought the war in a materialist way, supposing that military victory could be achieved by firepower, air power, the favorable body count ratio, and so on).

The Cao Dai is a syncretistic Vietnamese Church which was founded in 1926, with great éclat, by a Vietnamese intellectual called Ngo Van Chieu (1878–1932). It is highly eclectic, but may be said to be more than anything Taoist in inspiration. The name means "High Tower," which is a Taoist symbolic representation of the Supreme Being. In accord with the old Vietnamese tradition, the threefold religion of the Chinese-Vietnamese culture was incorporated into the beliefs and practices of the new religion, which nevertheless wove in other Western and nationalist strands. Its organization was modeled on the Catholic: having a Pope, cardinals, archbishops, and so forth. It is an interesting feature of Taoism – as of the Bön tradition, too, in Tibet – this tendency to mimic its rivals' organizational structures. In the old days it was Buddhist monasticism that was the model: here it was Catholicism.

In addition to the Supreme Being, the Cao Dai also reverence other spirits, such as the Buddha, Confucius, and Sun Yat-sen, not to mention Jesus and Muhammad, and great figures of the conquering French such as Joan of Arc and Victor Hugo (the task of one official was to continue the latter's writings; there is in the Cao Dai a strong spiritualist element, so communication with Victor Hugo and taking down further works by dictation presented no problem in principle). It sought the unity of religions, as may be gathered from this list of honored spirits. But in its nature it was destined to become a

A statue of Ho Chi Minh as hero in the Museum of Dien Bien Phu. Ho Chi Minh was a charismatic, secular leader of the Vietnamese Communist Party.

separate organization. It was too strongly organized to be an effective umbrella for other groups: until 1955 it even fielded its own army. It was in the North–South struggle emphatically anti-communist. Its hope was for an independent Vietnam which would follow a middle path between the super-powers. In this it was sympathetic to the growing Buddhist movement in the South.

That movement contributed to the fall of the government of Ngo Dinh Diem, a Catholic, who was better able to organize outside support than to mobilize loyalty within the country; and during the 1960s the United Budd-hist Association under the leadership of the monks Thich Tri Quang and Thich Thien Minh was prominent in the political struggle, but from a neutra-list perspective. The self-immolations of Buddhist monks and nuns on behalf of their ideas were moving demonstrations of commitment and helped to highlight the essentially divided character of South Vietnamese religious and ideological loyalties. The victory of the Northerners in 1975 led to the elimination of dissent; and it was to be abroad that the manifestations of indigenous Vietnamese religion were to be continued – in the United States, especially, whither many Vietnamese fled, and where there flourish centers such as those of the Cao Dai and relevant Buddhist associations.

And so, over much of the old Indochina, there reigns in effect the Chinese system: the realization of national independence through Marxism. But in the case of Vietnam, mindful of Chinese domination in the past, it has been advantageous to ally closely with the Soviet Union, and to survive through Russian economic and military support, while fighting an occasional border battle with the Chinese. The logic of nationalism dictates this. But the logic of nationalism dictates otherwise in Laos and in Kampuchea, and no doubt anti-Vietnamese nationalist ideologies will continue to surface there.

Conclusion

In Sri Lanka and Southeast Asia Buddhism has undergone troubles. It has had some difficulties living with minority groups, especially in the turbulent times in Sri Lanka during the 1970s and 1980s. Prevalent Marxisms have been damaging. But in its mainstream it has successfully created a Buddhist mod-ernism, which brings together the results of ancient spiritual insight and modern knowledge. The Sangha has revived, together with meditation prac-tices and social outreach. It has also made strong moves toward cooperation with other Buddhists, notably in the Far East and in the Tibetan tradition, in a flourishing Buddhist world. For all the tragedies Buddhism has undergone, it is showing new signs of health and vigor.

CHAPTER SEVEN

Islam in South, Southeast, and Other Parts of Asia

Islam's Presence in Asia

It may be surprising to many people to realize that the bulk of the world's Muslim population lives in South Asia and eastwards. The globe's most populous Islamic country is Indonesia. It is followed by three countries with almost equal Muslim populations – the Republic of India, Pakistan, and Bangladesh. Substantial Muslim populations inhabit Central Asia and China. There are Muslims also in southern Thailand, the south of the Philippines, the Maldive Islands, and most of all Malaysia and Brunei. Although the classic heartland of Islam is the Arab world, its center of gravity is South and Southeast Asia. So although its rise is closer to the ambience of Judaism and Christianity, Islam is an important Asian religion. Let us therefore look briefly at its origins and shape.

The Spread of Islam

Islam, the religion of submission (as its name indicates) to the one God, took off from the northwest part of Arabia in the seventh century and rapidly spread north and west. It went north into Palestine and Syria, Iraq and Iran, and into Central Asia. It went west into Egypt, Libya, Tunisia, Algeria, Morocco, Spain, and Portugal. Beginning with Muhammad's migration from Mecca to Medina in 622, the political rule of Islam expanded with amazing rapidity. By 664 the new empire had taken Kabul in Afghanistan and by 670 Kairouan in Tunisia. By 732 it was beyond Bukhara and Samarkand in Central Asia, and fighting at Poitiers in France (where, however, it was defeated). This first phase, till the establishment of the Abbasid dynasty and the shift of the capital to Mesopotamia, may be called the early period. From 750 to 1258, the time of the Abbasid rule over all or part of the Islamic territories, was what may be termed the classical period. Then from the mid-thirteenth century C.E. until the impact of Western powers in the colonial

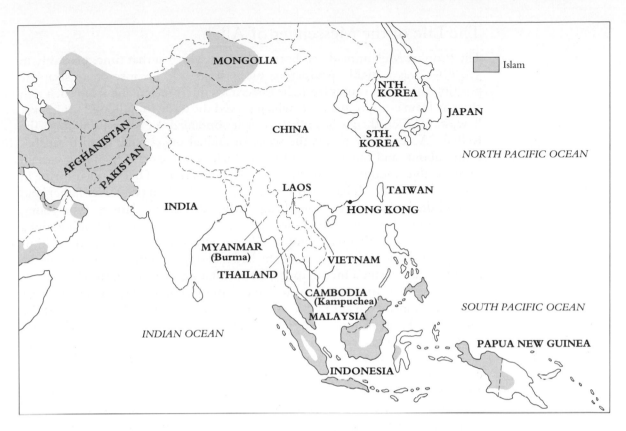

experience – until roughly the eighteenth century – we have what may be called the medieval or premodern period.

Map showing the approximate distribution of Islam in Asia in the world today.

Altogether Islam became the dominant religion over the whole of the Arab Middle East, along the shores of North Africa, across the Sahara in northern West Africa, through much of East Africa down to Kenya, through Iran, Afghanistan, and what is ex-Soviet Central Asia, in north and northeast India, in Malaysia and Indonesia, in Turkey and a part of the Balkans. It is a significant minority religion in the Indian subcontinent as a whole, and in Thailand, the Philippines, China, Madagascar, Yugoslavia, and Tanzania. Broadly, it stretches in a crescent from the eastern tip of Indonesia to West Africa. Though the religion has strong Arab cultural ingredients, above all in the use of Arabic for the Qur'an, the majority of Muslims come from other cultures. The most populous Islamic countries are in South and Southeast Asia: Indonesia, Pakistan, Bangladesh, and the Republic of India.

Islam established its main outline very rapidly, partly because it had a single founder, namely Muhammad, partly because it had a foundation document, namely the Qur'an, and partly because in having a political aspect it had to make rapid decisions on organization in view of its great success. The story of the religion turns of course very considerably on the life of the Prophet, and with that we begin.

139

The Life of the Messenger of Allah

The Prophet Muhammad was born in Mecca, which at that time, probably in 570 C.E., was a highly prosperous place. This was because of its strategic position across the routes from the eastern Mediterranean, and from such rich cities as Damascus, to the ports which served the trade to India and Sri Lanka. It was also even then a sacred city, for it contained the sacred building, the Ka'bah. Accordingly it was the scene of annual pilgrimage from the tribes round about; and the area round the Ka'bah was a sanctuary during certain months, thus moderating the impact of tribal warfare. The dominant tribe in Mecca, to which Muhammad belonged, was the Quraysh. His father and mother died when he was young, and he was raised by relatives. As a young man he found himself without the capital necessary to engage in trading; but a wealthy widow, Khadijah, employed him and subsequently married him. Though he became active in trade, he had had opportunities for reflection: he is said to have spent a month each year meditating in a cave near Mecca.

It was in 610 that he began to have some striking religious experiences which set him off in his career as a messenger of Allah. To begin with he mentioned his revelations only to his family and close associates; but after about three years he began his public career. His message was not altogether welcome for at least two reasons. First, in attacking polytheism, which he came to do with increasing clarity, he threatened the livelihood of those who depended on Meccan shrines; and in any case in such matters people tend to be conservative. Second, the ethic he pronounced was not fully in accord with the money-making policy of the rich merchants of the city: everyone would have to appear in the end before the judgment seat of the mighty God. Later, too, Muhammad would be involved in conveying revelations which altered the legal shape of society, especially in regard to marriage.

His message made little headway at first in Mecca, though he accumulated some fifty loyal followers. In 620 and 621 he received feelers from the city of Medina to the north, and in due course, in 622, he was invited to migrate there and take up the leadership. The city and area had been in a state of faction for a number of years, and the hope was that Muhammad, with his diplomatic skills and unifying message, would be able to bring harmony to Medina. This he did and came to control its political affairs. Then began an armed struggle against the Quraysh and the people of Mecca; and in 624 he defeated them in battle at Badr. After a few years of intermittent struggle Muhammad entered Mecca and became its leader. A battle shortly thereafter, at Hunayn, disposed of some of the outlying tribes, and Muhammad was master of a large slice of Arabia. Already he had plans for conquests in Syria and Iraq. But in June 632 he died.

He was a considerable military and political leader, magnanimous and decisive, and had behind him the assurance of faith, as a result of his prophetic experiences. To Muslims he is an ideal figure, someone to be admired and followed, and seen as virtually perfect – the finest of human beings, to whom

Allah entrusted his final revelation. Though Muslims are of course wholly opposed to any attempt to deify Muhammad – for that would be to set up another god beside God, which is the deadliest sin – in practice he is the supreme ethical ideal and more closely followed than Christ, partly because of the accumulation of biographical stories about him. These traditions, or *hadith*, are carefully sifted according to traditional methods, and constitute in effect a secondary source of revelation to that which is contained in the holy Qur'an.

The Qur'an

It is easy to think of the Qur'an simply as a book and to say that the Muslims have faith in the words of a holy book. But this does not convey the centrality and power of the Qur'an in Muslim eyes. If you were to look for a rough equivalent to the Christian Incarnation (the divine nature of Jesus) in Muslim piety, it would be the Qur'an. It is divine thought and divine law incarnated in words: it is mysterious sound which has everlasting life and existence, an emanation from the one Divine Being. One of the attributes of God is speech,

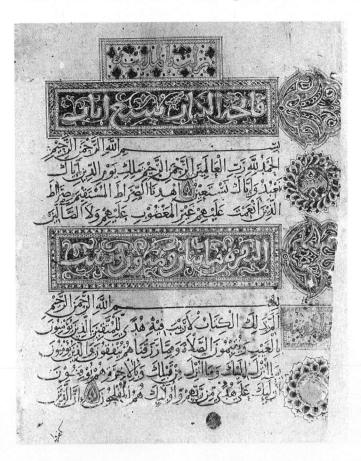

Page from a Qur'an, Baghdad, 1001 C.E.

and the Qur'an is God's eternal speech. Of course, recitations or written copies of the Qur'an are all created; but as divine speech what lies behind and within the Qur'an is eternal. All this gives it a much deeper meaning and a much higher status than that of the Bible.

Also, the Qur'an must be seen alongside the claims made by the faithful on behalf of Muhammad. He was not just the greatest of the prophets, in a line stretching from Abraham and Moses through Jesus to himself. But he was also the final Prophet, the "Seal of the Prophets," the *khatm al-anbiyā*. It was he who delivered the definitive expression of Allah's speech.

All this implies a divine plan. Abraham and the rest are God's means of communicating with the human race, and are part of his education of human beings in the process of *islam* or submission to his will. But it should be noted that the very process of looking back at previous religious heroes as being in the line of prophets made them exemplary figures also, so that Islam could claim to have ancient roots, though it was the last of the great religions to be revealed. It gave Islam a positive view of Judaism and Christianity, though this could also seem to adherents of those faiths to be somewhat patronizing.

The Transcendence and Immanence of God: Qur'ān

God is the Light of the heavens and earth;
  the likeness of His Light is a niche wherein is
    a lamp
    (the lamp in a glass,
  the glass as it were a glittering star)
  kindled from a Blessed Tree,
  an olive that is neither of the East nor of the
    West,
  Whose oil wellnigh would shine, even if no
    fire touched it;
  Light upon light;
  God guides to His Light whom He will.
And God strikes similitudes for men, and God
    has knowledge of everything.
In temples God has allowed to be raised up,
  and His Name to be commemorated therein;
  therein glorifying Him, in the mornings and
    the evenings,
  are men whom neither commerce nor
    trafficking diverts from the remembrance
    of God and to perform the prayer, and to
    pay the alms,
  fearing a day when hearts and eyes shall be
    turned about,
  that God may recompense them for their
    fairest works and give them increase of His
    bounty;

and God provides whomsoever He will,
    without reckoning.

And as for the unbelievers,
  their works are as a mirage in a spacious plain
    which the man athirst supposes to be
    water,
  till, when he comes to it, he finds it is
    nothing;
  there indeed he finds God,
  and He pays him his account in full;
  (and God is swift at the reckoning)
  or they are as shadows upon a sea obscure
    covered by a billow
    above which is a billow
    above which are clouds,
    shadows piled one upon another;
  when he puts forth his hand, wellnigh he
    cannot see it.
And to whomsoever God assigns no light, no
    light has he.

Hast thou not seen how that whatsoever is in
    the heavens and in the earth extols God,
  and the birds spreading their wings?
Each – He knows its prayer and its extolling;
  and God knows the things they do.

Muslims considered of course that Jews and Christians had tampered with the messages of the prophets, for instance by looking on Jesus as divine, which was blasphemous. This retroactive acceptance of elements of the other two traditions could be concretized in very particular claims, for instance that the Ka'bah was built by Adam and then rebuilt by Abraham and Ishmael (Isma'il). Whatever others may feel about the validity of such a claim, Muslims will see in this something which is part of the warp and woof of their faith, and so undeniably certain.

The revealed and everlasting nature of the Qur'an gives Islamic faith a great strength, especially because the book is not to be translated. It is only in Arabic: there can be no non-Arabic Qur'an, for it is primarily sound. The writing is like the score from which you perform. The non-Arab may use paraphrases as a kind of commentary to help her or him. But the true Qur'an remains the Arabic Qur'an. In this sense, God thinks in Arabic.

The Dimensions of the Faith Muhammad Founded

Thus, built on the rock of Muhammad's career and the revelations of the Qur'an, there arose the great edifice of a new faith which itself helped to define a new civilization, for long a glittering challenge to its neighbor Christendom. What were the dimensions of this faith?

The Ritual Dimension

First, let us start with ritual. Above all, Muslims have the duty of praying five times daily, facing toward the Ka'bah, according to certain formulae of words and bodily postures: before sunrise, early afternoon, late afternoon, straight after sunset, and before retiring. They should also keep the fast during the holy month of Ramadan, which is the ninth month of the lunar year: between dawn and sunset there should be no eating, drinking, smoking, or sex. And they should try to perform the pilgrimage to the Ka'bah at least once during their lives. These three rules constitute the second, third, and fifth of the so-called Pillars of Islam. The first is a duty to commitment: they should recite the credo in public: "There is no god but God and Muhammad is his messenger." The fourth is to pay the alms tax, or *zakat*. Thus the community should look after the welfare of the poor. Friday is a special day of prayer, with congregational worship and preaching in the mosque.

The fact that Muslims have to orient themselves toward the Ka'bah and are urged if at all possible to go there on the great annual pilgrimage (the *hajj al-akbar*) means that there are continual reminders of the unity of the whole community, however much from time to time it may be riven by political or religious conflict.

The Experiential Dimension

As to the experiential dimension of early Islam, obviously the Prophet's own visions and the numinous power of Allah left their stamp not only on the

143

The doctrinal dimension: "There is no god but Allah and Muhammad is his messenger," inscribed on a 16th or 17th century Turkish tile.

The ritual dimension: a plan of Mecca rendered on an 18th century Turkish tile.

Qur'an but also on the community's sense of the tremendous nature of God. The deepest sin known to Islam chimes with this sense: it is *shirk*, setting up some other god beside God. So we have a sense of the overwhelming presence of God, who yet in his mercy communicates with human beings to lead them on the right path. Later on, as we shall see, a different, mystical sort of experience appears: the sense of that which lies within, gained through the practice of contemplation. This was due to the Sufi movement.

The Ethical Dimension

As for the ethical dimension, we have to see that morality for the early Muslim was thoroughly woven into the political task of founding a good and just society under the guidance of God. Throughout the history of Islam there is recognition of the central place held by the law or *sharī'a*. The obedience due to God should lead to the recognition of human equality. Rights may vary, as with men and women. But in principle all are equal before God. Social legislation and the payment of *zakat* stress their religious duty to the

144

poor. Kindness should be cultivated, especially by husbands toward wives. Polygyny is allowed, but only four wives per man; and the rights of women are protected by the dowry system and legislation regarding divorce. The Prophet himself can be followed as an example, and the *hadith* are a vital source of moral inspiration.

The Social and Institutional Dimension

Institutionally, Islam organized itself as a state to start with, and only gradually did the total community – the *umma* – break up. In theory this should be unified under a leader, or successor to Muhammad, known as the *khalifa* or Caliph. From time to time in later Islam the Caliphate was revived. As for religious institutions more narrowly conceived, there were prayer leaders from early days, and later professional exponents of theology and law.

The Doctrinal Dimension

Doctrinally, the single most important strand in Islam is the unity of God, who is creator of the universe. He has human beings as his regents over the earth, which was made for their ultimate benefit. Though varying emphasis in the Qur'an can be found, the trend is to think of God as determining each person's destiny. As we have seen, the Qur'an was believed to be the eternal speech of God. The Muslims were strong in condemning what they saw as the tritheism, or three-God-doctrine, of Christianity; but God can be addressed through the rich notion of his Ninety-Nine Names, beginning with *al-Rahman*, the Compassionate. Among other popular names are *al-Hafiz*, the Preserver; *al-Haqq*, the Real; *al-Qadir*, the Powerful; and *al-Rashid*, the Director.

The Narrative Dimension

As to the narrative dimension, we have seen that the Islamic story implies a chain of prophets from Abraham, and indeed before that from Adam, down to Muhammad. The coming of the last Prophet is of course central to the whole narrative understanding by Muslims of human history. The amazing success of the community in its early days and the mighty conquests were a sign of Allah's grace and mercy. Eventually the final hour of the world will come with various signs, the descent of Jesus, and a fire which will drive people to the place of judgment.

The Material Dimension

Materially, Islam soon enough began to have its houses of prayer; it was only later that they became a glory of Islamic architecture. Since the ban on any concrete representation of God was extended to cover God's image in the human face and form, much came to be made of calligraphy as an art. But in the early days the chief material aspects of Islam were the cities of Medina and Mecca, and above all the pilgrimage sites in and around the latter. There were for instance the valley of Mina to the east of Mecca, where pilgrims spent a night, and the mount of 'Arafat, where Muhammad had his first visions.

The Formation of Classical Islam

The early decades after the death of the Prophet were marked with dissension over the leadership. Muhammad's father-in-law Abu Bakr was first appointed. He lasted two years and was succeeded by 'Umar, who organized the growing Arab empire along fairly simple lines: the Arabs looked after war and religion, and non-Arabs – and these were for the most part non-Muslims – paid taxes but rather lighter ones than they had been used to. 'Umar was followed by 'Uthman. His assassination led to the first civil war within Islam, when 'Ali's succession was opposed. 'Ali was assassinated in 661, and in 680 his surviving son Husayn was ambushed at Karbala in Iraq; he was to become the prime martyr figure for the Shi'i movement, which we shall come back to later. Under Mu'awiyah and his successors (661–750), the Umayyad dynasty, centered in Syria, carried on the successful policy of military expansion.

In the end, a revolution in 750 brought the 'Abbasid dynasty to power at Dar-es-Salam, a new capital constructed at Baghdad in Mesopotamia. A glorious new cultural phase of Islam was thus entered, though disintegration

---

Islam some key terms

Allāh The one true God.

Ḥajj Pilgrimage to Mecca, urged on all Muslims.

Imām Prayer leader, and in Shi'a Islam one of the twelve great leaders of the community, the last having gone into hiding or occultation, to return at the end of history.

Jihād The struggle for Islam, interpreted either as righteous war or as a spiritual striving.

Nabī A prophet, among whom are some of the great figures of the Jewish tradition, and Jesus; the final one is Muhammad.

Qur'ān The sacred revelation or word of God, being eternal, and revealed to the Prophet.

Salat Worship or prayer, enjoined on Muslims five times daily.

Saum Fasting, especially during the month of Ramadan between sunrise and sunset, enjoined on all Muslims.

Sharī'a Islamic law.

Sūfī A mystic within Islam, typically belonging to one of the various *tariqas* or orders.

Umma The whole Muslim community.

Zakāt Giving alms to the poor. One of the pillars of Islam, with the profession of faith, prayer, pilgrimage, and fasting.

occurred later through the establishment of rival Caliphates, in North Africa – where Cairo was conquered in 969, and became a brilliant capital under the Fatimid dynasty – and in Córdoba in Spain, ruled by the second Umayyad dynasty from 929. The Islamic community was divided, but it was a fine period of Islamic civilization. There were stresses, one of them being the disaffection of the Shi'i party, who were loyal to the descendants of 'Ali and who opposed the traditionalists of Sunni.

New religious forces were entering the body of Islam. One was the effect of Greek learning, and in particular philosophy, upon Islamic theology. Another was the mystical movement, the Sufis, who brought contemplative methods into the practice of Islam. Meanwhile the law or *shari'a* had to be interpreted, and diverse schools had been growing up.

The Spread of Sufism

The movement which is known as Sufism (from *suf* meaning the coarse wool worn by ascetics) was an attempt to introduce into personal life a kind of spirituality which would compensate for the excesses of Islamic culture after its notable successes. Sufism was involved with ascetic training, but it issued ultimately in mystical contemplation. Sufis aspired toward that purification of consciousness which leads to the feeling that ordinary consciousness, with its dualism (the distinction between me as subject and God or the world as object), disappears. They therefore often came to speak of union with God, and even being merged with or becoming God. Now this was not at all to the taste of mainstream orthodoxy. In Islam there has always been a very strong emphasis on the radical difference between God and human beings. Some Sufi claims could be thought blasphemous. The Sufis seemed to think that by the annihilation of their egos they could make a place for God and so in some sense become God. It was not surprising that the orthodox should resist such ideas.

The Sufi movement started with groups who would cooperate in the cultivation of piety. There grew up the custom of having a leader or *shaykh* who would act as a spiritual teacher and master. The groups not only pledged themselves to simplicity of life, but engaged in forms of meditation very similarly to the contemplative orders in Christianity and to much in Indian mysticism. Perhaps the most famous of all Sufis was al-Hallaj, who illustrated some of the tensions in the situation. An admirer and follower of Jesus (also of course an Islamic prophet), he reportedly said "I am the Real – *al Haqq*," which was taken as tantamount to saying that he was God. In his teachings he spoke most of the love of God, and he openly referred to his divine experiences. As a result he was accused of blasphemy and executed on the cross in 922 C.E.

But the strong piety and zealous teaching of the Sufis, "friends of God" as they called themselves, was too valuable to be sacrificed by Islam. Sufism was given a powerful defence, but in a moderate form, by the great philosopher al-Ghazali, from northeast Persia (1058–1111). He gave up his post as pro-

The experiential dimension: a group of angels help a Sufi ascetic.

fessor at the university in Baghdad to take up the life of a Sufi, and thus had both intellectual and spiritual preparation for the task to which he was called, which was to give an account of Sufism which would show its deep compatibility with orthodox tradition.

He argued that the language of Sufis, sometimes extravagant, need not be taken literally. The Sufi, when he reached his high state of union, was like a person drunk – and they themselves often used this metaphor. What they say during this state comes from their unawareness of any context: but once they are out of the state they can acknowledge that, however close they might have been to God, nevertheless a distinction between the Divine Being and the human soul remains.

Sufism was important in the spread of Islam. The holy person commands respect in many societies. In North Africa the *baraka* or mysterious power of the saint, in Central Asia features of shamanism, in India the prestige of the yogin – such manifestations were taken over by the Sufis. They had much, too, to do with the spread of Islam into Malaya and Indonesia.

Developments after the Mongol Incursion

Though Islam was well established through the middle ages in Central Asia it was destined to suffer greatly. The thirteenth century was a terrible era of devastation, because of the irruption of the Mongols, initially under the leadership of Genghis Khan. In the first years of the century the Muslim centers of Central Asia were destroyed, along with much of the Persian empire. In 1256 Hülegü Khan, Genghis' grandson, sacked Baghdad and slaughtered large numbers of Muslims. The Mongol successor state in Persia, the Il-Khan principality, was eventually won over to Islam, so that the Mongol rulers began to favor the faith. Later, Turkish power under Timur caused devastation across Central Asia and into India, where the Muslim capital of Delhi was sacked. But a descendant of Timur, Babur, established his rule in Delhi and founded the Mughal empire, which turned out to be a great patron of both Islam and the arts.

Meanwhile, though the Mongols had struck at the rising Ottoman regime, the latter was to make its way in Asia Minor. Turkish in texture, it ultimately conquered the Byzantine empire and established rule over most of the territories formerly ruled by it, in a kind of alliance between Muslims and Christians. In the fifteenth century, although Islam was driven out of Spain, in much of the rest of the world it underwent a renaissance. It was penetrating deeply into Indonesia and Malaya. It made its way through the patronage of the Mughals in India. It was busy crossing the Sahara and moving into Black Africa. Though the Middle Ages of Islam brought it into conflict with rising European power, it was nevertheless a constructive period. In Central Asia, in India, and in Ottoman territories, rich varieties of architectural style, calligraphy, and painting flourished.

Islam in Central and South Asia

During the reign of Timur, who was a pious Muslim, virtually all non-Muslim practice in Central Asia was wiped out. But a great part of the consolidation of Islam in the region was due to the work of the Sufi orders. As elsewhere in the Muslim world, the tombs of mystics became more potent often than mosques in the popular imagination, and the houses where adepts met and were to be seen in prayer became symbols of the new piety. It was in Bukhara that the influential Naqshbandi order was founded in the fourteenth century; it penetrated both intellectual and unlettered circles. The tomb of its founder, outside of the city of Bukhara, became a famous place of pilgrimage in the region. Other orders, by introducing shamanistic practices, also helped to bridge the worlds of Islam and indigenous religion.

The Mughals in India created a fine syncretic civilization, incorporating Central Asian and Indian motifs. Admittedly the emperor Akbar (1556–1605) failed in his attempt to found a pluralistic ideology for his rule, and there were also severe Hindu–Islamic tensions, especially during the reign of his successor Aurungzeb. Perhaps the most creative of all the Mughals was Shah Jahan, who came to the throne in 1627, and was the ultimate creator of the Red Fort and the Taj Mahal, blending Persian and Indian themes in a great new architectural synthesis. Also wonderful was Akbar's city of Fatehpur Sikri, which was eventually left empty because it had no assured water supply.

In India, as in Central Asia, a great part of the missionary activity on behalf of the faith was done by Sufi orders. The figure of the Sufi master was a familiar one, with echoes of guru, *sadhu*, and yogin. The Sufi orders were willing to move away into peripheral places, and not stick to the centers of power. They made use of vernacular languages, from Bengali to Tamil, and they also participated in the widespread *bhakti* style of religion of the period. They involved themselves in social rites to provide a counterpoint to Hindu society. Sometimes the Muslim wandering ascetics looked very much like Hindu ones, and were scarcely respectable by ordinary Muslim standards, e.g. in their relative nakedness, use of smeared ashes, and so forth. For some, becoming Muslim was socially advantageous, and the Hindu world had to pay penalties for untouchability.

At a more intellectual level, the influence of Ibn al-'Arabi (1185–1240) was great, since he presented a point of view congenial to the Hindu mystical tradition. Also important later on, from the time of Aurungzeb, was the spread of well-endowed teaching institutions or *madrasahs* which could create a class of indigenous scholars of Islamic teaching and law.

The period of the Mughal empire, especially during the sixteenth and seventeenth centuries, was one of great cultural riches: Islamic architecture, such as the Fort in Delhi and Agra's Taj Mahal, was strikingly beautiful. Mughal painting also reached considerable glories, and the contact between India and the Arab and Persian worlds stimulated literary and religious writings. The magnetism of Islam was strong among those Hindus and outcastes to whom the faith offered both devotionalism toward God and the promise of better social conditions. Often the country convert did not effectively change greatly the nature of his piety: Muslim saints were substitutes for Hindu holy men and gods. But the influence of Islam helped to stimulate not only the growth of Sikhism, but the general prevalence of *bhakti* or devotional religion. There were also, toward the end of the Mughal period, moves toward the revival of prophetic Islam, which had often been overlaid by cults which the reformers saw as little better than Hinduism. Islam in its sterner varieties of course was strongly anti-Hindu, but despite this the Mughal period contributed greatly to the richness of Indian life.

The Modern Period

Muslim Modernism in India

Because the British defeated Mughal power in the north and a number of powerful Muslim rulers such as Tipu Sultan in Mysore, and because the old Mughal emperor had let himself be drawn into the rebellion of 1857, the Muslims initially were less adapted to the values of British rule, and less favored by the British, than the Hindus. The first major Islamic thinker to adapt publicly to the new conditions was Sir Sayyid Ahmad Khan (1817–98), who had a traditional Delhi education in Arabic and Persian sources, and who was employed by the East India Company for over thirty years. He was profoundly impressed by the events of 1857 and 1858, seeing in them the inevitability of British rule. He saw the new scientific knowledge as good and ultimately proceeding from God: drawing on old Islamic philosophical principles, he saw reason and revelation as functioning in parallel. But he thought that Islam had been overgrown with foreign life, much of it unfortunately embodied in the *shari'a*, the law. He took in this matter a neofoundationalist view: that is, he distinguished between the teachings of the Holy Qur'an and the mass of *hadith*, which he considered to be very unreliable, having been orally transmitted over a long time. So he was a modernist in the sense that he urged legal and social reform, and in seeing harmony between Western science and Islamic religion. Besides, Western science owed its initial impetus to Islamic sources, through the transmission of Greek ideas and Islamic scientific developments to the medieval West. After a visit to England in 1878–80 he established the Mohammedan Anglo-Oriental College in Aligarh, thus beginning the process of opening up to young Muslims the possibilities of English-language higher education. He urged Muslims not to join the Hindu-dominated Indian National Congress, fearing that Muslim minority status in a nationalist movement would be perpetuated.

But though Khan's modernism pointed one way forward, it did not of course eliminate the causes of friction between Hindus and Muslims. In a revived Hinduism there was a call for protection of the cow: yet Muslims traditionally slaughtered cows at certain festivals. The Hindus agitated for Hindi, written in Devanagari script, to have equal status with Urdu (much the same language but peppered with more Arabic and Persian words), written in Arabic script. Such causes of conflict, in north India especially, must be seen as a constant background noise in the history of modern India. The drums of violence may at times have been muffled, but their beat is still to be heard.

Some Indians have blamed the British for a "divide and rule" policy, and there were undoubtedly some British actions which helped to fuel the conflict, notably the partition of the province of Bengal in 1905. It sparked off terrorist bombing and some degree of communal violence. But the religions were at the ritual level remarkably incompatible. Muslims considered *shirk* or idolatry as the most heinous sin, and they were surrounded by Śiva statues and Ganesh and all manner of representational sculpture among the impenitent Hindus. Every statue was an offense, especially when it was carried in procession in front of the mosque. For the Hindu, Muslim cow-slaughter was an offense against their very deeply felt veneration, from time immemorial, for the cow. And if Muslims should think it their duty to smash an idol, or if Hindus were to stop Muslim sacrifices, then mayhem would break loose. So there was a constant problem of the peaceful coexistence of these two great religions.

In so far as the tensions could be resolved by intellectuals, then Sir Sayyid Ahmad Khan's position, influenced by Sufism, could help in a better understanding with Hindus. But he himself was strongly attacked by many of the 'ulama, and his modernism was out of tune with the feelings, under threat, of many of his coreligionists. But we should note Sir Sayyid as being a forward-looking thinker who made the move to modernism with self-conscious confidence and strong educational interests.

Muhammad Iqbal and the Idea of Pakistan

In Chapter 3 we looked at Gandhi's campaign for an independent, united India. His vision was matched by those who foresaw problems for Muslims in such a state. The ultimate division between India and Pakistan led to bloodshed on a huge scale. But it would have been surprising perhaps if no one had sketched out an alternative to a united India, because of the strong Mughal heritage in the north and northwest. Also, for Muslims there was always the nagging question of how to arrange the law when under foreign or non-Muslim domination. Sir Muhammad Iqbal (1877–1938) was a noted poet who had been knighted by the British government for his works in Urdu and Persian. His philosophy was one which looked to a true, morally dynamic Islam, toward which Islam as it is must reach. He saw history and life in terms of an evolutionary process toward the higher ethical life. He also, significantly, in his presidential address to the Muslim League in Allahabad in 1930, urged the creation of a Muslim state in the northwestern parts of India. Only where Muslims were free to put the law into operation freely could a true Islam be realized.

Muhammad Ali Jinnah, though not a very pious Muslim himself, was concerned, as President of the All-India Muslim League, to protect the interests of Muslims, and took a large number of them out of India to form the new State of Pakistan.

152

His ideas on this front were a bit vague. It was Rahmat Ali, living in Cambridge, England, who gave them more precision. He invented a name for the new country, Pakistan, which consists of the first letters of some of the key provinces: Punjab, Afghan Province (or Northwest Frontier Province), Kashmir and Sindh, plus the last portion of Baluchistan. Later Rahmat Ali added the idea of another Muslim state in Bengal, far away to the east, which he called "Bangistan." Actually Pakistan at first included East Bengal, but after a civil war this did evolve into a new state, that of Bangladesh. Rahmat Ali's ideas at first put off the Muslim leader, Muhammad Ali Jinnah (1876–1948), but after 1936 he was won round, and it was his intransigence in fighting for this new state which meant that in 1947 partition was inevitable.

Pakistan turned out not to be a very stable country, even after the civil war in 1971 which led to the separation of Bangladesh. A succession of military regimes replaced the early civilian administrations, save for a period after the Bangladesh war. It has introduced Islamic law into its system, but is rather far from the vision of a revived Islam that Iqbal had looked to.

Mosque at Badshahi, Pakistan, fills for the festival to mark the end of Ramadan, the month-long fast from dawn till dusk.

Pakistan: an Islamic State?

One of the most difficult questions posed to the new State of Pakistan was set by the Jama'at-i Islami, created as a political movement by Mawlana Mawdudi (1903–79) in 1941. Mawdudi was suspicious of the secularizing Jinnah, but moved to Pakistan on the partition. He was often in bitter opposition to the government. His movement was devoted to the ideal of an Islamic state in which non-Muslims would not have full rights. He foresaw the use of Islamic law in public life and took a holistic view of the religion, which fused politics, economics, private life, and public worship into a single whole. He was jailed for his part in anti-Ahmadiya riots in 1951–3, and even condemned to death, though the execution was not carried out. His party remained a vital force in Pakistan, though it lost a lot of ground during the civilian rule after the war with Bangladesh; and it never had much support in what is now Bangladesh, especially because it supported the Pakistani state in its war there. But its agitation for an Islamic system did bear some fruit with the adoption by the Zia ul-Haq regime of Islamic law.

On the other hand Bangladesh, founded in 1971, never really has displayed enthusiasm for the idea of an Islamic constitution.

Islam in Central Asia

The Muslims of the ex-Soviet Union are found in three main areas, in the Caucasus, in the middle Volga region, and in Central Asia. During the time of Russian expansion to the east there were attempts to convert many Muslims, especially in the region of the Volga. And in a sense the Soviet state has continued a like policy, save that the religion being preached is Marxist atheism. However, in Turkestan under the Tsars there had been a hands-off policy in relation to Islam; proselytizing by Christian missionaries was forbidden, and so, even, was preaching by Tatar modernists (the Tatars having been much more directly affected by Islamic modernism). Such a policy was designed to foster Islamic backwardness and to make Russian rule easier to impose. The result was that when the Revolution occurred a revolt broke out in Turkestan, which was anti-Soviet and to some degree religiously motivated. It took ten years to suppress.

Thereafter the settlement of Russians in Central Asia and the promotion of atheistic propaganda proceeded apace. Despite this, Islam has survived and indeed in its own way flourished, despite the imposition of strict controls on the mosques and the educational system. Religious education and publication are virtually banned, with the exception of minor training schools run by the government for a limited number of clerics. Yet it is reckoned that some 80 percent of the non-Russian population still are believers. This is out of a Muslim population of some 30 million in Central Asia. It is reckoned that of the population 20 percent are "fanatics" (the Soviet category); that is to say, they are believers by conviction. Others are more traditionally oriented. But even of the 20 percent who are atheists, virtually all practice circumcision and Islamic burial. Yet in the whole region there are less than two hundred mosques, probably, which still function as such.

So on the one hand public Islam is more or less washed out; yet Islamic practice and belief still persist in a more private way. What is the explanation? It is partly of course due to nationalist sentiment – these peoples feel themselves somewhat under threat from what they perceive as Great Russian chauvinism – but the more immediate explanation is that the Sufi *tariqas* or brotherhoods still exist, and they are almost impossible for the regime to control, since they can operate secretly and by word of mouth, and they do not need to come into public conflict with the authorities. They represent a huge religious underground movement (the same applies in other regions such as the Caucasus).

Of the Sufi orders the Naqshbandiyah is the most important. It was founded in Bukhara in the fourteenth century and for long played a highly visible role in the politics of the region. It is moderate in its asceticism and well suited to playing its missionary role in the ex-Soviet Union. Also important is the Qadirīya, founded in the twelfth century by the saint 'Abd al-Qādir (1088–1166), from the Caspian area, whose tomb in Baghdad is a major center of pilgrimage (incidentally, this custom of pilgrimage to saints' tombs is a major complaint of reforming, neofoundationalist Muslims, who regard the practice as a medieval innovation). In much of the rest of the Muslim world there is a reforming prejudice against Sufism. It is often seen as one of the reasons for the corruption of the faith and its straying from the true way. But in Soviet Central Asia it has been a major cause of the persistence of Islam.

The attempt, moreover, of the Soviets to make their influence firm in Afghanistan, when they moved in forces in 1979 to help the beleaguered Marxist regime after the ouster of the king in 1973, generated strong though not very united resistance from mainly Islamic guerrilla groups in that country. It was not always possible for the Soviet government to rely on the loyalty of its Central Asian troops in these circumstances.

Southeast Asian Islam

In Malaysia and Indonesia, the consolidation of Islam as the religion of the area has occurred partly during the colonial period. During this time the Malay language became thoroughly impregnated with Arabic and Islamic borrowings and came to be written in the Arabic script. It is in the main this language that forms the basis of the national languages of Malaysia and of Indonesia. In the latter case it is also suffused with Sanskrit and Indic expressions deriving from the Hindu culture of Java. These tongues are now written in Roman script.

The impact of Islamic modernism in the area was great, as was that of the Wahhabi reform movement. In 1912 there was the foundation of the well-organized movement known as the Muhammadiya, which was designed to purify Islam, and especially that of central Java, of the folk elements of Javanese religion. In other words it was designed to root out aspects of the typical peasant worldview and some of the persisting aspects of the Hindu–Buddhist tradition of the area. But it came to be a pan-Indonesian movement, and it modeled itself organizationally on the methods of the Dutch Reformed Church in its missionary and publishing activity. It also did much in the reforming and modernizing of Islamic religious education.

There are also strong moves of a more conservative nature, both in Malaysia and in Indonesia. Thus in the latter country, three or four armed revolts on behalf of an Islamic state in different regions have broken out since independence in 1945. In Malaysia some of the states of the federation apply Islamic law, and there are moves to give it federal status. There is some dissatisfaction also in Indonesia with the ideology under which officially the state is ruled, which is summed up in the so-called Five Principles or *Pancasila*. This is of course originally the name given to the Five Precepts or Virtues of the Buddhist tradition.

Here Javanese influence is paramount, since Java is the hub of Indonesia and its values are often presented as applicable to the entire vast country. The formula seeks to create a pluralistic framework for Indonesia as a whole: the Five Principles are belief in God, nationalism, democracy, humanitarianism, and social justice. With the last four of these the Muslims have in principle no quarrel (though some see nationalism as itself something which has to be subordinated to the Muslim ethos). But belief in God is deliberately interpreted vaguely, so that the religion, say, of the Torajas of central Sulawesi is included under this head, even though from a Muslim point of view it is a polytheistic or animistic system. After all, Indonesia is a great concatenation of islands with people of many different cultures and languages and stages of economic development: for this reason the central government prefers a pluralistic ideology so as not to alienate various regional groups.

A Footnote on the Limits of Islam: Ahmadiya

Finally there does remain a question about the self-definition of Islam, which maybe we can illustrate through the Ahmadiya. This is a movement which originated in India, and which has been fairly successful in proselytizing in certain parts of the world, for instance in West Africa. It has had probably the greatest mission success of any Islamic organization, and has over 10 million members in various parts of the world.

The movement rests on the teachings of Mirza Ghulam Ahmad (1835–1908), who came from a village, Qadian, in the Punjab in north India. He was a Muslim revivalist who was drawn into making special claims for his own status. He regarded himself as a *nabi* or prophet, and it was this above all that alienated many orthodox Muslims, since for them there is absolutely no need for further prophecy after the career of Muhammad: this was why he was the Seal of the Prophets. Mirza Ghulam Ahmad also saw himself as Messiah in some sense, and as the returning avatar of Viṣṇu, predicted in the Hindu system. He did not think of Messiah-hood as having some kind of transcendent ontological status, since he argued that Jesus did not in fact ascend to heaven, but escaping from the cross departed on a journey which took him to Kashmir, where his tomb is to be found in Srinagar. This idea about Jesus of course offended both Muslims and Christians, the former because the usual interpretation of the Qur'an has it that Jesus was never crucified. But in most ways, the life of the Ahmadiya conforms to Islam, though it rejects the idea of military *jihad*.

A split in the movement led to a branch being set up with its headquarters in Lahore (now Pakistan), which denied that Mirza Ghulam Ahmad was a prophet but called him merely a reformer: this branch has stayed close to formal Islam. The more radical branch, the Qadiani, set itself up in Rabwah, in Pakistan, in 1947. Its successes in the mission area were due not only to the sincerity of its exponents, who emphasized the vital part of sincerity and not just outward observances in religion, but also because of the adoption of modern Christian methods of mission – street preaching, pamphlets and other forms of publishing, good organization, and sometimes aggressive propaganda. But it has attracted enmity from the orthodox, and in 1954 it was ruled in Pakistan that it was not a form of Islam and should not use claims which suggest that it is a kind of Islam.

It will be observed from this that the tendency in modern Islam is to place a close definition on the religion in terms of doctrinal orthodoxy: a non-practicing orthodox Muslim is much better placed than a practicing non orthodox person. By an irony the Ahmadiya movement is now much worse off legally in Islamic Pakistan than it would have been if it had stayed in Hindu-dominated India.

The Dimensions of Revived Islam

Despite the importance of the Iranian revolution, it may well be that the future lies more with the revival movements within Sunni Islam, such as the Brotherhood. At any rate in a number of countries, such as the Sudan, Pakistan, and Malaysia, Islamic law is required: and there are calls in a whole range of countries for similar legislation. This spirit of revivalism seeks to restore practice to what it was; but often its mission is conducted in most up-to-date terms. We can discern some of the dimensions of this Islam as follows.

Doctrinally it has a tendency toward more rather than less literal interpretations of the Qur'an. It is not hostile to science, but it rejects some of the philosophies of medieval and premodern Islam. As far as its *narrative* dimension goes, it of course accepts and focuses on the career of the Prophet: but it also sees Islamic culture as having betrayed the spirit of true Islam through various innovations, and it is because of all this that Islam has fallen into its relatively sorry current state. *Ethically* and legally it calls for the revived application of the *sharī'a*. It is strict about such matters as alcohol and the conduct of women: it usually favors the use of the veil. Since it is traditionalist but not quite traditional (for it arises from the very situation in which tradition is being challenged and overridden), its espousal of tradition is a matter of self-conscious commitment, so that there is a great emphasis on being "converted" to true Islam. It has a much more notable evangelical fervor than would be typical of simply traditional Muslims. *Experientially*, therefore, it is vigorous: but it is not much oriented toward the mystical meditation of the Sufis, since Sufi practices are often what has brought Islam (in its eyes) into disrepute. *Organizationally*, revivalist Islam is much indebted to the methods of Christian missionaries, while it also lays stress on Islamic education. *Ritually*, it is pious in reaffirming the importance of regular public

157

prayer worship. *Materially*, it is often at the forefront of the building of new mosques, especially where the Muslims are a minority; so in the lanes of Sri Lanka and the back streets of Liverpool, England, will be found new structures, often subsidized by oil money. Islam is at a vigorous global stage.

Islam in China

From toward the end of the seventh century onward there were contacts between Muslims in China, through trade along the Silk Route, and through seaborne trade via south China. There were also conflicts between the Arabs and the Chinese. But gradually a Chinese Muslim community was built up, though much of its history is obscure, since the first written works by Muslims in China date from the seventeenth century. It is known that two of the Ming emperors were favorable to Islam: the earlier of these, in the late fourteenth century, may have had a Muslim wife. On the whole, though, the opinion of the Chinese elite was hostile to them, considering the religion alien and barbarous; though Wang Tai-yu (1580–1650?) compared Islamic and Confucian ethics and another Muslim writer, Liu Chih (1662?–1736?), made a favorable impression also in presenting his faith by means of Confucian ideas. But under the Ch'ing dynasty during the eighteenth and nineteenth centuries there were a number of Muslim rebellions. The Ch'ing, in extending the empire westward into Central Asia, dominated more Islamic peoples, such as the Kazakhs. Altogether therefore by modern times there is a considerable body of Muslims in China, both Chinese and minority, including the Uighurs, Kazakhs, and Uzbeks: perhaps as many as 40 million. Generally, they are free to worship and have shown remarkable persistence in not being assimilated to Maoist values.

Conclusion

Altogether, then, there is a very large number of Muslims in Asia. While they have not yet imposed a fully-fledged Islamic regime in the area, they have moved somewhat in this direction in Pakistan, while there are elements of such a system in Malaysia (though here the situation is complicated by the presence of a substantial Chinese minority). Islamic revivalism is making itself felt in a number of countries, and tendencies to syncretism, for instance in Indonesia, are increasingly resisted. But we may note that Sufism has played a great part in the spread of Islam into South Asia and Southeast Asia, even if now it tends to be under criticism from the more orthodox.

CHAPTER EIGHT

The Sikh Tradition

Islam Meets Hinduism

The meeting of Islam and Hinduism in north India was one of the roots of the Sikh tradition. There were some obvious affinities between the *bhakti* movements – especially the *nirguṇa* form which stressed the imageless and formless God – and the Islamic heritage of devotion to the one God, Allah. The similarity was perceived with great clarity by Nānak (1469–1504), who came to be recognized as the first Guru in the Sikh tradition. In the traditional accounts of his life he underwent a dramatic experience when bathing in a stream, in which he received a call from God. When he reappeared after three days' absence, his first words were "There is no Hindu; there is no Muslim." Thereafter he became a wandering recluse and undertook long journeys, even according to Sikh tradition as far as Mecca. Before his experience, however, he had already moved in this direction of providing a faith which transcended external barriers between religions. He and a Muslim minstrel called Mardana had composed hymns together, which became a vital part of later Sikh worship. On Nānak's journey to Mecca he is reported to have fallen asleep in error with his feet pointing toward Mecca and so showing disrespect to the Muslim faith. A mullah had woken him angrily, but Nānak's comment was devastating: "Then turn my feet in a direction where God is not."

A feature of the religious movement set in motion by Nānak was the importance of the guru. The teacher, who is not thought of in any way as an incarnation or manifestation of God, is important for guiding people in the way of Truth or God. The framework of Nānak's theology was Hindu in that he affirmed reincarnation and that the best symbol of the divine was the mysterious syllable Oṃ, of Vedic origin. He referred to God as creator of Brahman and the Vedas. But he dispensed with the idea of a priesthood (he himself was a *kṣatriya*, of the warrior caste).

Nānak's successors as leaders of the new community were a line of nine further Gurus, culminating in Guru Gobind Singh, who died in 1708, and

159

A 19th-century lithograph from Amritsar, showing Nanak reciting poems to various Sikhs, ascetics, and others.

who nominated the scriptures of the community, the Adi Granth, henceforth to be the Guru. Of the other Gurus perhaps Arjun is the most important. He led the community from 1581 to 1606. He founded the Golden Temple at Amritsar, collected the scriptures, and came into conflict with the emperor Jehangir – a conflict which led to clearer self-definition of the Sikhs as a militant and outwardly distinguishable group. It may be noted that there has long been fluidity at the edges of Sikhism. Quite a few followers of the Nānak tradition – and that of his elder contemporary Kabīr (1440–1518), some of whose poems were incorporated into the Sikh scriptures – remain within the definitely Hindu framework, as followers of a path which emphasizes *bhakti* and the unity of religions.

The Formation of Sikhism

In the seventeenth and eighteenth centuries the Sikhs came increasingly into conflict with the Mughal power based in Delhi. The empire was suspicious of the rise of a new power in the Punjab. On the other side, the Sikh clash with Mughal dominance led to the fashioning of a new community cemented together by the turban and other external marks of male membership, and by loyalty to the religion of the Guru Granth. This community was fashioned, too, by an alliance of different Punjabi castes, notably the cultivators known as the *jāts* and the merchants who were strong patrons of *bhakti* or devotional religion, which the Sikh tradition embodied. The evolution of Sikhism from

160

a syncretic and peaceful way of combining Hindu and Muslim motifs – the religion of Kabīr and Nānak – to the militant organization which was finally fashioned by the Tenth Guru, Gobind Singh (1666–1708), has puzzled observers. But it is only the tendency of religions to represent themselves as unchanging, as though the religion of Kabīr were the religion of Gobind Singh, which causes this puzzlement. It was basically in the time of Gobind Singh that Sikhism as we know it was formed. It makes use of a past tradition and leadership, of course, going back to Nānak.

Already before the time of Gobind Singh the community was in the process of forming itself into a military organization, but it was his reforms which set Sikhism on the path of becoming both a military and a religious power. He is represented as being the very ideal of chivalry and loyalty and is an example held up to the male Sikh. This quality of chivalry combines both martial and spiritual dedication.

His father Tegh Bahadur, the Ninth Guru, was executed on the orders of the Mughal emperor in 1675, and before his death proclaimed Gobind as his

Sikhism some key terms

Amrit Initiation by baptism in sweetened water stirred by a two-edged sword, in which the initiate swears to abide by the code or Rahit.

Granth or *Ādi Granth* or *Guru Granth* The sacred scriptures of Sikhism which, since Guru Gobind Singh, serve as the teacher or Guru.

Gurdwara or *Gurudvāra* The Sikh temple housing, primarily, a copy of the Granth.

Guru One of the ten leaders and preceptors of Sikhism, from Nānak to Gobind Singh.

Janamsakhi Punjabi writings celebrating the life of Guru Nānak.

Khalsa The Sikh community or order, the "Pure Ones" started by Gobind.

Mool Mantra The "basic verse," a brief statement of belief composed by Nānak affirming the oneness of God.

Panth The community of the Sikhs, literally the "path."

Rahit The code of ethics and rituals laid upon Sikhs, including the wearing of the five K's: uncut hair, dagger, breeches, comb, iron bangle.

Sant A member of a devotional tradition of north India, picturing God as without attributes or *nirguṇa* rather than more personally as among Vaishnavas. The two most important members were founders of Sikhism, Nānak and Kabīr. A Sant is a preceptor or guru within the tradition.

Sat Guru The name most given to God in Sikhism, "Being, the Teacher."

Sikh Literally "disciple," member of the Sikh Panth.

successor. After some successful warfare against both the Hindu Rajputs and the Mughals, Gobind established his capital at Anandpur, and summoned his followers there for a ceremony on April 13, 1699. After the morning devotions he called for five men to offer their lives in sacrifice, and took them behind a tent, to reappear with a sword dripping with blood. However, he had killed five goats, and the men reappeared, to be nominated by him as founding members of the new community or *Khalsa* (literally "Community of the Pure"). He caused them to drink out of a common bowl, from a drink he had made called *amrit* or nectar, conferring immortality. Importantly, this sacramental act was designed to break down caste barriers within the new community. They were to change their names to Singh or Lion. So in theory every Sikh is called Singh. In practice, as we shall see, there are complications to the story.

Each Sikh man has to wear five badges of his belonging, the five K's as they are called: to keep his hair and beard uncut (*kais*); to carry a comb (*kangha*) to keep his hair tidy; to wear *kacchā* or knee-length breeches, then used by soldiers; to wear a bangle (*karā*) on his wrist as a sign of loyalty to the Guru; and to carry a short sword (*kirpan*). Sikhs are forbidden alcohol, tobacco (then being introduced into India), and meat slaughtered in the Muslim manner, that is, by being bled to death.

The final great reform of Gobind was to proclaim that after his death they were to have the Adi Granth, or sacred book, as their Guru. It is therefore referred to as the Guru Granth (Teacher Book), and is a central object of veneration in the typical Sikh temple or "Guru House," *gurudvāra* or Gurdwara. The Granth is a collection of writings going back in part to Nānak, including saints from before him, such as Namdev, Kabīr, and Ravidas. Its final recension was done by Gobind Singh. The original collection in this form was put into the Golden Temple at Amritsar in the Punjab, which became the spiritual center and focus of pilgrimage for the Sikhs.

With its great variety of languages from north India and its styles of poetry, the Granth gives a broad sense of the devotional life of the region. At the social level it lays a lot of emphasis on the irrelevance of caste and race. It condemns distinctions. It also underlines the vital role of purity of motives. One does not win God's grace by the performance of external acts but

Guru Nānak's Japjī

There is but one God whose name is true, the Creator, devoid of fear and enmity, immortal, unborn, self-existent; by the favor of the Guru.

The True One was in the beginning; the True One was in the primal age.

The True One is now also, O Nānak; the True One also shall be.

By thinking I cannot obtain a conception of Him, even though I think hundreds of thousands of times.

through the devotion of the heart. It emphasizes the performance of truth, sincerity, and the attainment of equipoise (*sahj*) and knowledge of the Divine.

Despite these teachings, Sikhism developed, as we have seen, its own battery of external practices. Maybe this was inevitable. But it creates a lively dialectic between loyalty to a particular, transcaste community and the realization of universal humanity.

The History of the Sikh Movement

The new community eventually established dominance in the Punjab under the leadership of Ranjit Singh (1780–1839), but shortly after was defeated by the British and incorporated into British India. The British harnessed the military expertise and spirit of the Sikhs by using them prominently in the Indian Army which they created. But not all Sikhs were actually oriented toward full incorporation in the Sikh community. As well as the "unshorn" ones who observe the external forms, there are many other followers known as *sahajdhāris*, who are regarded as taking longer to attain full membership. After all, the tradition of Nānak was a general *bhakti* form of religion, and so a cloud of devotional Hindus forms a penumbra of the Sikh movement.

There are also other movements which have relationships to Sikhism. On the one side are the followers of Kabīr, known as Kabīrpanthis (those who follow the path of Kabīr); on the other hand, more directly indebted to

The material dimension: Sikhs sell the Five K's outside a Gurdwara. Following initiation into the Khalsa, the "Saint-soldiers" are obliged to signify their pledge by the wearing of five symbolic objects: their names in Punjabi all begin with "K."

163

About 3000 Sikhs demonstrate at the major New Delhi shrine to protest against the army's siege of the Golden Temple in Amritsar.

Sikhism through the Adi Granth, are the Radhasomais, founded in Agra by a banker, Shiv Dayal (1818–78), who carry on the Guru tradition and stress the vital importance in God's communication to the world of the essence of sound, *shabd*, the Word. In this form of faith, which itself is split into differing groups, there is stress on the union of the disciple with the Teacher and the unity of the Teacher with the Divine. It is a kind of incarnational Hinduism, but it owes a lot to the Sikh connection. The name signifies the unity between the soul, symbolized by Rādhā the lover of Krishna, and the Master or *somai*. The Khalsa idea (see above) has remained strong, and in fact during the latter days of the British became more militant in a blend of Punjabi and all-Indian nationalism. Later still, in the 1980s, Sikh militants have gone further, agitating for an independent state which would be predominantly Sikh, in the Indian Punjab.

In a way the history of the Sikhs illustrates in sharp form a general point, that when religion A meets religion B it may turn out that a blend, AB, occurs, which becomes by the force of circumstances a third element – in effect a new religion. In the Sikh case this move also led to a marked transformation, of a sharp kind. In the circumstances Sikhism could easily have been counted as just a variant on Hinduism, as the Kabīr movement was, for Hindu religions have fluid boundaries. It could simply have learned from Islam and incorporated Islamic elements into its fabric. But by forming a political community its role has become less ambiguous. By and large, Sikhs

164

now feel themselves as belonging to a separate religion: and a modern complaint about the Indian constitution is that it does not recognize separate status for the Sikhs in terms of the law and the like.

The Sikhs had been involved in a struggle in the Punjab in the 1920s and 1930s over the matter of the control of their temples. The danger from a Sikh point of view was that an increasing number of them would drift back into the Hindu environment. In the late nineteenth century the Singh Sabha had been formed for educational and religious purposes, and had in some degree checked that drift. But the temples remained in the hands of the *udasis* who were not outwardly conforming Sikhs. This had come about in part from conservatism dating right back to the formation of the Khalsa by Gobind Singh: the pre-Gobind type of holy person was still in charge of temples. The struggle was promoted by a militant party, the Akali Dal.

During partition, the Sikhs found themselves existentially on the same side as the Hindus, and were regarded as such by Muslims. This gave most Sikhs a loyalty to the new Republic of India. However, as time went on there were problems, as the Sikhs saw it, in preserving their distinctive rights in law and elsewhere, and so agitation grew for a Sikh state in the Punjab, which the Indian central government has resisted. It was because of this that Indira Gandhi was assassinated by her own Sikh bodyguards in 1984. A few months previously she had ordered the Indian army to storm the Golden Temple complex in Amritsar, which a rather extreme young leader, Jarnail Singh Bhindranwale, had turned into a stronghold. He was killed during the Amritsar affair, but his ideas gathered some significant support from the diaspora Sikhs overseas, in Canada, Britain, and elsewhere.

The Dimensions of Sikhism

It is useful for us to sum up the Sikh experience by recapitulating the various dimensions of the religion.

The Social Dimension

First, the social dimension is somewhat complicated. There are those in the tradition of Nānak and Kabīr who, while retaining that loyalty and addressing devotion to the one God, nevertheless are not integrated into the full community of Sikhs who follow Guru Gobind Singh's reforms, with their accent on external signs such as beards, the wearing of bangles, and so on. We noted above too the Radhasomai tradition, which owes quite a lot to the Sikh connection. On the other hand, Sikhs in the full sense not only display the five badges of belonging, but have an institutional life, both in India and overseas, centered on the Gurdwara or temple, which houses the Adi Granth, or book of scriptures. In reverencing the book Sikhs make plain their loyalty to the prior sequence of ten leaders or Gurus. The life of the Gurdwara, which has both a social and educational function as well as a ritual one, gives Sikhs a communitarian solidarity. It is important too that Sikhs reject the Hindu caste system, though they are in a sense integrated into it, as are other minorities such as the Jains.

The Doctrinal Dimension

Doctrinally, Sikhs belong to that strand of north Indian devotionalism which emphasizes the ultimately indescribable character of God. One must attain to a pure love of God without relying upon myth and image. In this way there is a strong affinity with Islam, which likewise dispenses with images. Nānak defined God as Truth or Reality, pervading the whole cosmos, being unborn and omniscient. On the other hand, and unlike Islam, Sikhism affirms the whole notion of rebirth. But by devotion and self-transformation, the individual can gain release and unity with the Divine. This is possible even in this life, in the state of living release or *jīvanmukti*.

The Ethical Dimension

As to the ethical dimension, from the time of Guru Gobind Singh and even before, solidarity with the community was to be expressed if necessary in (for men) soldierly courage, in fighting against enemies. The turning of the Sikh tradition into a militant organization was the result of vicissitudes and persecution, and takes Sikhism far from the gentler *bhakti* of its origins. The wearing of the dagger and the soldier's short trousers are symbols of the lion-hearted character of the Sikh (the use of the name Singh or Lion for Sikh males is likewise symbolic of courage). But the rejection of casteism also means that there is a proud emphasis on the equality of men (and in theory women, though women's legal status is more problematic) in the community and beyond. The notion that God is Truth means that Sikhism lays stress on uprightness and honesty in language and conduct. The use of tobacco and alcohol is banned.

The Ritual Dimension

As to ritual, emphasis is laid on the formula of belief known as the *japji*. Congregational worship centers in the Gurdwara, where the Adi Granth is the focus of attention. While the Gurus are deeply respected, there is no question of worshiping them as incarnations of God: this is a consequence of the notion of God as *nirguṇa* or without qualities (that is, without worldly manifestation). In general the spirit of Sikh devotion is that it is what is felt within the heart which counts and there are various stories from the time of Nānak as to the inappropriateness of taking external ritual seriously in itself. Amritsar, with its beautiful Golden Temple, is the prime focus of pilgrimage.

The Experiential Dimension

The experiential dimension centers of course on the experience of God found in the religion of *bhakti*. There remains a difference between God and humans, and while God appears as personal he is conceived as a purely spiritual being. Typically such experience is conveyed through poetry, as with other north Indian *bhakti*. The tender feelings of the devotee combine with a sense of the quality of all before God to give Sikh poetry a strong humanistic character which reinforces a democratic sense of belonging to a single community.

The Narrative Dimension

The narrative dimension of Sikhism does not center on stories of the incarnate gods such as Rāma, as often with other devotionalism of the modern period, but rather on the heroic stories of the founding and subsequent Gurus. Consequently Sikhs have a strong sense of their own history from the time of Nānak onward. Not all the stories of course may be of equal historical validity – for instance the notion that Nānak met Kabīr is probably just an invention of later hagiography – though conservative Sikhs may well be upset at doubts cast on the saintly tradition. (The same phenomenon can be seen in other historically anchored faiths.)

The Material Dimension

The material dimension is represented principally by three things: the external garb and badges of Sikh males, the book of the Adi Granth, containing the essence of Sikh teaching but standing in, in a temple, for what in much of the

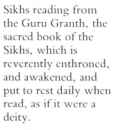

Sikhs reading from the Guru Granth, the sacred book of the Sikhs, which is reverently enthroned, and awakened, and put to rest daily when read, as if it were a deity.

Hindu tradition would be the image of the god or goddess, and the famous city and temple of Amritsar in the Punjab. There the fourth Guru Ram Das (1534–1581) had not only set up a new city, but also dug a large pool (the Pool of Immortality or Amritsar) for Sikhs and others to bathe in. The establishment of what in effect was the capital of the Sikh community combined with their increasing wealth, lying athwart trade routes to Central Asia, to consolidate Sikhism as a political religion, liable to be at loggerheads with the Mughal emperors. Ram Das' successor and son Arjun (1563–1606) built the present Golden Temple as the Temple of God, being in effect the counterpart both of Mecca and the city of Banaras for the Hindus. From his reign dated the strongly political role of the Guru: some considered that this was a move too far in the direction of Islam. At any rate, Amritsar has become the material center of Sikhism.

Conclusion

The story of the Sikhs expresses a remarkable transition from a peaceful devotional movement to a powerful military-style community, a transition which was perhaps forced on them by the need to resist suppression by the Mughals. Their military tradition was carried on after their defeat by the British in 1849, after which the Sikh state was annexed. Sikh regiments played a notable part in the British army and later in that of the Republic of India. In recent times the Sikh Punjab has been a prime beneficiary of the so-called Green Revolution. From this prosperity spring some of the tensions that have issued in the demand for a separate Sikh state.

CHAPTER NINE

Confucianism and the New Chinese State Ideology

A General Perspective on Chinese Religion

Westerners often assume that Chinese religious and philosophical ideas can be classified in a Western way, so that we can speak of three religions of China, namely Confucianism, Taoism, and Buddhism. However, often these are not so much three as parts of a single functioning system. Also, the words themselves which we use can be misleading. Is "Confucianism" a word meaning the philosophical stream of thought that started with Confucius? Is Taoism the teaching of Lao-tzu? If so, then the religions labeled by these nouns are something very different from the "philosophical" teachings, though overlapping with them. Moreover, the state cult which is sometimes labeled "Confucianism," though it rested on an ideology of ritual which can be traced to Confucius – and though temples to the memory of the sage himself were incorporated into it – was a rather artificial construction. It was not strictly speaking the religion of anyone, except that people were expected to observe it to further the continuing welfare of the state. Also there is so-called "popular religion," meaning the general and usually very localized religion of the people, which also is sometimes loosely referred to as Confucianism, but is actually a set of practices and ideas which draws on various aspects and institutions of Taoism, Buddhism, and the state religion. All this can seem rather messy and muddled. It should help to make some stipulations about words.

First, what we are dealing with as a single, but also localized and varied, phenomenon is Chinese religion. Now Buddhism and Taoism can be clearly distinguished by their well-defined monastic embodiment and a class of religious specialists, so we can refer to these traditions as separately embodied. In parallel with this we shall use "Confucianism" to refer to the official cult which disappeared with the revolution of 1911, and has had no basic significance since then. To refer to the philosophical tradition from the time of Confucius (and indeed before) we shall speak of "Confucian thought." This

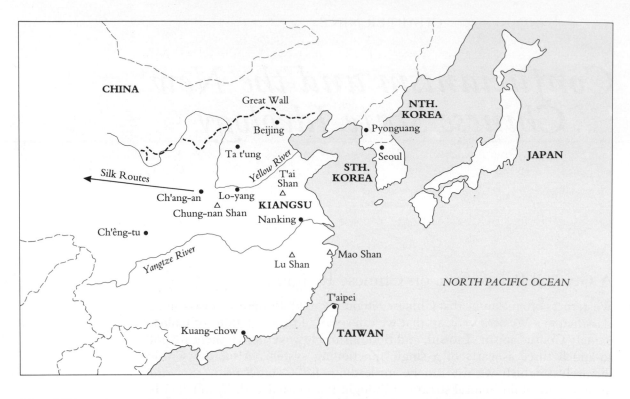

Map of China and Japan.

includes a strong strand of ethical theory and prescriptions. Similarly, in Chapter 10 we shall refer to the Taoist intellectual tradition, beginning with the anthology known as the *Tao-te Ching*, ascribed to the legendary Lao-tzu, and the treatise known as the *Book of Chuang-tzu*, as "Taoist thought." Themes from Taoist thought were to be incorporated, as one element, into "Taoist religion." But neither Lao-tzu nor Chuang-tzu, even if they really existed as historical persons, was responsible for the later faith, with all its complexities.

Although the Chinese in fact managed to integrate rites from the three strands into their local practice, there were of course also rivalries for state patronage between the three organizations. At different periods certain Western religions also made some impact on China: Nestorian Christianity, once quite powerful; Manichaeism; Zoroastrianism; Judaism; and Islam. Of these Islam remains the most potent (see Chapter 7). In modern times Christian missions have made an impact, especially in the educational field.

Important Periods of Chinese Religious History

Shortly before 1000 B.C.E. the old Shang dynasty came to an end, to be replaced by the Chou, under the regent who became an ideal figure in later times, the Duke of Chou. It was from the eighth century B.C.E., under the rule of the Eastern Chou (771–221 B.C.E.), that Chinese culture as we know it began to form. The classics which Confucius was to edit as part of his educational and philosophical task date from this time. Confucius himself, or

170

Master K'ung as his name says ("Confucius" being a Latinized reflection of K'ung-Fu-tzu), lived from 551 to 479 B.C.E. The legendary Lao-tzu was supposedly an older contemporary of his; but the anthology which he is supposed to have composed is doubtless somewhat later. The succeeding centuries saw some important figures in the traditions of Confucian and Taoist thought, such as Chuang-tzu and Meng-tzu (Mencius).

By the first century C.E. Buddhism was starting to establish itself in China. In the second century Tao as a religious system was founded by Chang Tao Ling. It seems therefore reasonable to look on the period before the second century C.E. as the formative or early period. Then we can look on the Sui and Tang dynasties, up to the tenth century, as the classical period, during which the three religious traditions took their main form. And finally, from the eleventh to the end of the eighteenth century we may call the medieval or premodern period, before the full and somewhat fatal impact of the West made itself felt in China.

During the classical period, particularly, the effects of Chinese culture were perceived abroad, especially in Vietnam, in Korea, and in Japan. China was the foremost world civilization, and was creating a new synthesis of cultures in Chinese Buddhism. In the nineteenth century substantial migrations occurred under the influence of a growing colonialist world economy, and in consequence Chinese culture and religion are to be found in the U.S.A., the West Indies, Indonesia, Malaysia, Singapore, and elsewhere.

Some Fundamental Ideas and Practices

Since we are dealing with a single civilization, it is reasonable to try to single out its chief ideas and practices, which can be seen as relevant to all three religions. At the *ritual* level, there is that most general and important concept of *li*, roughly meaning due ceremonial behavior, or ritual at the broadest, including music. This *li* played a vital role in K'ung's whole philosophy. Of immediate significance also were the offerings directed toward ancestors – a

---

Confucius: Analects

K'ung said, "The ruler who governs the state through virtue is like the pole star, which stays put while the other stars revolve round it."

K'ung said, "All of the three hundred odes in the Classic of Poetry can be summed up in one of its lines, 'Have no wrong thoughts.'"

K'ung said, "If you control the people by government acts and keep them in line with law and order, they will refrain from doing wrong, but they will not have a sense of honor or shame. But if you lead them through virtue and regulate them by the laws of propriety, then they will have a sense of shame and will attain goodness."

K'ung said, "At fifteen my mind was fixed on learning. By thirty my character had been formed. At forty I had no more confusions. At fifty I understood the Mandate of Heaven. At sixty it was easy for me to hear the truth. At seventy I could follow my desires without transgressing what was right."

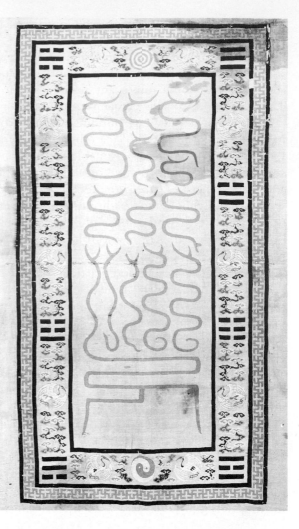

The doctrinal dimension: here various motifs important in Chinese thought are symbolized – the Yin and the Yang, the Buddhist swastika, the basic trigrams which when combined form the hexagrams of the I Ching, and stylized dragons, alluding to the fertility of nature and the Imperial entity.

kind of cult that occurred in the emperor's reverence toward his ancestors, in clan temples, and in the home. The cult of ancestors ties in with funerary rites, designed to transfer the dead happily to their resting-places, so that they are not consigned to the sad status of restless ghosts. A third important ritual motif was divination, extensively practiced from before the time of the classic *Book of Changes* or *I Ching*. Geomancy, or the practice of harmonizing human activity – such as building a house – with the spirit (and the spirits) of the landscape, is worth mention too. Chinese religion also made its contributions to forms of mysticism and yoga.

At the *experiential* level, a characteristic idea was the goal of experiencing harmony or identity with nature through following the Way of Nature, the Tao. Mediumistic religion in the form of being possessed by the god was important in popular religion, and much attention was paid to visions of the divine realm.

Doctrinally, importance was always attached to the concept of Heaven, sometimes treated rather abstractly as Providence, and sometimes more personally as God. Rulers were thought of as receiving, or not receiving, the Mandate of Heaven which justified (or failed to justify) their governance. In later thought there was also the notion of the Great Ultimate, a sort of God beyond God. In cosmology much was made throughout Chinese history of the interplay between the Yang and the Yin (the male and female principles, and active and passive polarities). There was a whole system of classifying phenomena according to the Yin and Yang and Five Elements or processes: wood, fire, earth, metal, and water.

The *narrative* and mythic dimension of Chinese culture was peculiarly rich. From our perspective we need to note the story of K'ung's life, the tale of Lao-tzu, and the stories of the divine immortals as especially significant. *Socially*, the ideal of the scholar or *ju* was important; but still more vital was the figure of the sage. Much of Confucian *ethics* revolved around family relationships, but at the same time Buddhist and Taoist monasticism provided an escape from the family's structures, through the monastic vocation. Throughout there is a corresponding ethical contrast between the morality to be displayed by the benevolent person in the world, summed up in *jen* or human-heartedness, and that of the Taoist or Buddhist who is concerned with *wu wei*, that is not-acting, or acting through not acting.

These then are some of the principal motifs of Chinese religious culture. If one were to point to anything at the *material* level it would perhaps be the

The social dimension: Chinese women mourning at a grave, and burning imitation money as an offering. Ancestors remain important members of the society they have left behind.

painting scroll. For the Chinese painter there is no frame. It is not as if nature can be framed: the scene painted wanders off beyond the dimensions of the scroll itself. And it is common to bind together the arts: the poem or inscription is an integral part of the painting and vice versa. A certain dynamic boundlessness gives fluidity to Chinese culture: it is less concerned with analysis than either Western or Indian philosophy and religion.

The Early Period

K'ung's Life and Teachings

Because of the total imprint which he placed upon Chinese culture, it is right for us to start with K'ung, whose discourse has come down to us in the book known as *Analects* and whose spirit was to be followed by many generations of China's scholars and administrators. K'ung was born, probably in 551 B.C.E., in what is now Shantung province, in the small state of Lu. He was perhaps from a minor aristocratic family. At any rate, he received an education, which until his time was normally reserved for the elite. One of the revolutionary aspects of his teaching was to throw open his academy to everyone; this helped, with his teachings, to create the notion of the true gentleman (*hsün-tzu*) whose high class is not a matter of birth but rather of moral behavior. K'ung was perturbed by the chaotic state of political and social life in his times. In theory the royal house of Chou was supreme in north China, but in fact there was a variety of independent feudal rulers. He saw that good rule should occur not by force but by moral persuasion: and for this reason he paid a lot of attention to rites and ceremonies, since he perceived in them a natural way of inculcating right behavior and loyal service. He pondered the meaning of tradition, and though he was a reformer he was also highly committed to older ways. He had a vision of the past, refined and redefined, as playing a vital role in shaping the nonviolent means whereby the good ruler maintains his power.

At about the age of fifty, by which time, so K'ung avers in the *Analects*, he "knew Heaven's decree," he took service as a minister or official in the state of Lu; but in the event his political intervention was not a success. He left Lu, wandering in exile for some thirteen years in neighboring states, with a band of his disciples. He went back to Lu about his sixty-eighth birthday. By seventy, he said, "he could follow his heart's desire without overstepping the line." He had reached full maturity of judgment. He died at seventy-three, saddened by the loss of his son and two disciples who predeceased him. But his influence lived on; and eventually his ideal of the scholar as administrator became the norm for about two thousand years.

He is credited (probably wrongly) with having edited the Six Classics, actually now five: the *Shi Ching* or Classic of Poetry, the *I Ching* or Classic of Changes, the *Shu Ching* or Classic of History, the *Li Chi* or Book of Ritual, the *Ch'un-ch'iu* or Spring and Autumn Annals, and the now lost *Yüeh Ching* or Classic of Music. At any rate, his name came to be associated with these major literary works, which together with some other writings came to form the curriculum for the imperial civil service examinations. And so, indirectly at least, K'ung was responsible for the creation of a class of bureaucrats who had deep literary skills, knew about the ceremonial side of life, and were brought up in the ideals not only of correct formal behavior but also of the necessary sincerity which has to lie behind it. They were also infused with the moral ideal of *jen* or human-heartedness. The official ruler must be correct, sincere, and humane. It was a fine vision, which placed classical education at the heart of politics. The Confucian ideals were to serve China well.

There was nothing greatly speculative in K'ung's thought. It is clear from various references that, although he did not talk about it much, he respected belief in Heaven as a kind of personal God. He did not talk about miracles and such events, it is reported; and he was not without a gently rationalistic tone in what he said about religion. It is partly from this that later "official" Confucians were often dismissive of what they saw as the superstitions of popular religion. There developed an elitist poise about the scholarly gentleman in China; but this seems to have been foreign to K'ung's own thinking. He underlined the importance of treating all people well and the sanctity of ancient rites, including offerings to ancestors and to Heaven. His was not a combative nature, but one of humility and grave courtesy, not without a sense of humor. A nice touch is that when he was out shooting he would not shoot at a sitting bird, thus showing his sense of fair play.

K'ung set the agenda of much later Chinese thought, concerned as he was with political rule, right conduct, and human nature. In the following century we see the pendulum swinging toward a much less formal view of virtue and government. Mo-tzu argued vigorously for the importance of universal love and applied utilitarian tests to all policies, which should be in the interests of the people, conducing to their wealth and safety. He found a sanction for his doctrines in the will of a Supreme God, Heaven (T'ien), who had under his command a host of lesser spirits. His personalist ethic and frugality in living did not appeal to all, and the movement which he founded gradually died out, though there was a revival of interest in the eighteenth century C.E.

Meng-tzu, Hsün-tzu, Han Fei-tzu

The greatest of the successors to K'ung-Fu-tzu was Meng-tzu, known in the West as Mencius, who lived *c.* 371–289 B.C.E. or perhaps two decades earlier. He advocated rule by a kingly sage, whose policies would be informed with virtue. His path should be the Wang-tao or Emperor's Way; and people were entitled to rise up against an evil monarch who would have forfeited the Mandate of Heaven. Despite this he was strongly pacifist, partly because of the disturbed and bloody period during which he lived. Conquest should only proceed by the desire of other peoples to join the country of a supremely benevolent ruler. The most important part of his teaching, however, has to do with his concept of *hsin*, or "heart," "mind." This is the power within each person which contains dispositions, which should be encouraged to sprout and grow, toward *jen* or humaneness, *i* or dutifulness, *li* or proper behavior, and *chih* or knowledge of right and wrong. This inner sense is essentially oriented therefore toward goodness. In other words human nature is essentially good. In this Meng was defending the Confucian tradition against those – Taoists, for instance – who saw the human heart as egoistic and obstructive of harmonious living, and on the other hand against those like Mo-tzu who had a superficial idea of goodness, defining it in outer and material terms. It followed also from his idea of *hsin* that both moral education and political policy should be designed to bring out the innate tendencies toward virtue. Especially we ought to develop *jen* or humaneness, which could be seen as a caring and benevolent attitude toward others.

By contrast Hsün-tzu (third century B.C.E.), who lived to see the unification of the states of China under the Ch'in regime (221 B.C.E.) and was upset to observe its harsh nature, especially since two of his own disciples served as officials at court, took a different and more pessimistic line from that of Mencius. In his view human nature was inherently chaotic and bad and needed the forces of education to tame it. He strongly emphasized the *li* aspect of the Confucian tradition: ceremonial and behavioral propriety was something that involved both inner feeling and outer act, but it was instrumental in teaching individuals how to act well, and was crucial therefore in moral education. Without inner feeling, *li* might be wooden and hypocritical. But rightly understood it gave outer expression to inner respect for others, including the ancestors. In practice, then, Hsün-tzu, though breaking with the moral optimism of the earlier Confucian tradition, adopted a very similar view of the shape and point of education. Some of his writings also give *li* a cosmic role. Thus he says:

Indeed it is through *li* that Heaven and earth are in harmony, that the sun and moon are splendid, that the four seasons succeed each other, that the stars follow their motions, that the rivers and streams maintain their flow, that all things and creatures enjoy prosperity, and joy and wrath are controlled.

He also rather movingly writes, in defence of reverence for the dead, so central a value in Chinese culture:

When man's end and beginning are both well treated, the Tao of humanity is fulfilled. Hence the superior individual respects the beginning and attends to the end. To treat them alike is the Tao of the superior individual and the refinement of *li* and *i*. To exalt the living and belittle the dead is to respect one who has consciousness and neglect one who has lost it – this is the way of the evil man . . .

Hsün-tzu came at the end of a creative period, that of the so-called "hundred philosophers." There were various schools apart from the Confucian, of course – Taoists, legalists or authoritarian writers, and others. The Confucian tradition had already established itself as an educational force, and it was not long before Confucian literature became the staple of a centralized education system through the establishment of a Great Academy. Yet this was after a traumatic period for Chinese thought and scholarship, when in 213 B.C.E. all controversial books were burned.

Confucianism some key terms

Ch'i Material energy which combines with *li* or principle to make up things in the world, according to neo-Confucian philosophy.

Chiao A religious movement, teaching, or sect.

Ching A classical text, usually referring to the five Confucian Classics.

Chün-tzu The superior person or morally advanced being: the ideal product of Confucian education.

Jen Human-heartedness or loving benevolence toward human beings.

Li Principle or the spiritual substance or energy which combines with *ch'i*.

Li Ritual, ceremonial, rules of propriety, good behavior: central concept of Confucian education.

T'ai Chi The Supreme Ultimate in neo-Confucian philosophy.

T'i Substance as opposed to use (*yung*).

T'ien Heaven or personalized God residing above, whose cult was that of the emperor.

Wu-hsing The five elements or agents: metal, wood, water, fire, and earth.

Yung Use: nineteenth-century Confucianism wondered how to retain the traditional substance (*t'i*) of Chinese values while adopting Western technology for use.

Legalism (Fa-chia) had as its chief exponent Han Fei-tzu, who had studied with Hsün-tzu but rejected the latter's Confucian morality. The main point about Fa-chia was what it rejected: it saw written law, as opposed to traditional moral values, as the best way of controlling people. Han Fei-tzu's book is a witty exercise in expounding for a ruler the best methods of dominating people and controlling a bureaucracy. A person's title should be defined in terms of the work he is expected to perform and his actual success in this should be measured. The central fact about government is the use of power, and Han Fei-tzu has a lot of good advice on this front. For instance, the effective ruler should not make his desires or prejudices known, or otherwise his ministers will distort information and advice to him. He should delegate action, and so should sit at the center of power without acting. The two handles of government are reward and punishment, and these should be used systematically. Method will triumph over virtue: you do not need to wait for a sage to get effective rule, since heeding Han Fei-tzu's methods will accomplish much, and mediocre talent will be able to make good use of them. But his rather cynical way of writing and his emphasis on humanly created law rather than traditionally sanctioned morality gave him a Machiavellian reputation.

The Classical Period: Confucianism Becomes Official

Despite the espousal of legalism by the emperor Shih Huang-ti (reigned 221–210 B.C.E.), there were greater attractions for a ruler in taking up Confucian thought – partly its traditionalism, which was important in the legitimation of rule; partly its ritualism, which could be taken up into the practices of the central government; and partly too its moralism (it is, for one thing, unwise to act the Machiavelli if you parade that that is what you are doing; it is better

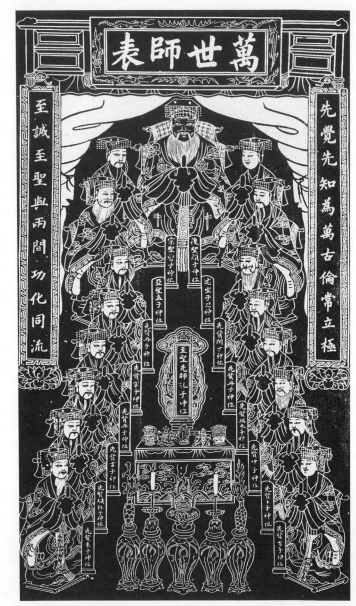

Confucianism idealized gentleman scholars, who became the highest class in China until the 20th-century revolution.

to conceal cynicism behind a mask of morality). And Confucian thought was believable. At any rate, it was under the Han dynasty, from the first century C.E., that Confucianism came to be an officially sponsored ideology and cult. Offerings were to be made to K'ung, and these were linked to state ceremonies in which the emperor made sacrifices to Heaven. Much later, in the seventh century, Confucian temples were established throughout the administrative system of the empire. Tablets inscribed to famous disciples and other prominent figures were included too, so that Confucianism came to be a kind of "civil religion" or national cult honoring those who had served the empire well.

The kind of Confucianism that became a state orthodoxy was the kind of view espoused by the highly influential thinker Tung Chung-shu (c. 179–104 B.C.E.). He expounded the doctrines of Confucian thought in terms of the generally accepted Chinese cosmology of the time, making use therefore of the notions of Yin and Yang, the Five Elements, and T'ien or Heaven, which he saw as a personal Lord. He made use too of the idea of the Mandate of Heaven, and evolved a theory of the succession of dynasties. If a ruler does not follow the Mandate by acting morally and wisely, then sooner or later the dynasty will break down. The Yin–Yang theory was applied by him to crucial human relations, especially the three bonds between ruler and ruled, father and son, and husband and wife. In each of these the Yang (ruler, father, husband) is superior. This hierarchical theory of human relationships was pervasive in Confucian China.

In effect, official Confucianism began the process of treating K'ung as an honored ancestor, together with other notables and the ancestors of the emperor. This was parallel to the cults which emerged systematically in classical China, especially in the south, of clan lineages. All this was in addition to domestic shrines in which the names of forebears inscribed on tablets came to be the norm.

The Medieval Period

The Neo-Confucian Revival

The religions of Taoism and Buddhism were sufficiently successful to present a serious threat to traditional Confucian thought. Its pragmatism and primary concern with political and ethical issues were oblique to the more intense spiritual interests of people, whether the devotionalism of Pure Land Buddhists and of Taoists (such religion the *ju* tended to despise as ignorant) or the quests for enlightenment and personal immortality of more mystically inclined followers of the faiths. It was to fill this gap in Confucian thought and practice that there arose the movement the West knows as neo-Confucianism. In Chinese it is known as *Li-hsüeh* or "Learning of Principle."

With this movement we are reaching out into the medieval period, after 1000 C.E., when Chinese religion took its final premodern form. Part of the revival was straightforwardly educational: for instance, Hu Yüan (933–1059?)

set up two curricula for the vast academy he founded – one had to do with matters of substance (*t'i*), i.e. the study of the classics, and the other with matters of function (*yung*), covering practical and scientific subjects including mathematics. Maybe a better translation of "substance" from a modern perspective is "values." Later, in the nineteenth century, the question was raised as to whether it was possible to borrow Western ideas for *yung* while retaining Chinese traditional *t'i*. But as well as a reinvigoration of education there was speculation about the nature of reality and the way to knowledge that gave Confucian thought a stronger metaphysical basis. The new thinkers were aware of the subtlety of Buddhist analyses of the world, and of epistemology or the theory of how it is that we know things. The first moves in the direction of a systematic worldview came in the writings of the so-called Five Northern Masters, during the Sung dynasty (960–1126). Their thought was summed up and used as the basis for a creative synthesis by the great scholar Chu Hsi (1130–1200). Behind phenomena are *li* or dynamic principles. These flow from the T'ai Chi or Great Ultimate, which we might also translate as "First Principle." It is beyond time and space, and yet it contains within itself the potentiality of all the principles which define the particular patterns in the created order. It is not like the Taoist Ultimate, Nothing, nor is it mere Emptiness; if we use negatives about it it is because it transcends the language which is adapted to life in space and time.

Everything is composed of *li* and of material force (*ch'i*), but the former is logically prior. The mind of humanity shares the creative power of Heaven or the Great Ultimate; and so our spiritual and moral practice should be to recover the original heavenly human nature in us and fight against those material forces which conduce to egoism and lack of concern for other people. Chu Hsi also advocated meditation or "quiet sitting," and in this we see a practical effect of Buddhist methods on the Confucian tradition. He made much of what he called "the investigation of things": the probing of principle, both external and internal.

Whether he could be called a theist has been much debated; sometimes he hinted at the personal nature of Heaven. Much of his life was spent in administrative service, and he was strongly activist. He also objected in strong terms both to the Buddhist theory of reincarnation and to the Taoist pursuit of longevity.

Wang Yang-ming – a Moral Idealism

Much later, during the Ming dynasty, the other towering figure in the rich tradition of neo-Confucian thought, Wang Yang-ming (1472–1529), was less concerned than was Chu Hsi with external learning in the investigation of things. For him, knowledge was an inner matter, though it could not be prized apart from action. He was interested above all in the "existential" nature of knowing (so one cannot know suffering without actually suffering). As he wrote: "Knowledge is the beginning of action; action is the completion of knowledge." Wang was very keen to defend the notion of the primordial goodness of human nature, and its identity with the Principle of all things. The sage by his self-cultivation extends his knowledge and his action in such a way that the whole world in effect becomes his body. The seeds of this universalism are there empirically to be observed. When we see a child about to fall into a well, we are immediately impelled to try to save it (this was Mencius' primary example to show the innate goodness of human nature); so we have analogous sympathetic feelings when we encounter frightened birds and animals, or see plants destroyed and crushed, or even when we see tiles or stones broken.

Such somewhat refined notions in the neo-Confucian tradition were a response in their own way to Buddhism. They set the scene for debates about the right interpretation of the Classics and of the Four Books – the *Analects*, the *Great Learning*, the *Doctrine of the Mean*, and the *Meng-tzu* – which formed the main substance of the educated person's basis for a worldview during the medieval period of Chinese culture.

The Dimensions of Medieval Chinese Religion

We may now sum up some of the movements and phenomena we have outlined by looking to some of the manifestations of the dimensions of religion during the medieval period in China.

Confucian ritual: priests are shown here burning incense at the tomb of deceased great scholars.

The Ritual Dimension

As to ritual, this occurred in varying ways at differing social levels. Local temples were the locus of particular gods with their own festival rhythms. At a higher level there were the official temples for the state cult, and notable Taoist and Buddhist shrines and monastic complexes, which were places for various ritual activities. But, as we have seen, a powerful impulse was devotional worship which would ensure a favorable afterlife. Funeral ceremonies, involving both Taoist and Buddhist practitioners, would involve the symbolic transfer of goods, fashioned of paper, and petitions, to the next world. There were also a pan-Chinese festival rhythm, with such special days as the New Year (according to the Chinese calendar), the Dragon-Boat Festival, and Harvest-Home; for the dead the Ch'ing Meng, in which graves are visited and cleaned and repaired; the feast of Hungry Ghosts, and so on. Another feature of ritual life was the prevalence of pilgrimages, especially to sacred mountains, which are often associated with important religious figures and events. All this was supplemented by household rites in which offerings were made to gods, whether Taoist or Buddhist, and to ancestors.

The Experiential Dimension

In the experiential dimension, not only were warm feelings developed in devotional religion, and so a sense of loyalty and gratitude to great Buddhas and the like; but also there were the various higher states of meditation cultivated in both a Buddhist and a Taoist context. Visions and shamanistic experiences were always taken seriously in traditional China. The pioneering of Ch'an Buddhism gave a new urgency to enlightenment and blended with the sense of harmony with nature which was always an ingredient of the Taoist tradition.

The Mythical Dimension

As to myth, the Chinese tradition is not as rich as the Indian in this; but the stories of the Duke of Chou and of Huang-ti, the histories and legends of K'ung, Lao-tzu, and other sages, all contributed to a sense of a sacred reality which found rich and complex manifestation in the decoration of temples. Because the Chinese had a strong historical sense, history itself loomed large in the narrative dimension.

The Doctrinal Dimension

Doctrinally the themes of Heaven developed into belief in the Great Ultimate, which had its more negative echoes in such notions as Emptiness and the ineffable Tao. The Yin–Yang polarity and the Five Elements were integrated into a metaphysics of the universe controlled by the rhythms of the Ultimate. There were rich views of the afterlife, but disagreement about the truth of reincarnation. To some extent, worry about the afterlife was transmuted in the Taoist strand into concern for longevity, achieved by a whole apparatus of personal discipline mingled with magical alchemy.

The Ethical Dimension

Ethically there was a most lively debate through most of Chinese history, revived during the medieval period through the resurgence of moral speculation in the neo-Confucian movement. The varied strands of Confucian, Buddhist, and Taoist ethics were not easily to be brought together; but in a rough and ready way they served to underpin a loose ideology and worldview that embraced the whole of Chinese society. There was a dialectic in it. The underlying menace and turbulence of the Taoist tradition, fueled sometimes by messianic expectations of a new order, strove against the orderly and elitist teachings of the Confucians; the otherworldly tendencies in Buddhism drew away from both the other traditions. But the whole gloriously eclectic pastiche of Chinese religion had much to offer people of different temperaments, and its medieval pluralism served to keep the wider society stable.

The Institutional Dimension

Institutionally the three traditions could exist side by side; Buddhist and Taoist orders were independently organized, and in effect the civil service was the institutional embodiment of the Confucian tradition.

The Korean Contribution

China had effects on its neighbors too. Chinese culture proved to be wonderfully attractive to Korea, Japan, and Vietnam. So many of the major features of Chinese religion and philosophy – as well as writing, technology, and printing – were exported and in due course transformed.

From very early times Korea was, naturally enough, under strong Chinese cultural influence, and occasionally it was directly under Chinese rule, for instance during the period from 193 to 37 B.C.E. For the next seven hundred years the peninsula was largely divided between the three kingdoms of Silla, Koryo, and Chosun. A characteristic view of religions and values was expressed by the founder of the Koryo dynasty (935–1392) in 918, Wang Kon, in holding that Buddhism was to govern spiritual matters, geomancy matters of prognostication, and Confucian thought social and political affairs. Various Buddhist schools were brought in during the Silla period (668–935); the most influential proved to be Ch'an or (in Korean) Son Buddhism. During the era of the Yi dynasty (founded in 1392 and lasting till modern times), Korean neo-Confucian thought flourished considerably.

Buddhist and Confucian teachings effected a merger with traditional Korean religion, with its emphasis upon shamanistic priests, both hereditary and chosen by vocation. Its various gods – such as the mountain god, and the household spirits – are somewhat like the Roman *numina*, deities to be dealt with in all kinds of daily encounters; but they were not traditionally arranged in a hierarchy. They predate the unification of the country and often have very particular local status. In some degree, too, this ancient set of religious practices merged with elements of Taoism imported from China.

Korean painting of
Amida Buddha with
two Bodhisattivas,
c. 17th–18th century.

Korean thinkers also made important contributions to the debates of the neo-Confucian tradition, especially in the sixteenth century, through the writings of Yo T'oegye and Yi Yulgok. Yo developed the thinking of Chu Hsi, arguing that the priority of principle to material force was ethical rather than ontological. Yi argued for the determining character of material force, and he objected to the notion that *li* is always unchanging and pure, since it and material force are correlatives.

These writers were active during the Yi dynasty (founded in 1392), which was itself committed to the neo-Confucian ideology. This was rather rigidly imposed, but it meant that all officials were heavily infused with Confucian values. It was in this frame of mind that the government of Korea had to face the problems of the modern era, including invasion by Japan and the interpolation of vigorous Western Protestant missionary enterprise.

The Chinese Predicament in Colonial Times

It was an irony that the eighteenth century in many ways was one of the most glorious in the history of Chinese civilization, particularly under the rule of the Chi'ien-lung emperor (1711–99), whose on the whole efficient administration (marred by later corruption) and wide patronage of the arts was the high point of the Ch'ing or Manchu dynasty. It was in the nineteenth century, though, that the real conflicts between China and Europe, and then America, were to develop.

The East India Company benefited from the British naval supremacy established in the Seven Years War (1756–63) by dominating the trade with China. China had various goods to offer, but the most important commodity was tea. The demand for it in Britain had taken off. There was no comparable thing which the Chinese wanted from Europe or from India. But in time the opium trade increased, though the sale of opium in China was illegal. When in 1839 an imperial commissioner terminated all trade through Canton (Kwangtung) and confiscated opium held in store, the British decided on war. By the Treaty of Nanking which brought the Opium War to an end in 1842, various ports were opened to British trade and British consuls permitted there, Hong Kong was ceded to Britain, and the way was open to a whole series of unequal treaties, whereby extra territorial concessions were granted to European powers in a number of cities along the coast of China. The Chinese gradually lost control over their customs operations, and the Western powers, later to be joined by resurgent Japan, had China more or less at their mercy.

There were other problems that China had to face: Muslim rebellions in Sinkiang, which was formally incorporated into China as a province; rivalry with an advancing Russia in Central Asia; persistent peasant rebellions; and problems in Manchuria from Russia and Japan. But it was mainly the problem of how to cope with the Western seapowers which exercised the imperial mind, especially after the burning of the Summer Palace in the Anglo-French war with China of 1856–60 and the flight of the emperor from Peking. It was also the time of the beginning of the main missionary era from the West, especially among Protestant missions. The Chinese traditional philosophies and religions were under pressure both from Western technology (through which European naval forces could be so successful) and from Western spiritual ideas. An attempt to resist these forces, but in an intuitive way and with little comprehension of what lay behind them, was the so-called Taiping rebellion (1850–65), a protean upheaval with millions killed in bloody conflict.

The Self-Strengthening Movement

The penetration of China by Western powers was such that by the early twentieth century there were over fifty treaty ports designated for foreign residence and trade, from Manchuria to Kwangtung and from Tientsin to

Yunnan. These places provided a kind of intellectual and commercial stimulus, though they represented an unequal balance of power. They initiated the process of industrialization and the growth of Chinese capitalism, but such that capitalists were often inextricably linked to foreign concerns. The capitalists were what the communists were to call the *comprador* class, using a Portuguese term (the "buyers"). Missions also played their role: although missionaries were often arrogant in relation to Chinese religion and culture, they did play, as in India, a vital role in the setting up of higher education on the Western model in China. This introduced some of the fruits of Western scientific education.

The basic problem for China was how to combine the insights of Western science and of traditional beliefs. Was it possible, as a famous tag had it, for Chinese learning to provide the basis and Western learning the practical use? There were various attempts to sketch possible approaches.

A movement known as "Self-Strengthening" was one outcome of China's weakness. It had been started by Feng Kuei-fen (1809–74) in the 1860s, following the words of an earlier scholar who had said: "Learn the superior barbarian techniques in order to control the barbarian." The movement was responsible for the starting of various programs and projects – the Foreign Ministry's language school, various arsenals, dockyards, sending students for education in America, merchant shipping, and so on. But such a piecemeal program was not enough. In this sense the instinct of the Taipings was right. You cannot bring modernity to an antique society without modernizing the society itself. The Chinese empire remained a centralized bureaucracy, resting on ancient Confucian and other values entrenched in a feudal society. It did not understand the link between science and the critical spirit and a new conception of the nature of human knowledge.

At the least, some reappraisal of the Confucian tradition, some neo-neo-Confucianism, was called for. This was a necessary preliminary to institutional reform. One may mention the frustrating effects of a more piecemeal approach in the life of China's great general and statesman Li Hung-chang (1823–1901), who took a leading part in the suppression of the Taipings and lent his influence to the Self-Strengthening movement. He wanted modernization and helped it, from a rather traditional Confucian base. He could not, for all his skill, stop the defeat of China by a resurgent Japan in 1895. When he died in 1901 he felt that the state of China was still weak, despite his efforts.

Part of the frustration no doubt arose from observing the failure of the Reform Movement of 1898 and the disasters attendant on the Boxer Uprising, an anti-foreign uprising in 1900. The 1898 reforms had much to do with the life and thought of K'ang Yu-wei (1858–1927). He was born in Kwangtung province in the south, and was educated chiefly by his grandfather (his father died when he was a child). As a young man he became disillusioned with Confucianism and explored Mahāyāna Buddhism and Taoism, as well as Western thought and knowledge. Eventually he became convinced that a new formulation of the Confucian tradition held the key to the process of modernization. He emphasized human-heartedness or *jen*, seeing it not only as a central value of Master K'ung, but also as the key to a philosophy of liberty, equality, and utilitarian reformism. History was to culminate in a time of selfless harmony, preceded by a time of emerging peace. In the great unity of the future, traditional Confucian values would be submerged in universal harmony, but the key to realization of the ideal was a gradualist and reforming approach. He considered that Confucianism should be the state religion, and indeed this came about under the Republic in a law of 1913.

In 1898 K'ang and his associates were admitted into government, and in a hundred days a whole set of reforms was promulgated. But the inept political behavior of the reformers let in a conservative backlash at court, and the repeal of the legislation. At least, however, an attempt at structural change had been made. In 1911 the collapse of military support for the imperial regime led to the proclamation of a republic, and in 1912 the last Manchu emperor abdicated (though he lived on, through various vicissitudes, to become a gardener in the imperial palace he had once occupied, under the communists).

Nationalism and the Various Options

The growth of Chinese nationalism in a modern sense was of course the result of the arrogant and damaging behavior of Western powers and Japan. On all sides China could feel encroached upon. In the west the British were gaining control in Tibet. In Central Asia and in Manchuria the Russians were advancing. In Korea the Japanese were consolidating themselves. In the treaty ports, some of them deep inland on the great waterways, Western powers were exercising control.

However, Chinese civilization did not provide an obvious ideological basis for nationalism. In the old days, China had no foreign ministry and did not expect to have to deal with foreigners as equals. They could come to petition the emperor and to recognize his suzerainty. The world outside China, except across the Wall, did not much engage the Chinese imagination: and only in that case because it was from the north and the northwest that invasions had come. Moreover, the Manchu dynasty itself was still felt to be foreign, so loyalty to it was not so easy to engage.

K'ang Yu-wei and his followers were in effect trying out a version of Confucian neoclassicism: a reshaping of the neo-Confucian tradition and an attempt to accommodate tradition to modernity. It was, however, unfortunate for this experiment that Confucianism was tied to the old education and examination system, which was abolished in 1905. Had the imperial family taken the option of modernization much earlier, as did the Japanese, then the outlook for a revived Confucianism would have been brighter. But this was not something to expect, because the whole imperial system was built on the assumption of Chinese superiority and of the barbarous nature of foreign culture.

Of the Western ideologies, liberalism was undoubtedly attractive and could be combined, for an elite, with Confucian attitudes: but the basis of liberal

The Kuomintang leader Sun Yat-sen in traditional dress. His blend of socialism and democracy with some traditional elements was destined to fail.

politics is a strong middle class, and this was wanting for various reasons in the fabric of China. One reason was that the Chinese bourgeoisie was somewhat entangled in a foreign system. It weakened their opportunities and political powers. Second, power in the first half of the twentieth century was controlled by naked military force, and it was a time when bourgeois politics were not widely feasible. Third, the educated Chinese were divided still between those traditionally raised and those who benefited from the new strands of Western education.

In some degree the ideology expressed by the Christian nationalist leader, Sun Yat-sen (1866–1925), might have supplied the answer; but this too had its limitations. He was, like a number of other prominent national leaders, a somewhat marginal figure. Born near Macao in south China, he was educated in Hawaii and at American colleges. Well known internationally through his writings, he was the obvious candidate to be president when the Republic was created in 1911, and was so briefly; but he was outmaneuvered by the warlord Yuan Shih-k'ai (1859–1916), who took over the post and suppressed Sun's party, the Kuomintang. It was not till the early 1920s that Sun's Kuomintang became fully established, and this was with Soviet Russian assistance: Moscow sent advisers, notably Michael Borodin (1884–1951).

188

The ideology of the Kuomintang was based on Sun's Three Principles of the People – namely nationalism, democracy, and popular livelihood – and on his work on "Fundamentals of National Reconstruction for the National Government of China." Sun envisaged three stages: military unification of China, a time of tutelage, and then full democracy. It was assumed that the Kuomintang would become the party entrusted with such tutelage. In this idea he was influenced by the communists, who joined the Kuomintang and became a constituent part of it. A military academy was founded in Kwangtung, the commandant of which was the young Chiang Kai-shek (1887–1975), whose later career was to confront China with the problem of having nondemocratic tutelage, even if it is thought of as being on the way to democracy: what happens when you are taken over by a military dictatorship? Sun died in 1925, when the future of his movement was much in doubt.

China was humiliated by foreigners, but it was not a colony. Had it been controlled by a single power, the political struggle would have been clearer. China in 1900 was half independent and half ruled by a committee of foreign powers. It was only on some occasions that nationalist passion could be clearly focused; for instance, during the May 4 movement in 1919, a great wave of chiefly student protest over what was seen as the betrayal of China at the Treaty of Versailles. This was so particularly because defeated Germany's rights in Shantung province were not restored to China but were simply assigned to Japan, which was a victor on the Allied side.

The enthusiasm provoked by this demonstration led to greater interest in new political options, among them Marxism. The Russian Revolution of 1917 made a deep impression across the world, and, as a kind of countercapitalism and countercolonialism, had obvious attractions for many of the peoples of Asia. The foundation of the Chinese Communist Party and its growth into a part of the Kuomintang were signs of an alternative means of regaining national prestige and independence. As it turned out, it was the thought and strategy of Mao Tse-tung (or Zedong, 1893–1976) which proved to be so effective in rebuilding China.

It was ironic that, in order to combat the West, China had to reach out and take up a Western ideology, one which had much greater contempt for traditional Chinese values and religion than the most radical forms of missionary Christianity. Admittedly Mao made changes to Marxism, making it more adapted to Chinese conditions. But the advent of his revolution saw the curbing of Buddhism, the closing of monasteries and temples, the suppression of Taoist practices, assaults on the cult of ancestors, and a strong anti-Confucian campaign – not to mention attacks on minority religions.

Mao and New China

Mao's Rise to Power and the Japanese War

In 1926 Chiang launched a largely successful military campaign from south China to unify the country. In 1927, after the capture of Shanghai, he had many of the leaders of the Communist Party executed there. This showed that the struggle would have to be undertaken rather in the countryside than in the centrally controlled urban environment. It was Mao who clearly grasped two facts: one, that the peasants of China were bound to be the backbone of any revolution owing to their great numerical predominance; and the other, that the way forward was through military campaigning. He was to become a great theorist of guerrilla war. In all this he was moving away from Marxist orthodoxy, which saw the urban proletariat as the vanguard of revolution, and which also saw a bourgeois phase as a necessary preliminary to a workers' revolution (for this and other reasons Joseph Stalin [1879–1953] went on supporting Chiang Kai-shek and the Kuomintang through World War II).

From 1927 to 1934, Mao found himself leading a Soviet government in Kiangsi province, and engaged in warfare with the Kuomintang, through various encirclement campaigns. Then the communists were forced to opt for a breakout, and there started the famous Long March, when their Kiangsi army and other groups marched to the communist enclave in northwest China, in Shensi. It was a march of heroic proportions, with many battles, struggles for food, deprivations, and over 6,000 miles covered. Only about one-tenth of those who set out made it to the end of the March: but its effect was to preserve the main communist leadership (Mao became chairman of the party during the affair), and to allow them to prosecute war against the Japanese, who invaded China in 1937 (by which time the communists had settled in Yenan). The successful prosecution of guerrilla campaigns during the Sino-Japanese War left the communists in a strong position in north China at its end, especially as the Soviets took Manchuria from Japan in 1945 and turned it over to Mao's forces. The communists then took on Chiang Kai-shek and won the civil war in 1949.

Mao's Thought and the Worldview of Red China

We have seen that Mao adapted Marxism in various ways. He was also much more voluntaristic in his thinking than most Marxists: that is, he emphasized the role of human willpower in shaping history. He became also more disillusioned with the intellectual life after the success of the revolution. He was to some extent inspired by Taoist ideals of anarchism and simplicity, and in the 1950s he began to turn his back on the Soviet model of development, which he thought might breed a centralized bureaucracy out of touch with the needs of the people.

Eventually, when he unleashed the movement known as the Great Proletarian Cultural Revolution (harking back to the events of May 1919, to which we have referred, known as the "Cultural Revolution"), much of the educational system simply disintegrated. Books and learning were no longer important. Millions of young people flooded into the streets and into the countryside to drag down much of the state and party apparatus. It was part of Mao's vision of keeping the pot boiling, and never letting revolution settle down. He had a fluid, restless vision of human betterment; and the Chinese, though blank and poor, yet could by their faith and efforts surpass others in building a new classless society in which men and women would join in the struggle to overcome faults.

It is not necessary here to recount the ins and outs of the power struggle during the years from 1965 to 1976, when Mao died and his Cultural Revolution formally came to an end. It had been a new, rather violent, experiment in social reconstruction. It involved, among other things, the intense adulation of Mao; the constant use of a selection of his thoughts in the so-called Little Red Book, compiled by Lin Piao (1907–71), who became his heir apparent but died after trying to escape to Russia when he allegedly plotted against Mao; and the rejection of traditional learning, both Western and Eastern, in the pursuit of intense commitment.

Particularly this phase of Mao's career, and of the history of China, presses us to ask whether here China had acquired a new religion. It is appropriate to think so. There were distinctively religious characteristics belonging to the Cultural Revolution. In one way, the question of whether Marxism-Leninism-Mao Zedong Thought is a religious worldview is not that vital: it is certainly a system of beliefs and practices which for a crucial period became, and still remains to some degree today, the norm for Chinese belief, and which has been used to try to wipe out rival worldviews which *are* religions, such as the traditional trio of Taoism, Confucianism, and Buddhism. It is useful to think of Maoism here in relation to the dimensions of religion.

The ritual dimension: the Little Red Book of excerpts from Mao Zedong's writings served as a sign and repository of faith. Here school children demonstrate their loyalty.

First, during the heyday of the Cultural Revolution the Little Red Book was used in a *ritual* manner, like sacred scriptures. The book was carried around, held aloft at rallies, consulted for insight and as a guide to action. Moreover, there were continued rallies, public confessions in which people who had made mistakes were expected to confess to them, and reverence everywhere for the Great Helmsperson, as he was called (Mao, a very strong feminist from his early days, might have approved of this translation!). Second, strong *emotions* were focused on the figure of Mao as a kind of Amitābha figure, and there was repeated talk of conversion experiences in which people came to see their lives purified and renewed by their new commitments. Third, at the *doctrinal* level, there were the principles of Maoism, and in a wider context Marxism, to master, for they defined not only the way the world is but also gave directions for action. Fourth, there was the powerful *narrative* of China's historic weakness and corruption, her prostration before the great powers, the formation of the Communist Party, the heroic struggle in Kiangsi, and the even more heroic Long March, the battles against Japan, the Liberation, the making of a new China. There was therefore plenty of myth, not to mention all those stories about people being cured through positive thinking (about Mao's thought), driven to great deeds, and the like. Then, fifth, there was the austere *ethic* of those times – the self-sacrifice which building the new China demands, the need to be along-

The social dimension: a collective farm. Chinese society was thoroughly reorganized after 1949.

side the peasants in their hardships, the ethos of the equality of women, the abandonment of hierarchical thinking (and even filial piety, that old Confucian virtue). It was a morality diametrically opposed to the orderly, respectful, traditional modes and etiquette of Confucian behavior. Sixth, there was a new *social* elite: the cadres, the young, those who, armed with the Little Red Book, would constitute a kind of counterculture and an organization against the big institutions of Party and State, a kind of new this-worldly monasticism roaring through the streets and the countryside. Seventh, there was the *art* of the new era: simple, propagandistic, largely Western in technique but without bourgeois ornament, serving the people, socialist realist, showing forth the heroics of the myth. All this added up to a kind of new religion. It was by passing through the crucible of this religion that modern China was formed, if often by reaction.

The effects on the traditions were devastating. Monasteries were closed and turned into granaries and the like. Many manuscripts and books were destroyed. Much of religious practice was stopped. Images were destroyed. Ancestors were no longer venerated. Graves were not swept, nor holy mountains climbed. Monks and nuns worked the fields. Bibles were confiscated; Muslims were discriminated against. It was, in short, a period of religious and ideological persecution; and even now there are strict limits to the cautious rebuilding of the traditional practices.

The Irony of the New Period in China

With the death of Mao in 1976, the power of the more extreme wing of the party, as represented by the group known as the Gang of Four, including Mao's wife, Chiang Ch'ing, came to an end. The country entered a more pragmatic era. Even so, it was of course still to be guided by the principles of Marxism. This being so, there have been debates as to how far it is possible to combine such orthodoxy with the borrowing of Western methods of scientific education, trade, and technology. The irony is that China has come to the same position it was in one hundred years ago, but in a new form. No longer is it a matter of Confucian values for culture and Western methods for function, but of Marxist ideas for values and Western technology for function. Thousands of young Chinese have been sent abroad to study in the West, and the whole educational policy of the Cultural Revolution has been reversed as China scrambles to make up for past losses and to build a new and more prosperous society. But can it do so without the freedoms which go with Western systems (including here the Japanese)? The contrast, of course, with Japan is remarkable, and for many Chinese it is painful. So now China is plunged once again into its old debate.

Reflections on Modern China

We have noted that Marxism will have changed the face of Chinese (and Tibetan) religion permanently. During the revival which has slowly begun in the time since Mao's death the place of religion is bound to be relatively private, in the sense that religious practices will depend largely on private decisions; so it is no longer possible to see the three religions of China as an integrated system, a kind of federation of ideas and practices. The Westernized concept of the three traditions as more or less independent religions is likely to become a reality.

Conclusion

Confucianism had a long and varied life in China. It was, however, unable to revive itself vigorously enough to become the basis of a new Chinese nationalism. Though the Kuomintang movement made alliances with Confucian practice and social institutions, it failed and persisted only rather feebly in Taiwan. The emergence of Maoist Marxism meant that a new state ideology hostile to the Confucian tradition, and to the other strands of Chinese traditional religious and philosophical thought, replaced Confucianism as a set of values for the governing class. Though Confucianism is somewhat revived in the Chinese diaspora, it will be some while before it can make anything like a vigorous comeback in mainland China.

CHAPTER TEN

The Taoist Tradition

Lao-tzu and the Taoist Tradition

Of the three main strands of Chinese religion, Taoism has the most elusive origins. Despite this it grew through various infusions of spiritual force into a major determinant of Chinese cultural values. It also interacted with Buddhism, with which it had some affinities. It provided a running critique of the more formal Confucian tradition. The main Taoist tradition of early China began to take shape in the book known as the *Tao-te Ching*, the Classic of the Way and its Virtue. This wonderful and mysterious text has exercised a fascination down the centuries, and not for nothing are there over forty English translations published. It is ascribed in the Taoist tradition to the sage Lao-tzu or Lao Tan, who supposedly was an older contemporary of K'ung (sixth century B.C.E.), whom he instructed in various matters, including *li*, according to later texts. Modern scholars are skeptical as to whether there was such an historical person; but he is vivid nevertheless in Chinese imagination, and for vast numbers of Chinese through the ages he has been real enough. Eventually he was seen as an incarnation of a transcendental Lao-tzu, supreme Immortal. But of such legendary developments we shall speak later, when we come to describe Taoism as a religion during the classical period. For the moment we are dealing with Taoist thought, in the *Tao-te Ching* and the later book the *Chuang-tzu*.

The justly famous opening words of the Classic of the Way and its Virtue have many resonances. They read:

The way that can be followed is not the eternal way;
The name that can be named is not the eternal name;
That which is without name is of heaven and earth the beginning;
That which is nameable is of the ten thousand things the mother
He who is eternally without desire perceives the spiritual side of it;
He who is permanently with desire perceives the limit of it.
These two things are the same in origin but different in name;
Calling them the same is a mystery –
Indeed it is the mystery of mysteries, of all spirituality it is the gate.

The mythic dimension: the legendary Lao-tzu, "founder" of Taoism, with his disciples en route to the far West (some Taoists thought of Buddhism as a distorted form of Taoism brought back into China).

These words suggest that the underlying but ineffable principle which pervades the universe (and is indeed the origin of the cosmos) is the Tao, the Way. It is a fundamental idea in the classical work that this Way is something to which we should conform: but since nature acts with complete spontaneity, so in conforming to her we need spontaneity and complete naturalness. It is not something which can be striven for. That is why it is not a way which can be followed. It is not a way which can be taught. From this perspective Confucian thought with its stress on complex and learned *li* was on the wrong track. This is why according to the legend K'ung needed instruction from Lao-tzu. So the person who lives in accord with the Way of all things sees the Way in all things – and so the nameable world is also an unnameable Reality. As was to be realized later, there are profound similarities between these teachings and those of Buddhism, especially Mahāyāna Buddhism in the works of the *Prajñāpāramitā* and of Nāgārjuna. These resemblances were to be exploited both by Buddhists, in their evolution of Ch'an or Zen Buddhism, and by Taoists, who saw Buddhism as deceptive and derivative.

There is in the *Tao-te Ching* an array of analogies which were used to suggest the power of the empty Tao, the power of *wu-wei*, of "acting through not-acting": there is the valley which is the "active" space between the mountains; there is water which is so strong in its formless fluidity; there is the space in the pot – the whole point of a pot is that its space should be filled, but that point is constituted by a kind of nothingness. In brief, Taoist thought emphasizes not-acting, naturalness, spontaneity, passivity. It is a quietist tradition, emphasizing peace and meditation and it looks, in its experiential dimension, to the achievement of a contemplative inner stillness. By contrast Confucianist thought is active, pragmatic, conventional. Taoist thought is quietistic, anarchistic, and intuitive: in fact, ultimately it is not thought.

These motifs were continued in the book known after its supposed author Chuang-tzu. He is supposed to have lived from about 369 B.C.E. to about 286 B.C.E. There are not many details of his life available, but we do have the fine and poetic book named for him. Again, he sees the Tao as the quiet spirit pervading everything. Since all the dualities which we use, such as health and sickness, life and death, pleasure and pain, brightness and darkness, are artificial – made up by us, and not ultimately true in telling about the Tao the way it really is – we should overcome them: we should treat sickness and health, good and bad alike. We should cultivate utter serenity. This mystical quest is finally something very private. Chuang-tzu's doctrines were thus viewed by Confucian thinkers with deep suspicion as being subversive.

We may note that Taoist thinking was important in later Chinese contexts in providing an ideology of rebellion, so maybe the Confucians were right in pointing toward its subversive nature as a movement. Chuang-tzu also, in describing the freedom of the Tao-conforming sage, writes of great flights through the air and immense longevity. Later in the Taoist tradition much attention is paid to the search for an elixir of life to stave off death, and to other miraculous powers that the Taoist follower might acquire. In these ways Chuang-tzu foreshadows later developments.

So the end of this period saw China moving toward unification. Various forces were arising which together would help to form religious Taoism. The scene was set, therefore, for what we have called the classical period, in which the three religions of China came to coalesce with varieties of local religion to produce the system which served China for a long time until its breakdown in the nineteenth century.

Taoism Emerges as a Religion

The early Taoist thought which we have looked at became an ingredient, though only one ingredient, of religious Taoism. The earlier tradition is sometimes known as "philosophical Taoism." Taken by itself it forms a body of coherent and profound thought. It also became part of the fabric of so-called "religious Taoism," which however was dominated by rituals and myths with a popular outreach and hierarchical organization. Important to

---

Taoism some key terms

Feng-shui Literally "wind and water": the traditional Chinese art of geomancy, to determine where best to place a building.

Hsien Immortal or perfected saint.

Shou-i Meditation on the One, a notable Taoist contemplative technique.

T'ai-hsi Embryonic breathing: a system of retaining the breath and in theory ultimately getting to breathe through one's navel.

T'ai-p'ing The great harmony: a golden age of the future and the inspiration of a number of Taoist political movements.

Tan-t'ien The Cinnabar Fields, or three vital alchemical centers within the body, located in the heart, in the head, and below the navel.

Tao The Way or Principle underlying the processes of the universe.

Te Moral virtue or psychic energy, that which flows from the Tao (as in the title *Tao-te Ching*).

Wu-wei Acting through not-acting: flowing with the nature of cosmic processes.

Yang The male or active power in the cosmos.

Yin The female or passive power in the cosmos.

Yü-huang Shang-ti The Jade Emperor, chief deity of the Taoist pantheon.

---

this religious Taoism were the experiences and organizational initiative of the legendary Chang Tao-ling. In 142 C.E. he received a vision of Lao-tzu, deified, who bestowed on him the title of T'ien-shih or Heavenly Master. A new scheme of worship was ordained, blood sacrifices were banned, and the faithful were to eschew their old gods. The movement became a highly organized sect, to which adherents were supposed to contribute five pecks of rice (the nickname of the movement became "The Way of Five Pecks of Rice").

A similar movement in eastern China was inspired by a prophetic book which was later included in the Taoist canon, the *T'ai P'ing Ching*, or Classic of the Great Peace. This idea of a future heavenly state in which harmony was to be achieved on earth was the inspiration of a number of messianic uprisings in Chinese history. The Yellow Turban, a religiously motivated rebellion, was eventually violently suppressed, but Chang Lu, Chang Tao-ling's grandson, who was also in conflict with the government, negotiated a surrender, and resided at the court of the Wei emperor, receiving patronage and protection for the Heavenly Master sect. The organization among other things supplied free food and lodging over a wide area, and in some respects replaced the official government. By now Lao-tzu was treated as the supreme

The Great and the Small: Chuang-tzu

In the question put by T'ang to Chi, there was a similar statement: "In the barren north, there is a sea, the Celestial Lake. In it there is a fish, several thousand *li* in breadth, and no one knows how many *li* in length. Its name is the *kun*. There is also a bird, named the *p'eng*, with a back like Mount T'ai, and wings like clouds across the sky. Upon a whirlwind it soars up to a height of ninety thousand leagues. Beyond the clouds and atmosphere, with the blue sky above it, it then directs its flight to the south, and thus proceeds to the ocean there.

"A quail laughs at it, saying: 'Where is that bird going? I spring up with a bound, and when I have reached not more than a few yards I come down again. I just fly about among the brushwood and the bushes. This is also the perfection of flying. Where is that bird going?'" This is the difference between the great and the small.

There are some men whose knowledge is sufficient for the duties of some office. There are some men whose conduct will secure unity in some district. There are some men whose virtue befits them for a ruler. There are some men whose ability wins credit in the country. In their opinion of themselves, they are just like what is mentioned above.

Once upon a time, Chuang Chou (Chuang-tzu) dreamed that he was a butterfly, a butterfly flying about, enjoying itself. It did not know that it was Chuang Chou. Suddenly he awoke, and veritably was Chuang Chou again. We do not know whether it was Chuang Chou dreaming that he was a butterfly, or whether it was the butterfly dreaming that it was Chuang Chou. Between Chuang Chou and the butterfly there must be some distinction. This is a case of what is called the transformation of things.

---

god Lao-chün, Lord Lao; as a human being he was an incarnate manifestation of the Supreme One. This form of Taoism has lasted until the present day, with the chain of Heavenly Masters continuing through the centuries. But other ingredients also went to make up Taoism as a religion.

One was a consequence of the failure of utopian rebellions. The T'ai P'ing or heavenly peace was to be sought within the individual through the practice of a shamanistic type of meditation which might result in a vision of heavenly beings, and even of Lao-chün. Meanwhile, the traditional concern with longevity was combined with the techniques of alchemy, a kind of magical chemistry which sought to find some substance which would prolong life. The process of healing was also important because it was thought that sickness was due to some moral fault or other. Some of the more practical concerns of Taoism were incorporated into a book by the important writer Ko Hung (283–343), the *Pao-p'u-tzu* or "The Master who Embraces Simplicity": by the pursuit of good deeds, breathing exercises, care not to lose sperm, and taking a sufficient amount of the elixir of immortality, one might aspire to become an immortal.

As a final main ingredient of religious Taoism we might mention the movement associated with Mount Mao or Mao Shan in Kiangsu, and based on revelations to Yang Hsi in the latter part of the fourth century: he was visited by supreme immortals. This visionary material was incorporated into further scriptures.

So what we have in the Taoist movements, increasingly coalescing into a single definable religion, is a combination of ancient quietism; a strong and fervent devotion to a heavenly Lord, believed to be incarnate in Lao-tzu himself, and to a lesser extent to other immortals; and the belief that the essence of divinity also resides in each individual, where it can be cultivated by meditation, breathing, diet, and alchemical experiments. Eventually the contemplative practices of Taoism became highly complex and bore some resemblances to high Tantra in Buddhism.

Indeed, in a sense Buddhism became a fifth ingredient in Taoism; its coming into China was a challenge to Taoism in particular. One of the ways the Taoists hit back was by describing how Lao-tzu went west and actually taught a kind of Buddhism to the Indians. But also to some degree Taoism created a kind of counterpart of Buddhism: by arranging its scriptures into three parts like the Tripitaka; by composing scriptures too from the late fourth century onward which are very much Buddhist in spirit, and which a writer on Taoism (John Lagerwey) has described as "pure Mahāyāna Taoism"; and by founding monasteries with Taoist nuns and monks. Their meditation methods and esoteric sexual practices, more ancient than Tantra, bore close resemblances to some Buddhist practices.

Naturally there was rivalry for imperial patronage, and during the T'ang dynasty (618–907) the issue was in doubt. But it was the emperor Kao-tsung (649–683) who decreed that there should be state-sponsored Taoist and Buddhist monasteries in each prefecture of the empire. This system of protection – and control – of the religions lasted until 1911. It did not interfere with the important role of ju or Confucian scholars as administrators. Thus a pattern was born of mutual support and toleration, even if many of the Confucians rather rationalistically treated the monks, nuns, and priests as presiding over superstitions fit for the ignorant masses.

The Taoist ethos

Taoism as a popular religion had much to offer on a number of fronts, which expressed typical Chinese and human concerns. It traditionally had been bound up with medicine and in particular the search for the secret of longevity. Here Taoism combined several motifs. There was the control of breath, accompanied by gymnastic exercises. Such practices were similar to those of Buddhism and of the Indian tradition more generally. It was supposed that an adept would eventually more or less cease to breathe, since a light feather placed beneath his nose would not in the least be disturbed (but it was alternatively supposed that the adept had begun to breathe through his navel or even the soles of his feet). Also somewhat like yogic ideas of the Indian tradition were special sexual practices, so that the practitioner would not ejaculate sperm during intercourse. It would recirculate internally, feeding the brain. Further, Taoism came to identify the body with the cosmos, the one being the microcosm of the other. The gods and heavenly bodies can be visualized and seen by the meditator within the body, illuminating it and purifying it. Exact visualization of these forces and their heavenly rotations could perfect the individual and enable him or her to climb up to paradise. But also the Taoists used contemplative techniques akin to Buddhist ones – emptying the mind: this facilitated the merger between Buddhist and Taoist values which gave rise to Ch'an.

Important too were more material methods – for instance, the use of diet to promote longevity and spiritual welfare. Most prominent of all was the practice of alchemy, attempting to convert cinnabar to gold, and by various combinations to find an elixir of life which, if taken, would make the body imperishable. All this experimentation was accompanied by complex rituals and purifications. The practice of alchemy hovered between science and magical religion, and the very esotericism of Taoist ritual conferred on it a mysterious and attractive power. Moreover, the Taoist ethos was popularly oriented. The religion promoted equality among people, for instance among men and women and between Han Chinese and members of tribal groups and outside nationalities. Its premise of a kingdom of heavenly peace (*t'ai p'ing*) played a messianic role in popular movements of rebellion. Although its gods were hierarchical, like a ghostly replication of the imperial civil service, Taoism had a populist air, and its sages stayed close to the people in spirit.

Partly because of the importance to the religion of the contemplative life, Taoism organized itself along monastic lines. Later it was influenced somewhat by Buddhist practice, though monks and nuns often lived in the same communities, and in T'ang days practiced sexual intercourse as a means toward higher insight and the hope of immortality. Sex without concupiscence was a symbol of the attainment of union with the Ultimate. During T'ang dynasty days (seventh to ninth centuries C.E.) Taoism attracted imperial patronage, and in the middle of the ninth century its rival, Buddhism, was temporarily suppressed. During this period Buddhism and Taoism were in frequent conflict, partly because Taoists insisted that on a famous trip to the west Lao-tzu had actually started Buddhism, which had then been reimported into China, and partly because Taoism imitated Buddhist scriptures and Buddhist practice. But by the second millennium the three teachings of Confucianism, Buddhism, and Taoism lived side by side, and incorporated many folk beliefs, as a single roughly complementary system of Chinese religion.

While Taoism emphasized popular sentiments and a certain spirit of anarchy, despite periods of imperial patronage, it also kept alive the serenity of the philosophy of the Tao. It remained an amalgam of many elements, but naturalness was always at its heart. It thus made powerful contributions to

Chinese art, nurturing the spirit of spontaneity and using emptiness artfully to fill out landscape. Taoism also made notable contributions to Chinese poetry and literature.

In modern times Taoism has had some slight philosophical success in the West, since its idea of the Tao chimes in with environmentalist concerns, and its fluid approach to natural events somewhat mirrors some contemporary notions in physics and cosmology. But under Maoism in China it has suffered severe repression and state control, now, however, pursued less vigorously; while in the late nineteenth and early twentieth centuries its alchemical and other concerns were considered to be superstitious and unscientific, its pacifism and anarchy were scarcely conducive to the reinforcement of Chinese nationalism in the face of colonial and capitalist inroads. However, in the last twenty-five years there has been a revival of Taoist scholarship, particularly in the West. Its philosophical heritage is perhaps its most powerful legacy, while religious Taoism has been in sharp decline.

The Dimensions of Taoism

The Doctrinal Dimension
As just indicated, the doctrine or philosophy of Taoism has had a perennial attraction, expressed above all in the books *Tao-te Ching* and the *Chuang-tzu*. The haunting words of the former point to the mysterious force unforcefully underlying the cosmos, the Tao, also figured as the Mother of all things, gently moulding events as they flow on in their harmonious and peaceful way. Nature acts by not-acting, and the sage is one who models his life on the empty Tao.

The Mythical Dimension
Mythically Taoism as a religious system saw Lao-tzu not just as a sage but as a supreme being, an immortal. In the complex hierarchy of gods Buddhist, Taoist, and traditional spirits blended with local folklore in a shifting system over the centuries, sometimes presided over by the Jade Emperor, a divine counterpart to the Chinese emperor. Various important deities include Hsi Wang Mu, the western Mother Empress, who rules a paradise in the Kunlun mountains, where she is visited by the Eight Immortals. Another important figure is the Vulcan of China, the Furnace Prince of Tsao Chün, the great alchemist. The myriad gods arose in different ways: some from Taoist sources, others from Buddhist Bodhisattvas and celestial beings, others from the deification of powerful mortals, such as the emperor Huang Ti (the third emperor) and Lao-tzu, and so on.

The interplay of the *Tao-te Ching* and the deification of Lao-tzu had some interesting consequences, notably that he is his own mother – thus fusing both the male and female strands of existence. For in the classic work the formed Tao, which has a name, is the Mother of all things: so Lao-tzu is identified with the body which evolves in creation. After a long period in his

The fluidity of T'ai-chi Chuan is practiced both for physical health and for teaching the mind to flow with change so that action is effortless.

mother's (that is his own)womb he appears in mortal form on earth. In later representations the Lord Lao's appearance increasingly resembles that of a celestial Buddha: the two religions in many ways converge.

The Institutional Dimension

Institutionally, Taoist priests played important local roles in the old China, since they served as a bridge between communities and the whole cosmos, as distinguished from local mediums, exorcists, and the like. A major factor in Taoism was the giving of offerings – paper, rice, and so forth – in gratitude to the Ultimate for the blessings of life. Priests might also perform healing rites, while certain rites of passage had a special significance in the Taoist context, such as marriage. Also rituals associated with helping individuals avoid hells and *post mortem* terrors were performed through the offering of paper money. Parallel to the priestly system is the network of Taoist monasteries, now clustered by the communist government under the National Taoist Association centered on the famous White Cloud Abbey in Beijing. This also contained the complete version of the Ming dynasty copy of the Taoist canon (in three main sections, echoing the typical arrangement of the Buddhist scriptures).

The Ritual Dimension

Ritually Taoism is not only characterized by such practices as those mentioned above, but also by a range of practices incorporating various types of visualization, alchemical ideas, astrological methods, and so on. But in modern times these have undergone large-scale suppression in mainland

The ritual dimension: inside a Chinese temple in Taiwan.

China. Not only were such "unscientific" practices repressed during the period of the Cultural Revolution in the 1960s and 1970s, but many temples and abbeys were closed down.

The Ethical Dimension

As to the ethical dimension, Taoism has historically been opposed to what it saw as the artificialities of Confucian proper behavior. Moreover, many of its more esoteric practices, such as alchemy and dietetics, were themselves thought of as means of enhancing natural processes. So ultimately, behavior should be in accord with nature. It should involve acting through not acting. This somewhat anarchistic ethos had political consequences which sometimes issued in violent rebellion: but the main themes of Taoist teaching were naturalness and peacefulness. While some degree of asceticism might be valuable in ridding oneself of artificialities, the tendency was to value this world and flow with it.

The Experiential Dimension

In regard to the experiential dimension, the most central act of Taoist meditation brings one to unity with the Tao, and it has close affinities with Mahāyāna Buddhist mysticism. But it is noteworthy that Taoism also encouraged the wide use of visualization as a means of inner manipulation.

For the ordinary worshiper there was much in Taoist ritual of a numinous character: indeed Taoism tended to deify all those humans and phenomena which had an awesome or strange quality. But more devotional religion, emphasizing warm personal interaction, was more vigorously taken care of through the Buddhist Pure Land tradition. Once again we can note the symbiotic character of the three religions of China.

The Material Dimension

Finally, regarding the material dimension, we may note the importance ascribed in Taoism to landscape, and in particular to mountains, notably the Five Peaks, such as T'ai Shan in Shantung province, as well as the mythic Kunlun on the western border, the Path to Heaven and the abode of the Mother Empress. Mountain pilgrimage was thus associated both with Taoist and Buddhist spirituality. And as well as temples and abbeys Taoism also, as we have noted earlier, manifested itself in the arts, such as painting and calligraphy.

Conclusion

Taoism has had an immense and multifarious influence on Chinese religion and society. But with rapid modern urbanization, especially among overseas Chinese, and with the crushing weight of the Marxist regime bearing down on it, its future will probably depend heavily upon a revival of interest in its philosophical roots.

CHAPTER ELEVEN

Buddhism in the Far East

Buddhism Comes to China

Buddhism, which as we have seen came to be a major force in Indian civiliz-ation, expanded beyond India in various directions, notably into Central Asia. There it lay on the trade routes leading toward China. Its missionary activity was due in large measure to the founding of new monasteries.

Buddhism infiltrated into China along the trade routes that ran north of Tibet; its spread was more by presence than by proselytization. Its earliest movement into China dates from the first century C.E., and by 166 C.E. we find a record of the emperor Huan installing statues of Huang-Lao (a god synthesized from the Yellow Emperor Huang-ti, a prehistoric immortal, and Lao-tzu) and of the Buddha within his palace.

The task of translation was immense, and often because of its suitability Taoist language was used, or alternatively some rather unintelligible phonetic attempts to render Sanskrit words. But Buddhism described itself as a path or *tao*: it had its immortal, the Buddha; it practiced acting by non-acting. It is perhaps not surprising that Chinese Taoists, prejudiced somewhat against what was after all a foreign religion (and foreign-looking, as in the garb of monks and the lineaments of the Buddha statues made before the religion was thoroughly sinified, made Chinese), should see it as a garbled version of the ancient teachings of the famed Lao-tzu, who had after all journeyed to the Western Pass and beyond, no doubt to spread the truth there.

Also foreign were the key ideas of *karma* and reincarnation. But these could be turned to fruitful use in China as time went on. The cosmology allowed for many heavens, and the Pure Land school in India had pioneered the attractive idea of a paradise whither those who call on Amitābha with faith would go. The notion was further developed in the Chinese scene. But the most original of the schools as developed in the Chinese context were the T'ien-t'ai, the Hua-yen, and the Ch'an.

The T'ien-t'ai School

By now we are reaching forward five centuries from the time that Buddhism first came to China. It had experienced both lavish patronage and some persecution (the main periods were 446–52 and 574–9 in north China and 842–5 throughout the empire). The T'ien-t'ai school was named after the mountain where Chih-i (538–97) founded his most important monastery. His was a masterly work of synthesis. The diversity of the texts and schools that came out of India was always something troubling to Chinese who were trying to understand the essence of Buddhism; Chih-i resolved the problem by assigning differing teachings of the Buddha Śākyamuni to different periods, because humans had to be introduced gradually to the grand teaching which is found most clearly and magnificently in the Lotus Sūtra.

In his developmental view of the Buddha's teachings he made use of the crucial idea of *upāya* or skill in means – the idea that the Buddha adapts his teachings to the psychological and spiritual condition of the hearer. Thus for instance in the Deer Park at Banaras he preached the Theravādin doctrines and practices; but once people had listened and had advanced to the state of saints or *arhants*, he could then teach them that sainthood was not the final or the highest aim. This was when the charm of the high Mahāyāna *sūtras* would

The philosophical dimension: the frontispiece to the Diamond Sutra showing the Buddha preaching to an elderly disciple. The Diamond Sutra printed in 868 is the world's earliest printed book.

207

beguile them and make them long for the Mahāyāna and realize the partial character of the Hīnayāna. As he lay dying the Buddha recited the Sūtra of the Great Decease, which was equivalent to the Lotus.

All this scheme was designed to unite the whole array of major Buddhist scriptures. Not only that but it was part of Chih-i's method of expounding scriptures to ask not just about the theory or the philosophy but what method of meditation a text laid down or implied. The school later was important in Japan, and certainly was influential during the classical period in China.

Hua-yen and the Interconnectedness of Events

The Hua-yen school is another school with a very Chinese flavor, though it only restates in another form a basic tenet of the whole of Buddhism. The school seems to have started before 600 C.E., but its great systematizer, sometimes counted as its third patriarch, was Fa-tsang (643–712). It is based on a vast and syncretic text which was probably put together in Central Asia, maybe in the fourth century, called the *Mahāvaipulya Buddhāvataṃsaka Sūtra* or *Hua-yen Ching*, or Flower Garland Sūtra. It represents in a very rich, prolix, and colorful way the thought of the Buddha immediately following his Enlightenment, when he was seeing things "as they really are." It ends with a long chapter, sometimes counted a separate *sūtra*, "On Entering the Realm of Truth," in which a young hero and seeker takes instruction during his immense pilgrimage through life from many teachers and completes the path of the Bodhisattva.

The Hua-yen teachings envisage that all phenomena and all the principles which underlie them are interconnected, and are seen to be without mutual obstruction: they interpenetrate perfectly without losing their individual identity. This is a restatement in positive form of the notion of *pratītyasamutpāda*, or codependent origination, which was part of the message of Buddhism from its earliest days. But while some Indian writers like Nāgārjuna, in taking this idea to its limits, had expressed their conclusions negatively ("Everything is empty"), the Hua-yen is positive. It likens the world to the famous mythic jewel-net of Indra, a net of jewels in which each one reflects all the others. Those who see this vision with clarity will see the essential Buddhahood of each living being and the presence of the Buddha Mind everywhere. The image highlights the purity deep down in defilements, the eternality of each moment, the sudden nature of enlightenment, and the supreme potential of all beings. It thus presents an optimistic and beautiful picture of cosmic interrelatedness, and represents a Chinese flavoring of central Buddhist doctrines.

For Hua-yen, other schools were incomplete. Hīnayāna noted the emptiness and egolessness of living beings but not of all phenomena. Early Mahāyāna stressed the unreality of things but not the equally important reality of them. Mature Mahāyāna saw the general truth but failed to stress the particularity of individual phenomena. Those who stressed sudden enlightenment failed to note sufficiently the need for effort, and neglected the

---

Mahāyāna and Far Eastern Buddhism some key terms

Amida Japanese version of Buddha Amitābha's name, creator of the Pure Land.

Ch'an Chinese version of Sanskrit *dhyāna* and Pali *jhāna*, and equivalent to Korean Sŏn and Japanese Zen: name of the Meditation school.

Jōdō The Pure Land, destiny of those who call on Amida in faith.

Koan Riddle used in the Rinzai Zen school to disturb conceptual thought as a preliminary to sudden insight (*satori*).

Kuan-yin Chinese name for the Bodhisattva Avalokitcśvara and usually portrayed as female. The Japanese version is Kannon.

Nirvāṇa Liberation from the round of rebirth and often identified paradoxically in Mahāyāna Buddhism with this world of rebirth, if we had the insight to see its underlying nature.

Prajñāpāramitā The perfection of insight: name for an important body of Great Vehicle texts.

Pratītyasamutpāda The codependent origination of events, the law which links together the events of the world.

Stūpa A mound for containing Buddha relics and the like, developed into the form of the pagoda in East Asia.

Śūnyatā Emptiness, the pervading character of all events, in that they are empty of self-subsistence and relative.

Trikāya The three bodies or aspects of Buddhahood—the transformation or earthly body, the celestial body, and the ultimate or truth-body (*dharmakāya*).

Upāya The Buddha's skill in means, in adapting his message to the differing psychological and cultural conditions of human beings, thus explaining the development of doctrine in the Great Vehicle.

---

importance of language (once we have seen through its pretensions) in guiding practice.

Ch'an as a Chinese Way

The shape of Hua-yen thinking had some influence on those who developed a uniquely Chinese (and later Korean and Japanese) form of religion, namely the Meditation school, called in Chinese Ch'an. This was a transcription into Chinese of the Sanskrit *dhyāna* – and nearly all of Buddhism is after all *dhyāna* Buddhism. But it was the style and boldness of Ch'an thinking which is impressive. In theory it was brought to China, maybe in 520 C.E., via Canton by the legendary monk Bodhidharma. At any rate he was retrospectively

A Tibetan version of
the Buddha-to-be
who looks down with
compassion, the Lord
Avalokiteśvara.

adopted as the first patriarch of the new movement, and also came to play a
wider role in Chinese folklore, getting in the process assimilated to a Taoist
immortal. To him was ascribed the brief statement of the nature of Ch'an
teaching:

A special transmission outside the scriptures;
No basis in words or writing;
Direct pointing to the mind of people;
Insight into one's nature and attainment of Buddhahood.

At first, Ch'an was a movement confined to wandering monks, but by the
seventh century it established itself in settled monasteries. It was the sixth
patriarch, Hui-neng (638–713), whose influence was the most profound. His
teachings, and a little about his life, are found in the Sūtra of the Sixth
Patriarch, otherwise known as the Platform Sūtra. The debate between Hui-
neng and Shi-hsiu, both outstanding pupils of the previous patriarch, partly
foreshadowed the drifting apart of the northern and southern schools of

Ch'an, the former emphasizing the gradualism of the approach to enlightenment or insight (*prajñā*), and the latter insistent on the sudden character of insight. Later both these schools came to be important in Japan, and we shall deal with them fully there (see page 220).

Hui-neng's Ch'an developed into a system with certain major features. First was the need for master–pupil transmission, rather than learning from scriptures (though of course the scriptures were valued too, especially the Diamond Sūtra, which sums up in short compass the whole teachings of the Perfection of Wisdom school). Second was the use of the so-called "public document" or *kung-an*, namely riddles of a seemingly nonsensical sort which the pupil had to try to solve. Third was the organization of monastic life round a meditation hall with fairly rigorous training under a master. Fourth was the creation of a vigorous tradition of Ch'an art.

Lying behind these practices and ideas was the taking of the Buddhist critique of language and concepts very radically. Since concepts are misleading and contradictory they have to be wiped away. We must learn to see things "as they are." A tree is not a tree: it is just that we categorize it as a tree. In itself it is – well, at this point words fail and we need direct experience. Such direct experience of nature reflected early Taoist thinking, and in Ch'an there is a fine fusion of Buddhist and Taoist thought (or nonthought). This is one of the powerful syntheses between the two cultures in Chinese history. But its danger is anarchy: if we cannot even rely on scriptural authority we have to strengthen the authority of the community – and thus Ch'an discipline came, paradoxically, to be rigorous. The emphasis was on the idea of transmission from master to pupil. In order to attain the spontaneity of enlightenment, people had to work hard at it. You need artifice in order to be natural.

Pure Land and Kuan-yin

The high Mahāyāna provided plenty of opportunities for piety. According to a traditional scheme the Buddha had three bodies. One is the transformation-aspect, in which he appears on earth to teach living beings. Another is the celestial-aspect, in which he appears as a Heavenly Lord, such as Amitābha; in conjunction with such god-like beings there are divine Bodhisattvas, such as, in India, Avalokiteśvara. Third, there is the truth-aspect of the Buddhas, their ultimate reality (or unreality): the Absolute, Emptiness, *nirvāṇa*, the Buddha-nature. The intermediate body or aspect, the celestial, provided a strong focus for piety. This was specially true of the Pure Land or Ch'ing-t'u movement, which was highly popular by the seventh century C.E. The great Bodhisattva Avalokiteśvara underwent a change, appearing in China as a feminine deity – Kuan-yin, a kind of Chinese Madonna.

These tendencies toward piety and faith, and concentration on the numinous, glorious, and worshipful aspects of the Buddhist tradition, provided a supplement to the Taoist pietism directed toward the immortals. It was a highly personalized and in many ways "easy" form of religion, suitable for an age when adherence to the severities of original Buddhism was weakening. The Buddhist theory of decline over time thus served the purpose of justifying easier and more pietistic forms of the faith. Meanwhile, similar devotional types of belief and practice were growing among Taoists. Thus the so-called Jade Emperor, Yü Huang Shang Ti, Supreme Being, was elevated to rule over lesser spirits, including Buddhas (according to the Taoists; the Buddhists argued the other way, subordinating the Jade Emperor and other spirits to the supreme Buddhas). But despite the rivalry of the differing traditions – culminating in the severe persecution of Buddhism in the ninth century, from 843 to 845, resulting in the return of over a quarter of a million nuns and monks to civilian life, the closure of over 40,000 temples and shrines, and the destruction of 4,600 temples – they nevertheless over most of the rest of Chinese history managed to achieve a symbiosis.

Buddhism in Korea

Of the creations of Korean religious thought and practice, perhaps the most original is the merger effected, in a highly imaginative way, between Hua-yen and Ch'an (Sŏn) Buddhism by Chinul (1158–1210). He had become dissatisfied with the rather degenerate form of Son which he experienced on entering the monastic order at a young age. There had over many years been a somewhat bitter bifurcation between Son and the more scholastic forms of Buddhism, and it was partly to bridge this gap that Chinul worked out his synthesis. He is regarded as the founder of a distinctively Korean school of Son, the Chogye school. He incorporated into his techniques the use of the *kung-an*, and sketched a version of the Bodhisattva path in which the adept starts with a sudden awakening at the intellectual level, and progressively advances through the ten stages of the Bodhisattva path to the final direct experience of the truth. He was able by this account to see Son methods as fully in accord with scripture; and the high valuation placed in Ch'an on harmony with nature made the more positive metaphysics of Hua-yen a good ally.

Japan: the Preclassical Period

Prince Shotoku and the Buddhist Revolution

Traditionally Buddhism is held to have been brought into Japan in either 538 or 552 C.E.; but it was primarily during the regency of Prince Shotoku Taishi (574–622) that Buddhism took root as part of the fabric of Japanese official life. In the second year of his regency, while still a young man (he was nineteen when he became regent), he issued an edict which commended the Three Jewels of Buddhism – the Buddha, the Dharma, and the Sangha, which were to be seen as indissolubly united. Later, in the Seventeen Article Constitution which he promulgated, he stated that these three treasures were to be revered by all beings. So he regarded Buddhism as the spiritual message which gave moral shape to the country. He sent to China for *sūtras* and other documents and himself wrote commentaries on three important Mahāyāna texts, including the Lotus Sūtra. This last work is preserved in the imperial archives, and it is claimed to be in Shotoku's own writing. Shotoku is credited with founding one or two important temples, notably the Horyuji Temple in Nara, later the imperial capital. But he also made use of the Confucian tradition, in establishing various ranks of officials at the court; and he did not see any incompatibility between his favoring of Buddhism and support for the cult of the *kami*.

After his death a brief period of chaos and bloodshed preceded the consolidation of his reforms, and a more centralized empire somewhat on the Chinese model was established. Law was proclaimed by imperial rescript – in other words, written law, rather than immemorial custom, was what counted, and the emperor himself was treated as a living *kami*. The emperor Temmu, who reigned from 672 to 686, ordered the writing of the *Kojiki* and *Nihonshoki*, and this helped to give a traditional justification for the new set-up. He is supposed also to have made Amaterasu's shrine at Ise the sacred focus of the cult of the imperial house.

The favoring of religion also meant its control. A law governed the activities of monks and nuns, and a ministry of *kami* was organized, which registered *kami* shrines and priests. Temmu also ordered the compilation of collections of traditional poetry. In 710 the court was established at Nara, which blended the glories of Buddhist faith and the pomp of imperial governance. In 741 the emperor Shōmu ordered the building of a state-financed system of provincial temples, and in 749 he had a vast statue in bronze of the Buddha Vairocana installed in the great Todaiji temple in Nara. Vairocana is

---

The Lotus Sūtra

The World-honoured One, in his tactfulness, told of the Tathāgata-wisdom; but we, though following the Buddha and receiving a day's wage of *nirvāṇa*, deemed this a sufficient gain, never having a mind to seek after the Great Vehicle. We also have declared and expounded the Tathāgata-wisdom to Bodhisattvas, but in regard to this Great Vehicle we have never had a longing for it. Wherefore? The Buddha, knowing that our minds delighted in inferior things, by his tactfulness taught according to our capacity, but still we did not perceive that we were really Buddha-sons.

Now we have just realized that the World-honoured One does not grudge even the Buddha-wisdom. Wherefore? From of old we are really sons of Buddha, but have only taken pleasure in minor matters; if we had had a mind to take pleasure in the Great, the Buddha would have preached the Great Vehicle Law to us. At length, in this *sūtra*, he preaches only the One Vehicle; and though formerly, in the presence of Bodhisattvas, he spoke disparagingly of *śrāvakas* who were pleased with minor matters, yet the Buddha had in reality been instructing them in the Great Vehicle. Therefore we say that though we had no mind to hope or expect it, yet now the Great Treasure of the King of the Law has of itself come to us, and such things which Buddha-sons should obtain we have all obtained.

The material dimension: the largest wooden structure in the world – the Todaiji temple containing a huge bronze Buddha statue, in Nara, the ancient capital of Japan.

especially associated with the Hua-yen (or in Japanese, Kegon) tradition, being the personalized form both of the universe and of what lies beyond it.

Saichō and Kūkai

The close identification of religion and government, and the lavish subsidizing of monastic life, had cloying effects. As a radical move at reform, the emperor Kammu (reigned 781–806 C.E.) moved the capital from Nara to Heian (Kyoto). The bonds between politics and religion were cut, and government by legal edict was revived. Various economic and military reforms gave the Heian period an energetic start. The severance of Buddhism from the affairs of state was healthy, and led to the creation of two new forms of Buddhism through the activity of the two most famous monks of the Heian period, Saichō and Kūkai.

Saichō, also known by his posthumous title Dengyo Daishi (767–822), was sent as a student to China, after having studied at the Todaiji in Nara. He brought back to Japan the teachings of the T'ien-t'ai, somewhat amplified, and known in Japanese as Tendai. Saichō established the headquarters of the

214

denomination on Mount Hiei, not far from the new imperial capital, and eventually after his death it was recognized as a place for the training of monks (the monopoly for this had been held by one of the Nara centers). His Tendai teachings were more syncretic than the Chinese, as he wove into them important Tantric motifs and the use of sacramental acts.

There was a place in the Tendai scheme of things for *kami*; and there was also a nationalistic flavor – Saichō believed that the Japanese were fully mature in their spiritual life and therefore ready for the consummate teachings of the Lotus Sūtra. He also elaborated the world-affirming theory of *hongaku* or "original enlightenment," which stressed that there was no difference between the Buddha's Enlightenment and that in ordinary men and women, and the identity between liberation and living in the world. Various new patterns of meditation were worked out, such as sitting ninety days in front of a statue of Amida (Amitābha), circumambulating a sacred statue for ninety days, and so on. These practices were introduced from China by Saichō's disciple Ennin.

Tendai, because it found a place for all stages of religious development, was popular; but its emphasis upon the magical and spiritual effects of ritual was sometimes to be a weakness. This ritualism was even more marked in the other new movement, Shingon, or Mantra Sect. Kūkai, known posthumously as Kōbo Daishi, had initially sought government service and studied Confucian classics, but switched as a young man to Buddhist studies; he had the opportunity moreover to go on a delegation to China and there spent three years studying Shingon in the then capital of Ch'ang-an. He introduced this form of Buddhism into Japan, on his return. He set up at Kongobuji, south of Nara, and also at Toji in Kyoto, as a springboard for propagating his message. He was influential in various directions: he founded the Imperial Academy of Arts and Knowledge, and was a senior religious adviser at the court. He had a warm attitude toward the way of the *kamis*. His teachings prepared the way for later syncretism between Shinto and esoteric Buddhism. He established the headquarters of the new denomination at Mount Koya, and after his death he was thought by his followers still to abide at Mount Koya, awaiting revived manifestation at the time of the coming of the future Buddha Maitreya.

The scheme which he evolved is a complex one. At its apex is the figure of the Buddha Mahāvairocana, conceived as identical with the Truth-body of the Buddha. That Ultimate Reality is described in typical Buddhist terms as Emptiness and as the "Suchness" of the Buddha as Tathāgata. But his Emptiness is, so to speak, a full one. The Truth-body is the creative force which is behind phenomena, and which embraces phenomena. In this Kūkai takes up the thought of Hua-yen. But because inner and outer are correlated (phenomena and ultimate Suchness; mind and body; and esoteric and exoteric Buddhism), the approach to attaining realization of one's essential Buddhahood is sacramental in character. Realization therefore occurs not just through mental meditation but through the use of mysterious powers – the *mudrā* or bodily gestures which also play a vital role in Tantric thinking in India; the sacred *maṇḍalas* or diagrams which he brought back from China with him; and the sacred syllables or formulae, *mantras*. For Kūkai, exoteric Shingon Buddhism was the highest form because it reflected the eternal Truth of the Body of Mahāvairocana and not the provisional and introductory teachings of the time-bound Buddha Śākyamuni.

The schools of Saichō and Kūkai represent the most solid achievements in the Buddhism of the preclassical period. They involved some adaptation of ideas and practices prevalent in the great T'ang capital of Ch'ang-an, which the two sages had the opportunity of visiting together. But it was basically at a later stage, after the coming of the Kamakura period, that Japanese originality in Buddhist religion really flowered, stretching Buddhism in the directions of fervid piety in the Pure Land interpretations, back toward the centrality of meditation in the Zen schools, and in a powerful nationalist direction in the teachings of Nichiren.

Japan: the Classical Period

The Pure Land Movements and the Mappō

Fundamental to the revolutions which took place from the twelfth century onward was the conception that we have reached the days of the final Dharma, the *mappō*. The present could be viewed from the standpoint of Buddhist orthodoxy as being a degenerate age in which the more rigorous Path could not be trodden effectively, but according to the new viewpoint it was a period of optimism and a more democratic way of looking at the Buddha's Path, for the tradition had of its nature tended to exclude certain people whose occupations grated against the Buddhist ethic – fishermen, warriors, hunters, peasants, prostitutes, and so on. But in the new age the faith was open to all. The success of the Pure Land movements in Japan was in great part due to their social widening of ultimate hope. The same, but in a rather different way, could be said of Zen.

The greatest figures in the Pure Land movements were undoubtedly Hōnen (1133–1212) and Shinran (1173–1263). Honen involved himself in extensive studies within the Tendai tradition, but was especially drawn to meditation on the Buddha of Infinite Light, Amida. He followed the sacramental method of meditation in which, by visualizing Amida, he would become unified with him. But through much arduous meditation, in the years he spent in the retreat of the saintly monk Eiku on Mount Hiei, he nevertheless felt dissatisfied: he could not attain a sense of utter liberation. Honen turned to the idea that those who cannot be freed by strenuous meditation can nevertheless gain Amida's favor and assure themselves of rebirth in the Pure Land simply through the repetition of his name in the formula *Namu Amida Butsu*, or "Homage to the Buddha Amida." This simple formula was for those who had to rely, as Honen came to put it, on *tariki* or "the power of the other," rather than upon *jiriki*, "one's own power." Sal-

The mythic dimension: the great Buddha (Daibutsu) Amida in Kamakura in southern Japan, whose size signifies his spiritual stature, who can help to save the faithful if they call upon his name.

vation had to come from another if one could not in this degenerate age rely on one's own strenuous efforts.

All this was in accord with the great vow of Amida Buddha to help all living beings in the world of suffering. His compassionate nature led to his projection of the Pure Land, where individuals could be reborn in conditions which were particularly suitable for the attainment of final liberation. In so far as this doctrine undercut the rationale for the extensive monastic training of the Tendai and other influential forms of Buddhism, Honen's rivals saw his new teaching as a threat. While they did not deny his own saintliness, they sought to suppress the new movement in 1204 and then again in 1205. Eventually the indiscretion of two of Honen's monks, in leading court ladies in an all-night worship service, enraged the emperor: they were executed, and Honen was banished for four years from the capital, from 1207. He returned in 1211 and died in early 1212, proclaiming his faith in Amida.

Honen's devotional pietism contained some possible inconsistencies which were the reason for the even more radical transformation of Buddhism that was to be attempted by Shinran. For one thing, Honen taught that *Namu Amida Butsu* should be continuously repeated by the faithful: but why so? Surely it was enough simply to turn once to Amida in faith. Repetition was no doubt creating a new form of practice, easier than traditional *jiriki*, but still a kind of *jiriki*. Second, Honen the monk had adhered to the forms of traditional Buddhism. His knowledge of the scriptures was comprehensive. His adherence to the monastic rules had been severe. But such practice was a hangover from the *jiriki* mentality. Pure Land Buddhism, or Jodoshu, ought to go in an even more radical direction. The man who imparted this new thrust was Shinran, founder of what much later came to be called the Jodo-shinshu – the True Pure Land school.

After many years as a Tendai monk, Shinran had been moved by a vision to follow Honen, and he was involved in the crackdown on the new movement, being exiled to Niigata province. There he had another vision, of the female Bodhisattva, Kannon (the Chinese Kuan-yin); and this implied to him that he should have a female helper. He married and had a number of children over the next few years. He lived the life of a poor householder and ordinary person. Since Amida did not require good works, but longed for the salvation of all beings, there was no point in such "good works" as becoming a monk or nun. By a logic similar to that of Luther, Shinran pioneered the move away from monasticism. Even calling on the name of the Buddha was not strictly speaking a condition of being saved, but rather the expression of a faith which after all had been implanted in a person by Amida himself. If the good were saved, how much more so the evil, said Shinran. The utterance of the Nembutsu, the formula, was an outflow of gratitude for the compassionate saving work of Amida.

Though Shinran's view is very similar to Protestant notions of the grace of God, there is a difference arising from the structure of the Buddhist myth. In the Christian case there is always maintained a differentiation between God and the human being, however tender the relationship and sense of communion on both sides. But in the case of True Pure Land, the destiny of those who go on to the Pure Land is to attain Buddhahood and indeed return to the world to help to save others.

Something of the spirit of Shinran's faith can be gathered from the following verses:

Too strong for me is the evil of my heart. I cannot overcome it.
Therefore is my soul like unto the poison of serpents.
Even my righteous deeds, being mingled with this poison,
Must be named the deeds of deceitfulness.
Shameless though I be and having no truth in my soul,
Yet the virtue of the Holy Name, the gift of Him that is enlightened,
Is spread throughout the world by my words,
Although I am as I am.

The humility of Shinran is the obverse side of the coin of the Buddha's goodness and tender love.

Shinran's teaching was to experience a second growth under the leadership of Rennyo (1415–99), who reshaped the community of the Jodoshinshu by developing new pastoral methods, including epistles in colloquial Japanese.

This period of Shinran's life was a turbulent one, with struggles over land and political power between the older aristocracy and the rising military class; some monastic foundations took part in the fighting, a sign of the decadence of the times. But the new rule of the Kamakura shogunate involved a simpler legal system than the complex *ritsuryo* system which it replaced, and this gave greater freedom to religion, which is one reason why the thirteenth and following centuries were so creative a period in Japanese religious history. Among the innovators of these times was Nichiren, who was unusual in having a school named after him.

Nichiren and Japanese Nationalism

Nichiren (1222–82) was a colorful figure, whose stormy life was in accord with his desire to stir up government to reconsider its attitudes to religion. It was a period of floods and natural disasters, and there was the threat of Mongol invasion (fortunately a typhoon crippled the Mongol fleet, a "miracle" attributed to Nichiren's stand by his followers). Though he studied – as did most other prominent leaders of the period – within the Tendai tradition, he came to condemn it as hollow and false to the true message of the Buddha. He was even more strongly critical of the Pure Land and of Zen. His heart was bound to the Lotus Sūtra, which he saw as the very incarnation of Buddhist truth. He rejected other accounts of Buddhism as false and dangerous, and coupled this fundamental stance on behalf of the Lotus with a strong sense of Japanese national identity. He was a prophetic figure and denounced the then ruling family, the Hōjo, for their toleration of wrong views, acceptance of pluralism in Buddhism, and devotion to Pure Land teachings. For his pains he was banished in 1261 for two years to Izu province and in 1271 for nearly three years to Sado Island.

His devotion to the Lotus Sūtra led him to replace the Nembutsu with the formula *Namu Myōhorengekyō*: in other words "Homage to the Lotus of the Perfect Law." He claimed to be a Bodhisattva to whom the Buddha Śākyamuni had entrusted the scripture, and whose reappearance was foretold. Zen Buddhists he denounced because they supposed that the transmission of truth occurs outside of scripture: scripture is needed if the truth of the Buddha's teaching is to be carried down to us. He attacked the Pure Land schools because by concentrating upon the next life they in effect turned people away from harmonizing their present lives. His attacks on the various other schools, including the Tendai that had nurtured him, were bitter and hurtful. He believed that by making people angry and pressuring them through evangelical insistence or *shakubuku* he could bring them to reflect more deeply about their own faith. This fierceness of the Nichiren tradition and its sometimes militant patriotism have raised questions in some minds as to whether it really is to be counted as Buddhist. But it came to play an important role at various stages of Japanese history, and it has always claimed to have the true interpretation of the Buddha's message.

The Formation of Zen

The classical forms of Japanese Buddhism emphasize in one way or another a this-worldly attitude. This is especially true of the kinds of Ch'an Buddhism which came into Japan and were developed well beyond the models that had dominated in China. Eisai (1141–1215) was the father of Zen Buddhism in Japan, though he met with quite a lot of resistance; in some measure he compromised, thinking of Zen as an extra ingredient which could be added to the establishment Tendai mix. But he set the tone of the movement.

Very important in the rooting of Zen was the settlement of Chinese teachers in Japan under the patronage of the ruling shogunate. Among them, four major figures in the thirteenth century established a pure form of Ch'an. Subsequently Japanese leadership gave special directions to the Rinzai movement of sudden enlightenment, to which most Zen exponents were loyal.

The monk Dogen (1200–53) brought Ts'ao-tung or Soto methods and teaching over from China. He experienced liberation in working with his Chinese master and so gained access to the line of transmission of the truth going back to the Buddha Śākyamuni – or so he saw it. The Soto Zen tradition restored the essential contemplative core to Buddhism.

Dogen's writings were massive. Most important was a 95-volume work called *Shōbogenzō*, or "Treasury of the Right Dharma Eye." This brought him much influence in the capital, Kyoto, and round about. But the latter part of his life he spent in the rugged mountain monastery of Eiheiji. There he urged what he took to be the true Zen monastic ideal – a life given to meditation, under fairly strict discipline, and in close contact with nature.

Dogen's thought was original and basic. He saw that attainment and practice are inseparable. By practicing meditation in the right way, that is, *zazen*, "sitting meditation," a person is brought into direct contact with reality. The most important Buddhist truth is that of impermanence. All beings, both living and nonliving, are always in flux, and it is not as if beyond the impermanence there were an unchanging Truth or Reality which could be attained independently of the world of impermanence. Rather it is that the impermanence of things is their true nature, and by the same token is Buddha Nature. In sitting meditation, we experience the flux directly and in doing so attain Buddha Nature. This attainment, it needs to be repeated, is not something extra, but is to be seen in the very particularity of the flow of things. So the substance of things lies in time: life is time, a series of "nows" flowingly linked together, yet each now there in its own particularity.

Both Soto and Rinzai Zen are keen to sweep away preconceived ideas. They emphasize the misleading nature of the concepts which we bring to bear in trying to classify and understand the world. A main reason for the strange riddles (*koan*, Chinese *kung-an*) which the Rinzai masters use is to bring our mental processes to a dead halt, so that we can disentangle ourselves from the language which acts as a fog to obscure our clear vision of the way things are in themselves. Consider for a moment. I am looking out of the window while writing this, and see among other things a large fir tree. But does the tree itself ask to be classified in this way? It is only human convenience that breaks up the scene stretched in front of me into discrete parts, such as trees and a lake. As for its being "large," does the tree ask to be compared, for example, with other fir trees? So although our language is indeed useful for communicating, it gives a particular slant to what I experience. It stands in the way of that visionary unitary kind of experience, sometimes known as "panenhenic" or "one-in-all-ish," which comes before all attempts to break things up into a subject–object kind of dichotomy, me here and the tree over there. Language casts, then, a screen over the flow of things, and so from a Zen point of view it needs to be scraped away. The riddle is one means of doing this.

Originally the *koans* or riddles posed to adepts were drawn from accounts of questions and answers with the masters of the past. This *mondo* or question-and-answer genre often incorporated paradoxes. A good instance is this: a Chinese master was sitting absorbed in meditation, and a monk asked him what he was thinking about. The master answered: "I am thinking of the

The ritual dimension: adherents of the Pure Land sect or Jōdōshu wearing Buddha masks enact a ritual in which saints from paradise, the "Pure Land," descend to this world.

221

absolutely unthinkable.'' ''But,'' asked the monk, ''how can one think what is absolutely unthinkable?'' The answer was: ''By not-thinking.'' In other words, you have to get beyond ordinary ideas of thinking.

The aim of using riddles and of sitting meditation is to attain to *satori* or realization in experience. Because of the doctrine of direct transmission by master to pupil it is usually thought of as something which has in a sense to be certified by a master. It is the master who can tell somehow that the pupil sees things as they really are. Because of the fusion of certain Taoist ideas and those of Ch'an in China, and because of the strong sense of nature in the Japanese tradition, stemming in part from attitudes to the *kami*, *satori* often came to be expressed indirectly by reference to natural events. Japanese art and literature became strongly integrated into the practice of Zen. As one brief poem in the Japanese style puts it:

Last year in a lovely temple in Hirosawa;
This year among the rocks of Nikko;
All's the same to me:
Clapping hands, the peaks roar at the blue!

Zen and the Arts, Martial and Otherwise
One of the main attractions of Zen during the classical period of the shogun-ates was its double virtue in reforming monasticism and in its appeal to the ordinary person engaged in lay life. It did the former by simplifying monastic life and insisting on both hard labor and the practice of meditation – both of

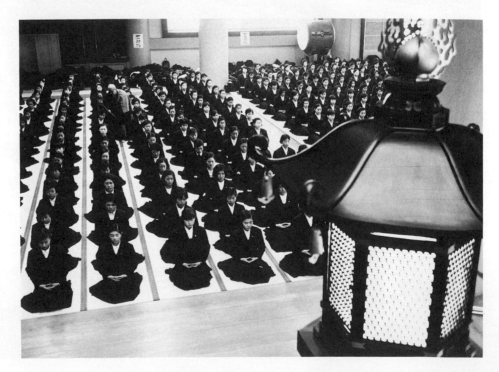

The ritual dimension: sitting meditation needs discipline, and here a monk chastises a girl for deviant posture.

which could be lost sight of in establishment circles. The movement appealed to the laity because it took seriously and in a practical way the Mahāyāna dictum of the identity between the empirical world or *saṃsāra* and the transcendental world or *nirvāṇa*. It took the idea expressed in the Latin tag *laborare est orare*, "to work is to pray," important for Western monasticism, in new directions. For it integrated the meditative task and the skills of ordinary life. In particular, it wove together meditation and the martial arts: archery and swordplay could be developed in a Zen way, hitting the target without aiming (highlighting spontaneity and the equation of means and ends in Zen training). Feminine arts such as flower arrangement and tea-making were also given a Zen mode and flavor. Zen ideals – sparseness, cleanness, control, and spontaneity – came to be influential in all the main arts, such as painting, arranging gardens, and calligraphy.

During the Ashikaga period (1338–1573) Zen's political influence greatly increased, and in effect it became the official religion. This position was enhanced by the fact that neo-Confucian thought was often blended with the Zen outlook, and Confucian ethics were commended for the laity. Confucian values harmonized with those of a feudal society presided over by a military aristocracy. The idea of the five relationships (father–son, husband–wife, ruler–subject, elder brother–younger brother, and friend–friend) provided a structure of thinking for a hierarchical society in which the system of subordinations is compensated for by the need for a paternal benevolence in the senior partner of any of the relationships.

The Dimensions of Buddhism in a Pluralist System

The Ritual Dimension

The picture which has emerged is of a vigorous and plural religious system. Its ritual dimension existed in different layers and varieties. There was the fervent use of devotional formulae, as in the Pure Land schools and Nichiren Buddhism. There was the return to orthodox meditation, but with a Chinese-Japanese twist, among the Zen schools. There remained the older ritualism of Tendai and Shingon. There were the ceremonies to the gods of Shinto, both associated with Buddhist temples and in disjunction from them. There were the domestic rituals combining Confucian, Shinto, and Buddhist motifs. There were pilgrimages such as the tour of the Thirty-Three Holy Places of Kannon, or that of the Eighty-Eight Temples of Shikoku (of over 700 miles [1,100 kilometers], no mean feat in the old days). There were pilgrimages to the Shinto shrine of Amaterasu at Ise, and to many others. Such rituals enhanced and formed religious experiences of various kinds.

The Experiential Dimension

The most prominent creation of the classical period was the opening up of the two basic experiences of religion – the numinous and the mystical. The devotion to Amida opened up the numinous sense of the glory of God and the

223

unworthiness or humility of the individual in the face of the Ultimate. Zen restored to Buddhism a vigorous concentration on the mystical quest. But here, as well as finding the blank and blinding light within, the adept could directly experience unity with nature, in a panenhenic type of experience. At the same time Shinto ritual reinforced the desire to experience purity and to remove impurity.

The Ethical, Social, and Institutional Dimension

The classical period reinforced traditional ethics in particular by drawing on the Confucian ethic. This helped to frame the values of the Way of the Warrior or Bushidō, combining Confucian directions and the spare Stoicism of the Zen tradition. Socially and institutionally, the classical period saw the spread and popularization of Buddhism and then eventually the reassertion of control by the shogunate. The imperial family and its Shinto connections also remained important, and there was a strong symbiosis between Buddhas and *kami*. The Confucian academic life was dominated by Zen monks, and though there were tensions between the old establishment of Tendai and Shingon on the one hand and the Pure Land and Zen forms of Buddhism on the other, by the Tokugawa period they were welded into a loyal collaboration.

The Doctrinal Dimension

In doctrine two outstanding developments of the Japanese tradition were the teachings of Dogen, giving fresh vigor to the *nirvāṇa-saṃsāra* equation, and the extreme but logical conclusions about salvation expressed by Shinran.

The Narrative Dimension

From the point of view of the narrative dimension the most significant concept was Nichiren's view of his own prophetic mission and the fusing of the destiny of Japan and Buddhism effected in his teachings. In fact the myth of a truly Buddhist Japan, taken in a rather strong and exclusive way, gives Japanese Buddhism some analogies with that of Sri Lanka.

The Material Dimension

But above all, Japanese creativity was seen in the seventh dimension – that of *artistic* creation. The Japanese had a wonderful spiritual aestheticism, a subtle blend of religion and beauty. No other culture has gone to such lengths as to imbue mundane skills with transcendental meaning. And above all it was Zen with its most original style which suffused so much of Japanese artistic creation with its spirit. Perhaps it is above all in the raked gravel, shaped bushes and rocks, the waterfalls, groomed trees, and cunning vistas of the Japanese temple garden that you can feel the grip of religion upon Japanese culture most profoundly, and the converse too. The cultivation of beauty is itself a kind of religious imperative.

Japan: the Premodern Era

The Tokugawa was a system of remarkable consolidation, which gave Japan breathing space until the next crisis, in the middle of the nineteenth century, when it became evident that seclusion would break down. It retained the imperial family as a sacred focus of the nation, but the administration was under the shoguns of the Tokugawa family – as it were, national and hereditary prime ministers – and devolved through a feudal system presided over by local warrior feudatories or *daimyo*. The social order was fairly rigorously defined by law and etiquette. The hierarchy in broad terms was: warrior, farmer, artisan, merchant (with one or two impure groups below). Though merchants were at the bottom, by the end of the Tokugawa period commerce and cities had expanded so that their status had improved with the accumulation of wealth.

As far as religion went, the Tokugawa system not only integrated the population with Buddhism, and Buddhism itself with the *kami*; but it expected the various ranks of society to conform to the proper norms. The warrior class had to follow the Bushidō, for example: the Way of the Warrior. As a concept this surfaced at the start of the Tokugawa era, and as it came to be expounded by Confucian scholars it combined the twin ideals of learning and the martial arts. The new warriors of the era had to get involved

Art and religion fuse into the orderliness of this raked garden with natural rocks and trees in Kyoto.

in administration and the running of society, and so their education became important. In fact as the Tokugawa period went on they came to fill many professional positions, as administrators, lawyers, doctors, as well as soldiers. This was one of the ways in which Confucianism was blended into the Tokugawa ethic. Another was by the combination of Zen and Confucian thought; and Zen also played its part in giving the martial arts a spiritual meaning and basis.

Theoretically it was a good period for Buddhism, but criticism of the regime was not allowed, and the only new form to emerge was Obaku Zen, brought in from China by Ingen (1592–1673) near the beginning of the Tokugawa period. It combined elements of Pure Land and Zen practice. Ingen's stricter practice was a challenge to the other schools and contributed to their reform and revival. But the Tokugawa period also saw new views of Shinto tradition and Confucianism being developed. The Tokugawa shogun Mitsukuni (1628–1701) caused a great historiographic enterprise to be undertaken, which was the reinterpretation of the history of the imperial family according to Confucian principles. This work, the *Dainihonshi*, played a part later in the ideology of the Meiji restoration (the restoration of imperial government).

Also of some significance in the eighteenth century was a revival of nationalism through the so-called *Kokugaku* or National Learning movement, under the leadership of such intellectuals as Motoori Norinaga (1730–1801). This saw the history of Japan as having three periods: a first pristine period, then a period of corruption by foreign influences, and finally a period of restoration and rediscovery of the ancient past. This stream of ideas and feelings helped to reinforce national sentiment during the closing years of the Tokugawa shogunate.

Japan: the Modern Era

The Impact of the Modern Era on Buddhism

At first the Meiji restoration seemed disastrous to Buddhism. The support which had been part of the Tokugawa system was withdrawn. The loss of patronage and membership was severe. The campaign to separate Shinto and Buddhism damaged many temples and institutions. But in the new opening up to Western knowledge there were new opportunities.

Some elegant syntheses of Eastern and Western thought were attempted, the most luminous of which perhaps is that of Nishida Kitara (1875–1945). His first important book was published in 1911, and set forth a philosophical method influenced by Kant, Bergson, and William James, in which he pioneered a method of examining experience. For him pure experience, that is experience unmixed with concepts and self-consciousness, is without the subject–object dichotomy by which we usually interpret experience. His relation to Zen ideas is obvious here. He gave a new slant on the Mahāyāna notion of nothingness, through his conception of absolute nothingness as the

226

mirror of all individual existence. He was in such ways trying to blend some Western enquiries stemming from Kant's time, and the search for what lies beyond experience, with Buddhist categories of thought.

A not altogether dissimilar attempt was made at a later time by the famous Zen scholar D. T. Suzuki, or more properly Suzuki Daisetz Teitaro (1870–1966). The two men were friends, and from their correspondence can be discovered the closeness of their general thinking. But Suzuki's chief contribution was in editing and translating Zen works and writing about Zen in a way which related it to both science and mysticism, and so sparking a general interest in Zen in the Western world. He was an important figure in making Japanese thought global in character. The fact that Westerners have become interested in aspects of Japanese Buddhism also has stimulated a revival of Japanese concerns with Buddhism.

Nichiren Shoshu and the Soka Gakkai

A revival of an older tradition which had been set in motion by Nichiren of the thirteenth century was due to the work of Makiguchi Tsunesaburo (1871–1944), who wove into his philosophy some elements of Western thought – notably utilitarianism and pragmatism. He dispensed, therefore, with the concept of truth as a separate category but stressed the attainment of benefits by present practice in accord with the general tenor of Nichiren's teaching. The supreme goal of human beings is happiness, and in his reforming of the Nichiren message Makiguchi founded an organization later to be reshaped by his most famous disciple, Toda Josei (1900–58), as the Soka Gakkai or Value-Creation Society.

This aimed at increasing benefit to members in accordance with beauty and altruistic desires – the foundations of art and morality respectively. This is seen within the framework of a vigorous faith in the benefits of repeating the invocation to the Lotus Sūtra and in other ways following the general life and precepts of the Nichiren Shoshu. Because of the group's deviation from the nationalist norms of the war period, Makiguchi and Toda were imprisoned, and it was in prison that Makiguchi died. The Soka Gakkai is a lay organization, and it came to have considerable success in the period after World War II. It did so partly because of its rather aggressive style of proselytization, called the *shakubuku*, which can be translated as conversion by breaking the person down. Toda's reconstruction of the movement, after its banning and during the time of renewed spiritual hope after the war, was a marked success, and it went on to play an active role in politics through its political wing, the Komeito Party.

The aim of the Soka Gakkai is benefit here and now and the promotion of a worldwide organization which will eventually issue in world peace. Its rituals concentrate on the invocation of the Lotus Sūtra (or *Daimoku*). This should be chanted daily, morning and evening. Replicas of the sacred scroll inscribed by the founder Nichiren and placed in the temple at Taisekiji near Fuji-san are the focus of devotion, and Nichiren is seen as the very embodiment of

Buddhahood, even beyond the Buddha Śākyamuni. But the modernization of philosophy undertaken by Makiguchi gives the Soka Gakkai essentially an up-to-date air, different from the more traditional forms of Buddhism.

In its organizational style and philosophical underpinning, the Soka Gakkai has taken Western models. In its myth and ritual it is the successor of the older Nichiren school. It is from this point of view a successful syncretism, preserving the essence of this older tradition in the changed circumstances of modern Japan.

Conclusion

While Buddhism has suffered terrible vicissitudes during the last hundred years, mainly because of the effects of Marxist regimes in Asia, it has also attracted a lot of attention in the West. In some ways it is the most successful Asian religion in America and Europe – fairly small in numbers but powerful intellectually and in practical, meditational outreach. There are signs of re-vival in China, and it has continued unbroken in the Chinese diaspora. It is vigorous in Japan and Sri Lanka and Thailand. It is likely that it will resume its place, during the twenty-first century, as one of the world's three great missionary religions.

CHAPTER TWELVE

The Shinto Tradition

The Term "Shinto"

Shinto as a name was given to the indigenous and prehistoric beliefs and practices of the Japanese with the coming of Buddhism to Japan in the sixth century C.E. It is based on two Chinese words, *Shin* or spirit, and *to* or way: literally therefore it means the Way of the Spirits or the Way of the Gods. The Japanese word for god or spirit is *kami*. While Buddhism distinguished itself from the primordial system of religious belief and practice it encountered in Japan, it also, as elsewhere in Asia, developed a symbiosis with the tradition. *Kami* were not denied, although Buddhism regarded them as irrelevant to ultimate salvation. But they could be treated as supernatural protectors of the Buddha, or even later as incarnations of the Buddha. They were subordinated in such ways to Buddha, who retained, so to speak, the commanding heights of religion.

While this relationship lived on in one form or another until modern times, the Meiji restoration in 1867 led to the forcible separation of Shinto and Buddhism. Often the *kami's* shrines were incorporated into Buddhist temple complexes, and the separation caused considerable upheaval. Moreover, the previous Tokugawa regime (see page 226) had instituted a universal system of Buddhist parishes, so that citizens were officially attached to one temple or another. But the Meiji made the attempt to make Shinto the official ideology. However, in the event what they did was to establish Shinto as a ritual and ethical system of practice, focusing in part on loyalty to the imperial family, which was obligatory on all Japanese as good citizens; but ideological or doctrinal claims were forbidden, and Shinto priests were commanded not to preach – for fear that ideological utterances might be divisive. In short, Shinto was made obligatory, not so much as a system of truth but rather as a system of practice. Such State Shinto even so ran into some opposition from various groups, including some revivalist Shinto denominations of the nineteenth century. For in addition to regular Shinto there were various new religions based on mainly Shinto values which helped Japan to cope with the rapid social and political changes of the nineteenth and twentieth centuries. The State Shinto idea was abolished after the end of World War II, when the U.S.-imposed constitution firmly separated religion and the state. Shinto was allowed to continue as something inextricably woven into the culture and tradition of Japanese society. It may be noted that during the nationalist period (from the Meiji restoration till the end of World War II) the Japanese maintained constitutionally that there was freedom of worship and religion, except that everyone had to respect Shinto. The apparent contradiction was overcome by affirming that Shinto is not properly speaking a religion.

Kami and Foreign Influences

The main center of Japanese power in the misty early centuries of the Common Era was the central region occupied by differing clans in a loose confederation under a Yamato kingship. Differing clans had different *kami*,

---

Shinto some key terms

Amaterasu The goddess of the Sun, leader of the celestial gods and ancestress of the Japanese imperial family.

Gagaku Sacred and solemn music supposedly pleasing to the gods and used in ceremonial contexts.

Haiden The worship hall in a Shinto temple complex where, in the most sacred inner sanctum, the icons and symbols representing the *kami* reside.

Kami Traditional nature god or spirit.

Kojiki Record of Ancient Matters, a sacred text dating to the early eighth century C.E.

Kokugaku Early seventeenth-century movement to revive the ethos of ancient Japan.

Kokutai The national essence: the State Shinto of the period before World War II is sometimes referred to as Kokutai Shinto.

Magokoro A central Shinto virtue, meaning sincerity or a bright, pure, upright mind.

Nihongi Ancient Chronicles of Japan, dating from 720 C.E. and a major source of Shinto myth and values.

Norito Prayers according to ancient formulae offered to the gods.

Shinto The Way (*to*) of the Gods (*Shin* = *kami*).

Torii The double-linteled gate typical of the entrance to a Shinto shrine, demarcating sacred from profane space.

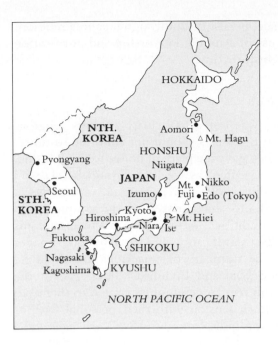

Map of Japan showing key Shinto sites.

but gradually a central core of myths of origin came to play a role in the centralizing ideology of the Yamato emperors. This group of myths in part focused on the great goddess of the Sun, Amaterasu, divine ancestress of the royal family. The complex myths were drawn from differing cultures, from Polynesia, China, and elsewhere, and were in due course codified in the books *Kojiki* and *Nihonshoki* in the latter part of the seventh century. They helped to justify imperial rule, granted absolutely to her descendants through the goddess. There was no Japanese theory of the "Mandate of Heaven" in relation to the royal family, and the fact that for many centuries actual rule was exercised by shoguns, while in theory people deferred to the emperor, is a significant comment on the ultimate sanctity of the imperial lineage. In the early period there was also a gradual infiltration of cultural elements from Korea and China. The Japanese fought and settled in southern Korea in the fourth century, though disastrously defeated by the northern state of Koguryo. The foundations, however, were laid for the decisive entry of official Buddhism into Japan in the mid part of the sixth century.

The multitudinous *kami* of mountains, streams, rocks, and the sea blended with ancestral and tutelary *kami* who were integrated into the life of particular clans. Broadly, the *kami* occupied differing planes of existence: Takamano-hara or "high heaven"; Nakatsukuni or "middle land," i.e. roughly the earth; and Yomi, the underworld. Though the heavenly *kami* were important, the *kami* of the middle region often had more immediate interest in human and clan affairs. There were shrines to various spirits, which later in the early imperial period multiplied significantly as a result of state patronage.

The *kami* were important for agriculture and hunting, and ancient practices of shamanism, both male and female, persist right through Japanese religion. Later commonplaces, such as the use of clapping in worship and purification with water, seem to date from prehistoric times.

Shinto and Popular Religion

Buddhism, in Japan as elsewhere, was not a particularly jealous religion. There was no reason why Japanese Buddhists should not continue to reverence Shinto deities, provided that they gave the place of honor to the Buddha, and prime place to Buddhist values. Often, as we find during the classical period in Japan, Shinto and Buddhist holy places merged. Sometimes a Buddhist monk might marry a Shinto shamaness, and the couple could jointly run a temple. Sometimes traditional *kami* places in the mountains would become imbued with Buddhist significance, and so sacred pilgrimages could combine. The increase in the numbers of *yamabushi*, or Buddhist mountain ascetics, helped to blend *kami* and Buddhist values. As for the emperors, they continued to perform regular ceremonies related to the myth of their divine descent, without much tension with their personal faith as Buddhists. At the domestic level it was quite natural to have a *kamidana* and a *Butsudan*, that is a god-shelf and a Buddha-altar. These could happily exist side by side. The Buddhist control of funeral rites and cemeteries gave the religion a high profile in ordinary life; but as Japanese typically had their marriages blessed by a *kami* ceremony, there was a synthesis in the treatment of rites of passage. Confucian values would inspire everyday ethics, while diviners and sorcerers of Taoist origin would also play their part in society.

Amaterasu and the Unification of Japan

The unification of the main part of Japan occurred essentially in the seventh century and therefore Amaterasu, the goddess-patron of the imperial family, acquired supreme status among the *kami*. The scriptures reciting various myths of ancient Japan, the *Kojiki* (Records of Ancient Affairs) and the *Nihonshoki* (Japanese Chronicles), divide the spirits into two classes, the high gods and the nature and ancestral gods. Generally *kami* represent strange and supernatural phenomena, like the Roman *numina*. Amaterasu's myth includes not just creative acts but also her retreat into a rock cave: the retirement signalized the withdrawal of reproductive power. But 80,000 *kami* gathered outside, and on hearing their laughter Amaterasu came out to see what was happening. The myth was no doubt coupled to spring fertility rites. Amaterasu is also associated with mirrors, seen as awesome in early Japan and suggestive of the notion that a person's spirit is contained in his or her reflection. In due course the mirror came to stand for Amaterasu herself.

Because of the association of Amaterasu with the royal family special attention was paid to her in the Meiji period, which saw a revival of reverence for the royal family in accordance with new nationalist sentiment.

While the *kami* were numerous and so reflected a polytheistic worldview, they were and are this-worldly in activity and emphasis. The Shinto system is world-affirming, and the *kami* are a frequent reminder of the numinous and beautiful aspects of the Japanese environment. In early times they were worshiped at natural sites rather than constructed temples, though today the temple-cult is typical. Partly under the rival influence of Buddhism, Shinto has grown a priestly class and a system of humanly constructed temples.

The Revival of Shinto in Premodern Japan

Preparing the way for the nationalism of the Meiji period was the eighteenth-century movement known as the Kokugaku or "National Learning," expressed through various intellectuals and most notably through Motoori Norinaga (1730–1801). He underlined the authority of the *Kojiki* as the scriptural basis for a reanimated Shinto. He and colleagues rejected the artificialities of Confucian and Buddhist thought, and drew on the naturalistic themes of Chuang-tzu to defend obedience to the *kami*. The reinforcement by the Kokugaku school of reverence for the imperial tradition helped to stimulate the restoration of the emperor's rule under the Meiji revolution.

The military dictatorship known as the shogunate had become too dependent, from the point of view of Shinto revivalists, on the Buddhist parish system and their critique of Buddhism came to underpin, a little surprisingly, the modernist regime which replaced the shogunate. Actually, Buddhism was nearer in spirit to modern science than ancient Shinto. But the latter suited the new nationalist emphasis, whereas Buddhism did not, and nationalism in the nineteenth and early twentieth centuries was a main engine of modernization across the world. All this lay behind the somewhat violent separation of Buddhism and Shinto in the early years of the Meiji period.

Shinto as a State Religion

The violence resulted in damage to Buddhist temples, and there was more to come after the constitution had been established. This was based on French and German models (the Parliament was called, for instance, the Diet). It guaranteed freedom of religion. What the Japanese did was to formalize what was implicit in nineteenth- and much of twentieth-century nationalism. They made all Japanese observe the rituals of official Shinto, because these related to the dominant ethic of the constitution, loyalty to the nation. In order to ensure this, however, and at the same time guarantee religious liberty, they hit upon a fine expedient – declaring Shinto not to be a religion. In a way the situation was not unlike that in Marxist countries, where the constitution declares the freedom of religion, and Marxism, which is the compulsory ideology of the state, is not of course a religion.

The original thought had been to make revival Shinto a kind of doctrinal ideology which was to be subscribed to by all citizens; but with the failure of

The Emperor Akihito in full court attire goes to an imperial sanctuary to inform his ancestors of the date of his coronation (1990).

the campaign to proclaim the ideology, fostered briefly among mostly unwilling Buddhist monks, in the early 1870s, State Shinto in effect got slimmed down. Priests were in fact forbidden to preach during ceremonies, so that Shinto could end up as a universal system of ethics and ritual, with of course myth attached, but not as a set of teachings which could divisively challenge other systems of ideas. To clarify matters, various new religious movements, such as Tenrikyo, which had some Shinto overtones, were reclassified by the state as being Sect Shinto. The consequence is that in modern times three or more kinds of Shinto are referred to: Shrine Shinto, which is Shinto as typically to be found in today's Japan, a set of practices rooted in the shrines (now separated from Buddhism); State Shinto, which existed from 1882 till 1945, when it perished as part of the aftermath of World War II; and Sect Shinto, which covers a number of new movements. Reference is also sometimes made to Buddhist and Confucian Shinto, covering syncretic forms of worldview.

In nominating Shinto as a necessary part of the ethos of Japan, the Meiji government was giving formal expression, as we have said, to the overriding importance of the nation over other values. Actually the same tended to apply in Western countries – through, for instance, the rituals surrounding the American flag or the British monarchy – even if in theory the nations in question counted themselves as Christian.

In brief, State Shinto – and the same is largely true of Shrine Shinto in the period since World War II – was a partly truncated religion, since it did not develop a set of doctrines. It did, however, form the emotional heart of a nationalist ideology which saw the expansion and the defence of the nation's power as the sacred duty of all Japanese. Its ethos linked up with a modern reinterpretation of Bushidō as the Way even of the conscript soldier. The stoicism and valor with which so many fought in successive wars is a testimony to the grip of such ideals.

Japanese New Religions

Contrasting with the revival of Shinto as expressing nationalist sentiment were new religions with some sort of Shinto background. Let us look at two of them as examples: Tenrikyo and Omoto.

Tenrikyo: the Center of the World and a New Community

Tenrikyo has in origin a Shinto ambience; during the reorganization of religion in 1888 it was treated as one of the so-called Sect Shinto movements, and in due course nationalistic values were forced upon it. But after World War II, under the Constitution of 1947 which ensured genuine religious freedom, it purified its teachings and resumed its onward course as a fairly successful missionizing religion both at home and in various areas abroad, including the United States.

It was started by a woman, Nakayama Miki (1798–1887), during the stormy years of the collapsing Tokugawa era. She was in early life devoted to Pure Land Buddhism, and wished to become a nun. But in deference to the wishes of her parents she married, and subsequently was dedicated to Shinto deities. It was in her forty-first year that she received a vision which formed the center of the divine revelations to her and later to her close disciple Iburi Izo (1833–1907). Her mission was to prepare the way for a perfect divine kingdom in which human beings will share a life of joy united with God. This messianic element in her teachings led to clashes with the state, both during her lifetime (she was imprisoned on several occasions) and after her death. As a revelatory figure she was thought of as *Kami no Yashiro*, that is, the Living Shrine of God, who descended into her. The revelations were characterized by having three predetermined characteristics – being the right soul, the right place, and the right time.

The place is very important for Tenrikyo religion, since it functions as focus of its most important practices. It is the *jiba* marked by a pole installed in the shrine at what is now Tenri City, near Nara, the old capital of Japan, which is the place that the revelations indicate as being the point of origin of the human race. The large shrine there contains the space necessary for the performance of the dance ritual which sums up and reenacts the story of God's creation.

Miki the foundress showed her humility and chosenness through her compassion for others (her habit of giving greatly impoverished her family) and in healing powers. The teachings she left outlined the essentials of the new faith, while those she ascribed to her disciple Inburi contain quite a number of directions about the organization of the movement. The Church is today under the leadership of a chief priest, descendant of Miki. It has grown somewhat and has about three million followers, and a very flourishing center at Tenri City, including the *jiba* shrine, a university, a remarkable library with some most valuable first editions and ancient manuscripts from both East and West (including Adam Smith's *Wealth of Nations*), a hospital, a publishing house, a mission headquarters, and a whole series of large dormitories for members returning to visit the *jiba*. Thus a city has grown up around the shrine.

The Dimensions of Tenrikyo

The Narrative Dimension
The narrative dimension of Tenrikyo centers both on creation and on the life of Miki, who is thought to have remained in a spiritual state at her sanctuary, to help the faithful. Hers is held up as a model life (a contrast, incidentally, to the male warrior virtues which are so much held in esteem in Japanese society).

The Doctrinal Dimension
As for the doctrinal dimension: God is seen as the true God and divine Parent who pervades his creation but at the same time is specially present to devo-

The ethical dimension: reverence for ancestors is part of the ethic of respect for those who have preceded you in life – seniority is important in Japanese society.

tees. His desire to create is so that he may see human joy and harmony, but this is prevented by selfishness, and the revelation is designed to overcome this. Human life is treated as something lent by God (borrowed by the human being), and this provides an ethical motif to Tenri teachings, which we shall come to shortly. Salvation also requires the purification of heart, and this can be achieved over a period of lives, through reincarnation. This softens the impact of the particularism of the *jiba* as the holy center where one should prepare for final union with God, since good conduct and purification can help one to receive the divine gift of being reborn at the *jiba*.

The Ritual and Ethical Dimension

The ritual dimension centers on the sacred dances in the central shrine. Pilgrimage to the center is a vital ingredient in the organization of the faith. As to the ethical side, we have noted how taking one's life as being on loan spurs devotees to be selfless and to use their talents on earth for the divine cause. Using Shinto-like language, where the image of dust obscuring a mirror is prominent, the faults of humans should be wiped away as being the so-called "eight dusts" covering up the human heart, one's true nature. They include hatred, anger, greed, arrogance, and so on. The general ethos is this-worldly, concerned with building up the visible life of the community.

The Material, Social, and Experiential Dimension

On the material side we have noted the importance of Tenri City. The actual main shrine is beautifully built with expensive wood, but it is without icons, unless one counts the *jiba* pole toward which the celebrants face. There are some patterns used on priestly robes which are reminiscent of Shinto modes, but basically the rites are separate from those used in Shinto.

The religion focuses strongly on the experience of parental love: God is loving Parent, and the creation saga of Miki emphasizes this idea. It leaves out of the story the complex of motifs associated with the goddess Amaterasu and the myth of the imperial family. This was one of the causes of friction between Tenrikyo and the State Shinto that the Meiji system put in place. Tenrikyo has a lot to say to those who belong in nuclear families in the postindustrial age, in a Japan which has undergone headlong industrialization and other vital social changes, including the defeat of World War II.

Omoto and Related Movements

Omoto (Great Source) never recovered from being disbanded on the orders of the government before World War II. However, it was very effective in stimulating other movements. It stemmed originally from the shamanistic visions of Deguchi Nao (1837–1910), a peasant woman. She saw in the talents of Deguchi Onisabiro (1871–1948) proof of his being a messianic messenger from God, whose coming she had predicted, and he was adopted into her family, becoming her son-in-law. The theology promulgated by the new religion was that souls descend from the divine world of spirits into this material world. It prophesied the coming of Miroku (Maitreya Buddha) with whom Onisabiro identified himself. The movement saw the present state of Japan as evil and in need of divine reconstruction, which would come with the new age. It tended to look on that new age as involving a return to rural harmony: in such a life religion would be lived as art, with an aesthetic beauty and harmonious feelings.

The movement was a reaction against industrialization and the whole modernization of Japan, and though it professed patriotism in accord with the dictates of State Shinto its myth and doctrine were in many ways in continuing opposition to the route which the state was taking. It was right-wing in politics, but with an emphasis on village life and the repair of agriculture. Because of these heretical politics it was suppressed in the 1930s. But it had an influence on other new groups, including Perfect Liberty Kyodan or PL Kyodan as it is known, created by Miki Tokuchika (b. 1900) in 1956. Its especial theme was that of life as art. Thus the first three of its twenty-one principles read as follows: "Life is Art. The whole life of the individual is a continuous succession of self-expressions. The individual is a manifestation of God."

We may see in Omoto a somewhat turbulent attempt to explain the present problems as being due to the withdrawal of the original *kami* from Japan, and the hope of a new age in which many of the evils of our time will be swept away by a messianic figure. The appeal of the message lay in its revolt against the times: against capitalism, against the constitution, and against both world wars. It argued, too, for the essential unity of all religions and for world harmony. It was thus a strange mixture of peaceful and extreme authoritarian views.

Both Tenrikyo and Omoto have a background of Shinto, but both in effect have fashioned alternative myths. Neither conformed to the State Shinto or the official Shinto of the imperial family. But they went in different directions: Tenrikyo toward a building up in a practical way of a city and a center here on earth, Omoto back to an earlier vision of a rural paradise. They both testify to a period when the Shinto framework in a broad sense was exceptionally dynamic, and breaking out from under the newer Shinto which was being shaped both before and during the Meiji era (and then the Showa era, from 1912). This was a newer Shinto which, while professing antiquity, nevertheless was self-consciously forming itself into a separate tradition rather than a functional correlative of Buddhism and Confucian values.

Just as China had the three religions which over much of its history served as a loose federation of spirituality and ideology, so Japan traditionally had a working combination of Confucian ideology, Buddhist doctrines and practice, and the *kami*. These forces were becoming separated out in the new Japan. Basically, Western institutions and ideas were taking the place of Confucian values; Buddhism was becoming self-consciously separate from the state; and Shinto was being formed into a separate system. In the nationalist period, up to World War II, State Shinto did not strictly teach any doctrines, as we have seen, but it had its imperial myth.

The disturbing thing about the new religious movements was above all their teaching of alternative myths. This harmonized with their origins in visionary experiences embedded strongly within folk culture. It would be only at a later stage that the need for more abstract and analytic doctrines would appear.

Nationalism in Japan and its Aftermath

The elevation of State Shinto into a sphere above religion, as it were, involved a blend of religion and the state. This was perhaps made inevitable in the Japanese case by the special role assigned to the imperial family in the reconstruction of Japan. The shogunate had already prepared the way by keeping the emperor as a sacred monarch, separate from the business of actual administration. The Meiji restoration superficially gave back power to the emperor, but as the polity was evolving toward a European-style constitution, the emperor's status was never ambiguous.

For the most part he functioned as a kind of sacred oracle, to be informed and consulted in matters of state but not to be involved directly with particular policies. This was a special mechanism for the conduct of affairs – with the imperial family hitched to the Shinto ritual and the myth of its own descent from Amaterasu – which gave a powerful focus to national loyalty. The emperor became the personalized form of the *kokutai* or national essence. The latter was a kind of Absolute, and the emperor the manifestation of that Absolute in personal form. The various religions of Japan, including Christianity, which had emerged from secrecy and oppression after the Meiji restoration, were necessarily subordinated to the national Absolute. All this might have seemed antique, save that nationalism was the very political arrangement under which nineteenth-century capitalism had chosen to organize itself.

The warpath which took Japan on its various stages to World War II was of course the path of imperialism. This had been fashionable among the White powers. Britain, Russia, France, Germany, Italy, Holland, and in a limited way the United States, had all engaged in it in the Pacific area in recent times, and, earlier, Spain and Portugal had taken a hand. By the late nineteenth century this had come to be justified by more than bare chauvinism. It was supposed to bring the benefits of Western civilization, usually conceived as Christian, to the "natives" of the areas conquered. Japan in her actions up to the time of Versailles had acted in harmony with the overall assumed imperialism, save in so far as she could hardly represent "Christian" civilization. But the ethos changed radically thereafter. In the 1930s her attempts to take over Manchuria and her war with China were severely condemned (as indeed was Italy's attack on Ethiopia). Evidently the nineteenth century was the time to do these things, which became criminal in the twentieth! Moreover, Japan

239

backed the wrong side in the lead-up to World War II, entering into an alliance with Germany and Italy. The penalties she paid were severe: most of her cities burned and blasted out by huge air raids, culminating in August 1945 in the atomic bombs on Hiroshima and Nagasaki (the latter, ironically, the most Christian city of Japan).

These tragedies did not in fact halt the whole process of modernization. On the contrary, they helped, in that the true capital was in the brains and skilled hands of the Japanese rather than in the factories and shipyards already in place: bombing enforced modernization on the material side. The Western models of life which had been presented to Japan were three in number, at least: there was the liberal democratic option, largely tied to capitalism, though it could be modified with welfare socialism; the Marxist model, with central state control and a totalitarian system of regulating ideas and behavior; and the fascist model, which was totalitarian hypernationalism. It was this last model which Japan had slid into following, and it was this that was decisively defeated in 1945. Since America was the chief force of occupation and had a decisive role in shaping the new constitution, it was the liberal model which was to prevail. At the same time the emperor was left in place as a constitutional monarch (but with undertones of sacrality, nevertheless, which remain in Japanese attitudes).

In October, 1945, the Allied Occupation abolished State Shinto, and on New Year's Day, 1946, the emperor announced that he was not divine. The result was the dispersal of Shinto into Shrine Shinto. The transition was calm enough. The legislation, which abolished counting by families in affiliation to religious organizations, such as the Buddhist parish system, produced a more individualistic stance in relationship to membership, but religious allegiance has grown. Thus, as far as Shinto goes, it is reckoned that the association connected with the great Meiji Shrine in Tokyo is over a quarter-million strong. There are about 80,000 shrines in the country, most of which are joined in the Association of Shinto Shrines, devoted to the training of priests, general education in religion, the development of shrines, and so forth. The associations or clubs of believers concern themselves with general mainten-ance, the fostering of Shinto music, boy scout activities, and so on. So religion has moved on to a voluntary basis. Membership of Buddhist temples has changed in similar ways.

A Summation of the Dimensions of Shinto

As we have seen, there has been little of a *doctrinal* dimension in Shinto, though there have been occasional attempts to wed it to Taoist and neo-Confucianist ideas. *Mythically*, of course, the religion is rich in its collection of narrative material about the gods and goddesses. As we have noted on page 232, Amaterasu emerged as a dominant figure linked to the imperial family and to the birth of Japan. The number of spirits is, according to tradition, vast – as many as eight million. Human life itself springs from the *kami*, not only

because humans receive it ultimately from the creative power of the spirits but also because the blessings of life come from spiritual forces. *Ritually* the existence of many shrines provides a large number of festivals and processions, and the opportunity for purification and the adoration of the *kami*. Shinto ceremonial comprises games and celebrations, adding color to local life, while Shinto music provides a solemn joy to please the gods. Most Japanese weddings and various other rites of passage (into adulthood, for instance) are Shinto, though typically funerals are Buddhist. The solemn rites associated with the access of a new emperor are Shinto also. Although officially disengaged from the state, Shinto thus commands a residual place in the life of the imperial family.

As to the *ethical* dimension there is a powerful emphasis upon purification. This in turn promotes sincerity, truthfulness, and upright conduct. *Emotionally* Shinto promotes a calm and sublime concern with nature, much in accord with the general spirit of Japanese aesthetics. We have noted too how shamanistic experience can characterize the founding of new Shinto movements. At

Priests at the Meiji Shrine in Tokyo, which is dedicated to the emperor Meiji and is a reminder of Japan's great period of Westernization.

241

Shinto: portable shrines (or mikoshi) are carried from the Futaaren Shrine at the Yayoi festival. Mikoshi are said to be the abode of the guardian deities.

the *social* level Shinto has undergone extensive development since World War II with the formation of parish associations, as we might call them, attached to the shrines, as well as other more specialized groups, e.g. for the cultivation of sacred music. The new Shinto sects are even more adept at organizing themselves. The various Shinto shrines, however, have formed themselves into an association, which serves among other things to train priests. Generally the great shrine at Ise is looked upon as the most prestigious Shinto center. *Materially* the most vital manifestations are found in the myriad temples of Japan, marked typically by an entrance gate of characteristic design, called a *torii*. Often a shrine is in a beautiful place, so that the ambience is part of its charm and calm. The main building is a worship hall, in the recesses of which may be kept a statue of the *kami*. Such statues are a relatively late response to the Buddha statues of Shinto's rival religion.

Does an Overall Japanese Worldview Exist?

The multiplication of new religions, especially in the period after World War II, the separation of religion and the state, the voluntary nature of affiliation with the religions, and the onset of extensive Japanese immersion in Western thought have led to an apparently very fragmented and confused state of affairs. Because of the possibility of belonging to more than one association, and the old tradition of combining different strands of faith and cultus, the total number of registered believers in Japan greatly exceeds the total population. The liberal basis of the constitution, and of an open society dedicated to the pursuit of capital success, has a vital place in the Japanese worldview, but how does it fit in with the traditional religions? Indeed, is there a single Japanese worldview at all?

If there is a central conception which prevails, it is probably that of harmony. A number of the new religious movements are keen to stress the unity of the world's religions; and, though the Nichiren Shoshu is aggressive, most Mahāyāna Buddhist groups seek harmony. Shinto, too, has an interest in maintaining its harmony with other religions, partly because it does not possess any rigid system of doctrines which might bring it into conflict with them. From this point of view democracy is a method of defusing rifts, especially between religious groups, in so far as the separation of religion and the state gives a peaceful basis for the voluntary pursuit of values. It also is in consonance with the Japanese ideal of gaining consensus before any serious line of policy is undertaken.

Religion has a role in promoting national harmony, and there is some hankering for the outward displays of royal religion in which some other countries, most notably Britain, can still indulge. But though religion has something of this public role, it is primarily concerned to satisfy the existential or emotional and physical needs of people. This is done through meditation and devotion, and to some extent philosophical insight, in the case of Buddhism; through self-purification and the harmonies of nature in the case

242

of Shinto; through moral improvement, as in the case of Confucian values; through tolerant attitudes, in the espousal of Western-style humanism.

In contrast to what happened in India and China, Japan's course in the face of colonialism and capitalism has been remarkable. She did not, as did the mainstream Indian nationalists, reach down into her own past for a philosophy from the classical period to adapt to the modern world and to give new shape to the anticolonial struggle. She did not, like China, reach out for a Western ideology to adapt against the West, and to express nationalism in a masked way. She did use elements of her tradition, but with a clear recognition of the role of nationalism in the modern world. By taking the Shinto motif, violently wrenching it from its previous entanglement with Buddhism, and promoting it as a ritual of national solidarity, the Japanese Meiji reformers attempted to give an explicit and sacred basis for the pursuit of the national ideal and conformity with the national essence. At the same time they took up as much in the way of liberal constitutionality as seemed necessary. The fact that there was no doctrinal baggage attached to Shinto left it apt for promoting unity in the nation but not in any way for teaching things which could seriously come into conflict with modern ideas and scientific thinking.

But from two angles the reformers were not able to conflict with religion – first because some of the new movements offered powerful alternative myths to the stories of Amaterasu that formed the ultimate basis of the authority and sacredness of the imperial family; and second because religions tend toward universalism and so are not simply ready to bow to the absolute demands of nationalism. The path to war – both in World War I and even more in World War II – led to the absolutizing of the national essence, the *kokutai*, and the clear subordination of religions to patriotism (similar things in practice had occurred elsewhere, in Europe for instance).

The basis that had been created in the nationalist phase could, however, remain, and Japan took (was virtually forced to take) a move toward liberalism. This has evolved into a different sort of attempt to take over some Western ways and blend them into an overall Japanese synthesis. While this remains largely unexpressed, it centers on a vaguer notion of national harmony, to replace the more concrete feeling for the *kokutai*. Religions can fit within this harmony through a pluralistic framework of thought and practice. In these conditions, Shinto has undergone considerable revival as a focus of yearnings for harmony both within society and with nature.

Western culture, with its heavy stress upon the arts, has some echoes in Japanese aestheticism. The Japanese have retained a strong affinity with nature, even despite the creation of a very powerful and often dirty human environment in the course of the headlong economic revival from the time of the Korean War onward. Society remains very crowded and formal; and the shrines and temples remain important outlets which allow human beings to see beyond their immediate milieu, the exigencies of correct social behavior, and the relentless pursuit of a growing Gross National Product.

243

Pilgrims ascending Mount Fuji, the great sacred mountain of Japan.

Conclusion

Though Shinto had its period of manipulation by the state, it has tended to continue as a natural and not too highly organized expression of traditional Japan, merging from time to time with Buddhism, Taoism, and Confucianism. It also fulfills a domestic function, since many Japanese houses contain a "spirit-shelf" or altar, dedicated to a presiding *kami*. This complements a Buddhist shrine, dedicated to a Buddha and to ancestors. This points to a generally Japanese emphasis upon harmony. Overt conflict is played down, and Shinto also reflects a desire to live in accord with nature, however much the modern industrial and technological world interferes with the beauties of old Japan.

CHAPTER THIRTEEN

Asian Religions and the Modern World

Differing Patterns of Response to the West and Modernization

Let us begin to estimate the power of traditional values by looking at the rather diverse destinies in recent times of India, China, and Japan.

We have already seen how Britain, in imposing a single order on the Indian subcontinent, helped to create a sense of Indian nationalism. That sense, however, was greatly modified by the fact that in the decades leading up to Indian independence an increasing unease felt by Muslims eventually issued in the demand for a separate, Islamic, Pakistan. Though the Republic of India contained and still contains a large Muslim minority, now over 100 million, and roughly equal to the population of Pakistan and Bangladesh (which split from Pakistan in 1971), nevertheless the main ethos of the Republic was Hindu. But in the main its Hinduism, at least among much of the ruling elite, has followed the new Hindu ideology fashioned by Vivekānanda and others, stressing the all-embracing and tolerant character of Hinduism. This provided an ethos for a pluralistic and democratic constitution. However, the separation of religion and the state began to fray with the rise in the early 1990s of the Bharatiya Janata Party, with its general commitment to a Hindu India.

But Hinduism has been able to modernize most effectively, incorporating ideas of science and liberal philosophy, without sacrificing much if anything of its traditional past. Of all the major countries of Asia there can be little doubt that India is the one that genuinely retains the most of its traditions. Yet it has a large university system, nuclear engineering, high-grade technology, modern forms of government, a relatively open society, and creativity in the arts, television, and journalism. In short, it has succeeded in marrying the new to the old. There remain, of course, vast problems of social justice, poverty, and so on, partly because the growth in production has been more than matched by growth in reproduction.

The social changes of the last half-century have been matched by religious changes – the growth of new religious movements, such as that of the charismatic Sai Baba, who attracts many middle-class Hindus (a class which has undergone phenomenal growth, up to about 150 million members). Regional nationalisms have helped to highlight pilgrimage centers in the various states of the Indian Union. The emergence of diaspora Hinduism as a force has helped to reinforce the vigor of such modern religious organizations as the Ārya Samāj and the Ramakrishna Vedānta movement.

Maybe the fact of having been conquered simplified India's course of national action. By contrast, the Chinese quandary was in part that her growing middle class was too much tied to the foreigner. As we have already noted, traditional Chinese values for various reasons were unable effectively to cope with the thrust of the West, Japan, and modernism. It turned out therefore that the Chinese spiritual response was to be Marxism, as adapted by Mao. We have seen already the quasi-religious character of Mao's version of Marxism. It was utopian, evangelical, organized, philosophical, strong on military prowess and expertise, ethically rigorous, economically promising, disciplined. Its first tasks were performed effectively: China was made strong and was able to hit back against the West during the Korean War (1950–3). It assured itself of a large degree of economic independence. It was able to navigate its own path, diverging from that of the Stalinist Soviet Union. To a great extent it reconstructed the internal composition of China. Much of the old Confucian feudalism was dismantled. With it Buddhism, Taoism, and folk religion were controlled and suppressed. A different state religion, Mao Zedong Thought, was substituted for the old ideologies. Oddly, it was a Western creed, admittedly adapted to Chinese conditions by a Chinese thinker, which came to replace the old values. In short, if India had grafted Western thought onto the great banyan of Hinduism (a relatively easy thing to do since Hinduism was used to grafting and loved to add further branches to its already luxuriant growth), China cut down its own trees to plant something new.

In adopting a Western anti-Western ideology China thus hoped to be modern. But forty years began to show, by June 1989, a fateful and ominous time for all sides, that Marxism was not as scientific as it claimed to be. Also, Mao's conscious flouting of learning could have left China with too few trained scientists to be able to take full advantage of the new possibilities opening up with new relationships toward the capitalist West. In fact, by opting for a foreign and aggressive ideology, China had sacrificed most of its historic and cultural past while failing to create a very vigorous new society. China's experience proved to be almost the opposite of India's. In the Chinese case a foreign ideology was taken over to counter the enemy, because it was seen as revolutionary and therefore one's enemy's enemy (but one's enemy's enemy is not necessarily one's friend). In India's case an ancient resource, namely Hindu ideology, was used to express a revolutionary spirit, but one in which the worldview was presented as one's enemy's friend. At any rate the enemy had good things to offer: the problem was how to appropriate them without losing strength in resisting Western pressures.

The Japanese solution was to draw upon its ancient resources, but at the same time to make a planned attempt to take over Western techniques. The Japanese saw that it is not possible just to take over science and modern education. Changes in society and therefore in spiritual outlook are also necessary. However, the Japanese also drew upon Shinto in order to express their nationalistic spirit, so that less than forty years after the Meiji restoration they were able in 1905 to defeat the Russians at the Battle of Tsushima, a major naval reversal. The change to Shinto was antagonistic to the spirit of Buddhism, so important in Japanese civilization. It also proved ultimately disastrous, in that the nationalist phase went beyond resisting the West (in order to defend the Japanese way of life) to an imitation of Western imperialism, culminating in the attack on Pearl Harbor in December, 1941, and in vast military operations throughout the Pacific region.

Nevertheless, the Meiji formula of adapting Japanese Buddhist and Shinto values to modernism and liberalism was ultimately successful. The U.S. and Allied occupation assigned Japan a new constitution, building on the old, reducing the imperial succession to a constitutional monarchy, and removing some of the militaristic tendencies of the Japanese state. The Japanese economic success is eloquent testimony to the new system. The end result is that Japan has evolved a society half Japanese and half Western: a midpoint between India and China.

Southeast Asia has seen in some areas the rise of a modernist Buddhism, notably in Thailand, relying on the new foundations laid in the nineteenth century by a forward-looking monarchy; in others the development of various and mostly unsuccessful socialist experiments, sometimes blending with Buddhism, and sometimes antagonistic to it. In Burma the blend encouraged a kind of collective withdrawal from the world economy: Burma practiced a kind of Buddhist socialism, but one committed to a kind of collective *nirvāṇa*. In Kampuchea the Khmer Rouge also preached a collective withdrawal from the world, but through a brutal system ordaining the purification of the country through the elimination, that is the murder, of all people contaminated by Western-style education (except some of the Khmer Rouge elite, influenced by Marxism). In Laos and Vietnam Buddhism suffered under communist oppression. In Sri Lanka, a largely liberal or modernist Buddhism has predominated and has promised much in the development of a new Buddhist ethos, except that tensions have grown with the Tamil and non-Buddhist minority, culminating in a complex civil struggle since 1979.

South Korea, Hong Kong, Singapore, and Malaysia have in differing ways harnessed traditional values to modern capitalism. Especially in Singapore there emerged a brilliant new Confucian welfare capitalism. In Indonesia the regime has successfully compromised between Islam and the need to hold a highly complex and decentralized state together, through the ideology of the *Pancasila*, somewhat reminiscent of Vivekānanda's ideological prescription

A Chinese Communist leader stands amid a crowd gathered in front of the Dalai Lama's Palace in Tibet as he reads a proclamation from Peking to the Tibetans, April, 1959. The often violent confrontation between the Buddhist and Marxist forces in the region remains unresolved.

for Indian unity. The notion that all groups are free to, and indeed even obliged to, worship the Ultimate in their own way allows of a middle path between Islamic rigorism and pluralistic toleration.

Islam in Pakistan and Bangladesh has on the whole taken a modernist tack, though Pakistan has experimented somewhat with the imposition of *sharī'a* or traditional law. But Islam on the whole has yet fully to resolve the question of how to adapt its rich past to the new demands of the contemporary world.

Asian Religions in One World

The Asian region has become immensely more significant in the cultural and economic life of the globe in the last fifty years. The phenomenal success of Japan and a string of post-Confucian countries around the western rim of the Pacific has been matched by the growth of Oriental influences on the Western world, through California and the growing diaspora of Asian populations in America, Europe, and elsewhere. Thus Asian ideas are taking a modest place in the array of Occidental worldviews – ideas such as reincarnation (believed in by 15 percent of Western populations), yoga, Eastern holism, vegetarianism, the multiple nature of the divine, nonviolence, etc. As organic traditions some groups are making converts well beyond traditional Asian areas:

notably Buddhism, neo-Hinduism (for instance through the Ramakrishna Vedānta Mission), Hindu *bhakti* (through ISKCON or the "Hare Krishna" movement), Taoist philosophy (in a rather diffuse way), Zen practice, Nichiren Buddhism, and so on. And because of the diasporas, traditional forms of Asian religions are practiced in virtually all the major cities of the Western world – Los Angeles, Sydney, Toronto, New York, Rio de Janeiro, Buenos Aires, Berlin, London, Rome, Marseilles – to name a few.

All this points to the need for more informed empathy, if groups are going to live together with understanding and some degree of harmony. Moreover, as we all enter rapidly into a new global civilization we need to perceive all our ancestors as ancestors of all of us. We should look back, in the West, not just to Moses, Jesus, Plato, Aeschylus, Goethe, Mozart, Shakespeare, Cervantes, Luther, Leonardo, Chopin, Beethoven, Dickens, Tolstoy, and Dostoyevsky as our spiritual ancestors, but to Confucius, Lao-tzu, Chuang-tzu, Mencius, the Buddha, Shankara, Caitanya, Gandhi, Mongkut, Milarepa, Akbar, Nānak, Gobind Singh, Buddhaghosa, Shinran, Honen, Wang Yang-ming, and Chinul too. This in turn means that we need to face the importance of worldview analysis – or religious education in the broadest sense – in our global education systems. In a way religious studies is too vital to be left to the religious traditions, which have often had a record of mutual denigration or of fostering ignorance of the other, by silence. I would hope that in both East and West the exploration with sensitivity and dispassion of the world's religions will figure centrally in education for a new world civilization.

Bibliography

General
Mircea Eliade, ed., *The Encyclopedia of Religion*, 15 vols., New York, 1987.
E. E. Evans-Pritchard, *Theories of Primitive Religion*, Oxford, 1965.
John R. Hinnells, ed., *A Handbook of Living Religions*, Baltimore, 1985.
Lescek Kolskowski, *Main Currents of Marxism*, 3 vols., Oxford, 1978–1981.
John Macquarrie, *Twentieth Century Religious Thought*, 2nd edn., New York, 1981.
David Martin, *A General Theory of Secularization*, San Francisco, 1979.
Peter Merkl and Ninian Smart, eds., *Religion and Politics in the Modern World*, New York, 1984.
Rudolf Otto, *The Idea of the Holy*, London, 1950.
E. G. Parrinder, *Worship in the World's Religions*, London, 1961.
Eric J. Sharpe, *Comparative Religion – A History*, London, 1976.
Ninian Smart, *The Religious Experience of Mankind*, 3rd edn., New York, 1984.
Ninian Smart, *Worldviews*, New York, 1983.
Ninian Smart and Richard Hecht, eds., *Sacred Texts of the World*, London, 1982.
G. van der Leeuw, *Religion in Essence and Manifestation*, Princeton, 1987.
R. J. Z. Werblowsky, *Beyond Tradition and Modernity: Changing Religions in a Changing World*, London, 1976.
R. C. Zaehner, ed., *Concise Encyclopedia of Living Faiths*, 2nd edn., London, 1971.

Hinduism and Jainism
A. L. Basham, *The Wonder That Was India*, London, 1971.
Cromwell Crawford, ed., *In Search of Hinduism*, New York, 1986.
S. N. Dasgupta, *A History of Indian Philosophy*, 5 vols., Delhi, 1976.
Louis Dumont, *Homo Hierarchicus*, Chicago, 1970.
Mircea Eliade, *Yoga: Immortality and Freedom*, 2nd edn., Princeton, 1969.
Clifford Geertz, *The Religion of Java*, Glencoe, Illinois, 1960.
Friedhelm Hardy, *Viraha Bhakti*, London, 1981.
P. S. Jaini, *The Jaina Path of Purification*, Berkeley, 1979.
Wendy Doniger O'Flaherty, ed., *Karma and Rebirth in Classical Indian Traditions*, Berkeley, 1980.
Ninian Smart, *Doctrine and Argument in Indian Philosophy*, London, 1964.
Benjamin Walker, *Hindu World*, 2 vols., London, 1968.
R. C. Zaehner, *Hinduism*, New York, 1966.
Heinrich Zimmer, *Myths and Symbols in Indian Art and Civilization*, Princeton, 1972.

Buddhism
Kenneth Ch'en, *Buddhism in China*, Princeton, 1973.
George Coedes, *The Indianized States of Southeast Asia*, Canberra, 1968.
Edward Conze, *Buddhism: Its Essence and Development*, New York, 1984.
F. H. Cook, *Hua-yen Buddhism*, Philadelphia, 1977.
H. Dumoulin, *History of Zen Buddhism*, New York, 1965.
Richard Gombrich, *Theravada Buddhism*, London, 1988.
Raymond J. Hammer, *Japan's Religious Ferment*, London, 1957.
Winston L. King, *Buddhist Meditation*, Philadelphia, 1980.
Trevor Ling, *The Buddha*, London, 1978.
S. Murakami, *Japanese Religion in the Modern Century*, Tokyo, 1980.
Walpola Rahula, *What the Buddha Taught*, New York, 1962.
Melford E. Spiro, *Burmese Supernaturalism*, 2nd edn., Philadelphia, 1978.
D. T. Suzuki, *Shin Buddhism*, New York, 1970.
Donald Swearer. *Buddhism and Society in Southeast Asia*, Chambersburg, Penn., 1981.

Giuseppe Tucci, *The Religions of Tibet*, Berkeley, 1980.
A. K. Warder, *Indian Buddhism*, Delhi, 1970.

Islam
Clifford Geertz, *Islam Observed*, New Haven, Conn., 1968.
Ernest Gollner, *Muslim Society*, Cambridge, 1981.
S. Hussain and M. Jagri, *Origins and Early Development of Shi'a Islam*, London, 1979.
Bernard Lewis, *The Emergence of Modern Turkey*, London, 1963.
Richard C. Martin, *Islam: A Cultural Perspective*, Englewood Cliffs, New Jersey, 1982.
Marmaduke M. Pickthall, *The Meaning of the Glorious Koran*, New York, 1930.
Fazlur Rahman, *Islam*, 2nd edn., Chicago, 1979.
Joseph Schacht, *An Introduction to Islamic Law*, Oxford, 1974.
Anne-Marie Schimmel, *Mystical Dimensions of Islam*, Chapel Hill, North Carolina, 1975.
Wilfred C. Smith, *Islam in Modern History*, Princeton, 1957.
H. Montgomery Watt, *Muhammad: Prophet and Statesman*, London, 1974.

Sikhism
E. O. Cole and P. S. Sambhi, *The Sikh Tradition*, London, 1978.

Confucianism and Taoism
Theodore de Bary and JaHyun Kim Maboush, eds., *The Rise of Neo-confucianism in Korea*,
    New York, 1985.
D. Bodde, *Festivals in Classical China*, Princeton, 1975.
Chang Chung-yuan, *Creativity and Taoism*, New York, 1963.
H. G. Creel, *What is Taoism*, Chicago, 1970.
Joseph Needham, *Science and Civilization in China*, 5 vols., Cambridge, 1954–83.
Stuart R. Schram, *The Political Thought of Mao Tse-tung*, rev. edn., New York, 1969.
D. Howard Smith, *Chinese Religions*, New York, 1968.
D. Howard Smith, *Confucius*, New York, 1973.
L. C. Thompson, *Chinese Religion: An Interpretation*, 3rd edn., Encino, California, 1976.
Arthur Waley, ed. and trans., *The Way and Its Power*, London, 1934.
Holmes Welch, *The Parting of the Way: Lao Tzu and the Taoist Movement*, London, 1957.
Holmes Welch, *The Practice of Chinese Buddhism*, New York, 1967.
Holmes Welsh and Anna Seidel, eds., *Facets of Taoism: Essays in Chinese Religion*, New Haven,
    1979.
Feng Yu-lan, *A History of Chinese Philosophy*, 2 vols., Princeton, 1952–3.

Shinto
H. Byron Earhart, *Japanese Religion*, 3rd edn., Belmont, California, 1982.

Credits

The author, publishers, and Calmann & King Ltd wish to thank the following institutions and individuals who have provided photographic material for use in this book.

Frontispiece: Barnaby's/Rudy Lewis

Chapter One
page 14: The Nelson-Atkins Museum of Art, Kansas City. Gift of Bronson Trevor in honor of his father, John Trevor.
page 19: Novosti Press Agency
page 21: Alan Hutchison Library
page 22: Victoria & Albert Museum
page 24: Calmann & King archives
page 25: Topham Picture Source
page 26: Popperfoto
page 27: Victoria & Albert Museum
page 29: I.W.M/Robert Hunt Library
page 31: Barnaby's/Ger Cubitt

Chapter Two
page 38: Ann & Bury Peerless
page 43: National Museum (New Delhi)/Mansell Collection
page 49: Alan Hutchison Library
page 52: Douglas Dickens
page 54: Victoria & Albert Museum
page 55: W. Forman/Barbara Heller Archive
page 57: MFA Boston (Charles Amos Cummings Bequest Fund)
page 59: Calmann & King archives
page 60: Topham Picture Source

Chapter Three
pages 73 and 78: Christine Osborne Pictures
page 75: Popperfoto
page 77: A.P./Topham Picture Source
page 80: Douglas Dickens

Chapter Four
page 85: Victoria & Albert Museum
page 87: Douglas Dickens
page 88: Topham Picture Source
page 90: Ann & Bury Peerless

Chapter Five
page 93 (left): Government Museum, Mathura/Calmann & King archive
page 93 (below): MFA Boston (Seth K. Sweetser Fund)
page 96: Freer Gallery of Art, Washington/Calmann & King archive
pages 97 and 102: Christine Osborne Pictures
pages 107 and 113 (left): Ann & Bury Peerless

page 111: © Tharpa Publications 1989
pages 113 (right) and 114: Victoria & Albert Museum

Chapter Six
pages 120 and 126: Douglas Dickens
pages 122 and 123: Barnaby's Picture Library
page 130: Christine Osborne Pictures
page 132: British Library
pages 133 and 134: A.P./Topham Picture Source
page 135: Popperfoto
page 136: Photo © Tim Page

Chapter Seven
page 141: Chester Beatty Library, Dublin
page 144 (both): Victoria & Albert Museum
page 148: Bodleian Library, Oxford
page 152: Topham Picture Source
page 153: Christine Osborne Pictures

Chapter Eight
page 160: Victoria & Albert Museum
page 163: Barnaby's Picture Library
page 164: A.P./Topham Picture Source
page 167: Barnaby's/Richard Gardner

Chapter Nine
pages 172 and 184: Victoria & Albert Museum
pages 173 and 181: Topham Picture Source
page 178: Archiv Für Kunst und Geschichte, Berlin
pages 188 and 191: Alan Hutchison Library
page 192: Douglas Dickens

Chapter Ten
page 196: Mansell Collection
page 203: © Al Huang Living Tao Foundation
page 204: Barnaby's Picture Library

Chapter Eleven
page 207: British Library
page 210: Victoria & Albert Museum
pages 214 and 225: Douglas Dickens
page 217: Barnaby's Picture Library
page 221: A.P./Topham Picture Source
page 222: Topham Picture Source

Chapter Twelve
page 234: A.P./Topham Picture Source
page 236: Robert Hunt Library
pages 241 and 242: Barnaby's Picture Library
page 244: Topham Picture Source

Chapter Thirteen
page 248: Topham Picture Source

Index